Contact Zones

CONTEMPORARY APPROACHES TO FILM AND TELEVISION SERIES

A complete listing of the books in this series can be found online at wsupress.wayne.edu

General Editor
Barry Keith Grant
Brock University

Advisory Editors
Patricia B. Erens
School of the Art Institute of Chicago

Lucy Fischer
University of Pittsburgh

Peter Lehman
Arizona State University

Caren J. Deming
University of Arizona

Robert J. Burgoyne
Wayne State University

Tom Gunning
University of Chicago

Anna McCarthy
New York University

Peter X. Feng
University of Delaware

Lisa Parks
University of California-Santa Barbara

Jeffrey Sconce
Northwestern University

Contact Zones
Memory, Origin, and Discourses in Black Diasporic Cinema

SHEILA J. PETTY

Wayne State University Press   Detroit

© 2008 by Wayne State University Press, Detroit, Michigan 48201.
All rights reserved. No part of this book may be reproduced without formal permission.

Library of Congress Cataloging-in-Publication Data
Petty, Sheila.
Contact zones : memory, origin, and discourses in Black diasporic cinema / Sheila J. Petty.
p. cm. — (Contemporary approaches to film and television)
Includes bibliographical references and index.
ISBN-13: 978-0-8143-3099-9 (pbk. : alk. paper)
ISBN-10: 0-8143-3099-1 (pbk. : alk. paper)
1. Blacks in motion pictures. 2. African Americans in motion pictures. 3. Slavery in motion pictures. I. Title.
PN1995.9.N4P43 2008
791.43'652996073—dc22
2007035463

Some material from this volume appeared in an earlier article as "The Metropolitan Myth: Assimilation, Racism and Cultural Devaluation in *Soleil O* and *Pièces d'identités*" in *L'esprit créateur* 41, no. 3 (Fall 2001): 163–71. Reprinted by permission.

∞ The paper used in this publication meets the minimum requirements of the American National Standard for Information Sciences—Permanence of Paper for Printed Library Materials, ANSI Z39.48–1984.

Designed and typeset by Maya Rhodes
Composed in Dante MT

For Vaughn

CONTENTS

Acknowledgments ix

Introduction 1

1. Africa and the Middle Passage: Recoupment of Origin in *Sankofa* 16

2. Collision of Cultures: Occulted Caribbean Histories in *Sugar Cane Alley* 52

3. Reclaiming Africa: Black Women's Discourses in *Daughters of the Dust* 80

4. Disjunction from Self: The Politics of Arrival in *Soleil O* 104

5. Arrested Memory: The Problematics of Return in *Testament* 127

6. Slippage and Mutable Histories in *Deluge* 154

7. Transnational Gazes in *Frantz Fanon: Black Skin, White Mask* 176

8. Locality, Memory, and Zombification in *The Man by the Shore* 196

9. Mapping New Boundaries: Discourses of Blackness in *Rude* 224

Notes 259
Bibliography 269
Index 287

ACKNOWLEDGMENTS

I would like to express my sincere gratitude to the artists whose films inspired this book project. During the research for this book, it was my good fortune to have collaborated in early 2000 with Dunlop Art Gallery in Regina and Mount Saint Vincent University Art Gallery in Halifax on a film series and catalog titled "The Archaeology of Origin: Transnational Visions of Africa in a Borderless Cinema." The series and catalog led to this book, and I especially thank Joyce Clark, Ingrid Jenkner, Anthony Kiendl, and Helen Marzolf for their enthusiasm and support of the project.

I also greatly appreciate the work of the people at Wayne State University Press, in particular Annie Martin, acquisitions editor, and Carrie Downes Teefey, production editor. I am indebted to copyeditor Jennifer Dropkin and indexer Jane Henderson for working so closely with the manuscript, and I am especially indebted to Barry Keith Grant, whose editorial suggestions were extremely helpful in the final draft of the manuscript.

For financial support to complete this project, I am grateful to the Social Sciences and Humanities Research Council of Canada, the Humanities Research Institute at the University of Regina, and the University of Regina President's Fund/SSHRC General Research Grant Fund.

Finally, I thank Vaughn Borden, Chris Cunningham, and Donna-Lynne McGregor for their encouragement, insight, patience, and support.

Introduction

It has become axiomatic to assert that the world is shrinking, connected as we are through computer, transportation, and telecommunication technologies. It seems, too, that cultures are dissolving as borders appear redundant in a world where thought and people can travel from here to there with the seeming speed of imagination. All this blurring of nation and identity has spurred debate on whether these concepts can stand unchallenged or pure in light of the pressures and fissures created by globalization. Are we defined by origin through (geo)political and (geo)economic forces, or are we shaped by (global) political and (global) economic forces that render origin and nation as outmoded concepts of a past analog age? Perhaps it is travel that defines identity, and we exist in some (not-here/not-there) state oscillating between arrival and departure, global and local, nation and (non)nation. Although this may appear to be a recent preoccupation in the West, for persons of the black diaspora, this inquiry has been alive and ongoing since Africans and peoples of African descent crossed the Atlantic through slavery, political exile, and/or economic exile. Compelled into transnational existences, survivors of these experiences have, down the generations, devised unique strategies of remembrance as devices to recoup, reconstruct, and go beyond origins and histories forged in and between shifting concepts of nation and identity. As such, the artistic and theoretical journeys of the black diaspora have much to offer in the current debate surrounding globalizing cultural spaces.

This is not a process of absolutes, for the black diaspora itself is one of the most complex and diverse spaces ever conceived, bringing together many differing layers of maps, histories, oppressions, and resistances that intersect and diverge in terms of goals and experiences. This view is supported by Paul Gilroy, who observes that "the fundamental, time-worn assumption of homogenous and unchanging black communities whose political and economic interests were readily knowable and easily transferred from everyday life into their expressive cultures has, for example, proved to be a fantasy" (1993b, 1). His position, which celebrates the existence of multiple black experiences and communities, underscores the inherent paradox of the black diaspora: how can any one theoretical or aesthetic system hope to circumscribe experiences that are at once different and the same?

As both a real and imaginary space, the black diaspora is governed by a multiplicity of journeys impelled by an infinite number of historical, economic, political, and personal factors. In addition, many of these journeys are directly affected by questions of race, creating, as Henry Louis Gates Jr. suggests, "a trope of ultimate, irreducible difference between cultures, linguistic groups, or adherents of specific belief systems which—more often than not—also have fundamentally opposed economic interests" (1986, 5). Thus, othering in the black diaspora often generates experiences of loss, alienation, oppression, racism, and survival that are as different as the peoples experiencing them.

Although this creates a complicated landscape in terms of theoretical geography, it also presents a unique richness and diversity of voices and debates, a state that has not gone unnoticed in theoretical writings and imaginings of the black diaspora. The difficulty with defining the black diaspora—or any diaspora, for that matter—is the fact that they are conceived in and through movement across borders and cultures, and as a result, any set of definitive terms has the tendency to rule in one subset of diasporic experiences while excluding another. It is this very multiplicity that James Clifford grapples with when he observes that "an unruly crowd of descriptive/interpretive terms now jostle and converse in an effort to characterize the contact zones of nations, cultures, and regions" (1994, 303).[1] If, as Gilroy argues, the conflict between local and global forces have compromised the concept of nation-state as a primary locus of economic, political, and cultural action, it is not surprising that terms, concepts, and even identities in the black diaspora reflect that state of flux (1993b, 192). With journeys that began in slavery, exile, or migration, it is understandable that an inestimable number of endpoints and methodologies of survival have arisen in this contested space.

While any attempt to categorize black diasporic experiences must be viewed as purely artificial, an argument can be made for distinguishing between those rooted in slavery and the Middle Passage and those rooted in exile and migration. Edouard Glissant frames this distinction by arguing that slavery, with its obliteration of cultural history, results in the rise of a new people in a new context, whereas exile or migrancy may generate change in a subject, but the subject remains connected to origin through the persistence of a singular history (1989, 14). Given this context, each of these experiences has left distinctive imprints within the black diaspora.

Slavery's forced migration of individuals under circumstances that deprive them of freedom and culture created survival strategies and resistances aimed at restoring basic human rights, identities, and dignity. The disruption of cultures, languages, and histories created by bringing together myriad African cultures into a slave population in which family units were routinely torn apart by sale made affirmative links with origin impossible to sustain. Furthermore, as Cornel West observes, the effort to control, confine, discipline, and dishonor Africans was supported by the development of racist strategies that denigrated African cultures in order to justify slavery and therefore protect the white economic interests that depended on slave labor (1997, 8). The result of this systemic racism is, as Sylvia Wynter describes, a condition of uprootedness that is "the original model of the total twentieth century disruption of man" (1976, 130). The distortions created by histories, both obscured by and written within the auspices of systemic racism, place a special emphasis on "reappropriating the past" in order to transform identities and the portrayal of histories (Lionnet 1989, 4–5). Thus, memory, valorization of oral history, and the challenging of racist precepts become driving forces in reassembling and reconceiving fractured histories (4).

INTRODUCTION

Although Middle Passage experiences possess certain commonalities based on a shared historical event, exile and migrancy cannot be traced to a single event. The multiple border crossings of both create new displacements and new diasporas that challenge the concepts of border and diaspora in new and multiple ways (Brah 1996, 179). Fueled by political and economic oppression, both exile and migrancy involve dispersal from a clearly identifiable and traceable origin. In contrast to those whose histories are fractured by the Middle Passage, migrants and exiles face their new realities with the full force of their cultural histories and identities behind them, although they often experience disjuncture and alienation from their origins. This being said, it is also accurate to observe that, certainly in the case of exile, satisfactory definitions are still elusive (Rosello 1993, 177). Furthermore, although both migrancy and exile suggest the possibility of return, the process involved is highly problematic: as Iain Chambers comments, "Such a journey acquires the form of a restless interrogation, undoing its very terms of reference as the point of departure is lost along the way" (1994, 2). This position underscores the inevitable processes of cultural change undergone by exiles and migrants that ultimately alter their relationship with the cultural locus of origin. As in the case of the Middle Passage, discourses of exile and migrancy access memory and recuperate histories as a means of defining identity. Because dispersal occurs with intact cultures and histories, however, the articulation of these discourses often occurs within very distinct maps of experience. This is not to privilege discourses of the Middle Passage over those generated by exile and migrancy or to suggest that one is more representative of black diasporic experience but, rather, to acknowledge that differences in the beginnings of a journey can have profoundly disparate results.

Yet, despite underlying differences, these are not totally divergent paths. Given that economics and politically motivated power disparities often compel exile and migrancy, it is possible to see that they share with slavery a racist emphasis on commodifcation of labor (Clifford 1994, 313). Thus, the journey from origin, whatever the reason, is invariably confronted by racism, "systematic exploitation and blocked advancement," creating a sense of displacement and alienation (312). This underscores the paradoxical nature of black diasporic experience: although these identities may be forged in specific circumstances, there is also a sense that shared histories of oppression both supersede and are delimited by boundaries. Rinaldo Walcott describes this connectedness of black diasporic cultures as a matter of circuitous routes or detours that bond black expressive cultures to their "rhizomatic nature." A reflection of an "improvisatory and an in-between space," it is this connectedness that causes diasporic experience to escape encapsulization in either generalizations or specifics (Walcott 1997, 18). Whether inscribed within Gilroy's black Atlantic (1993a, 3) or Clifford's specific maps/histories (1994, 319), it would seem that slippage between origin, journey, arrival, and remembrance plays a significant role in the creation of black diasporic identities. Therefore, it is not surprising that black diasporic theorists offer a multiplicity of viewpoints and contexts. Origin is both constructed and deconstructed as an element of identity, thus challenging static constructions by underscoring the positive and negative consequences of lives spent within transnational frameworks.

Gilroy suggests that there is a seemingly insoluble conflict between two distinct but symbiotic relationships to origin: the monolithic position presents diasporic experience as pan-African, and therefore privileges African origin as a defining feature of identity, while the pluralist view foregrounds race as a social and cultural construct, in which origin functions as one strand in a complex and varied cord of experience (1993a, 31–32). Set into frameworks of the Middle Passage and exile/migration, however, each of these positions is potentially valid because, as Clifford observes, "contemporary diaspora discourses retain a connection with specific bodies, [and] historical experiences of displacement that need to be held in comparative tension and partial translatability" (1994, 324). Ultimately, the efficacy of each depends on whether primacy is given to difference or similarity. Since black diasporic cultures evidence both simultaneously, it may be more fruitful to recognize that they are complementary, rather than conflicted, viewpoints.

Whether embedded in histories and/or maps, the proliferation of terms and concepts such as journey, arrival, origin, "creolization, transculturation, hybridity, and diaspora"—to mention a few—all contribute to the theoretical discussion of what constitutes the black diaspora and its myriad experiences (Clifford 1994, 303). Clifford's acknowledg-

INTRODUCTION

ment that slippage exists between terms and states of being seems to underscore the polycentric nature of black diasporic experiences that are, at their most fundamental level of expression, both collective and individual (302). Therefore, it seems that encapsulation of the black diaspora is futile, which is not surprising, as much of this work resists essentialism in all its blatant and subtle forms. The plethora of theory may seem daunting, or even impenetrable, but rather than viewing it as a competition in which the validity of one stance should triumph over another, one can find it worthwhile to recognize that the multiplicity of theories generated by, and within, the black diaspora is emblematic of its vitality and diversity.

How then, can these maps and histories be effectively navigated? Ultimately, as Gilroy perceptively notes, the question must be answered by considering "what is being resisted and by what means" (1993b, 120). In this light, my goal is to apply this question through an examination of a wide variety of theories and concepts in relation to the aesthetic and narrative concerns of selected black diasporic films. Like the rich tradition of black diasporic literature, black diasporic cinema demonstrates a breathtaking range of cultural critique from an amazingly innovative array of identities, voices, and cultural influences, each interrogating the notion of identities within often hostile contexts. A truly borderless cinema, the films chosen for this book reflect a wide sampling of issues, cultures, discourses, contexts, and spaces in between, each bringing a unique aesthetic and narrative perspective to the black diasporic experience. As a result, each chapter is structured to the unique demands of the film under discussion with the aim of providing opportunities to consider the ways in which maps and histories contribute to the interstitial dialogue between filmmakers and thinkers of the black diaspora.

Black diasporic film shares with black diasporic theory a focus on the complexities of constructing identity against transnational backdrops. Like its theoretical counterpart, black diasporic cinema oscillates between similarity and difference and resists easy categorization on the whole. Hence, although each film in this book shares a common interest in origin, history, survival, racism, and journey, the myriad ways in which they engage these broad parameters differ greatly, attesting to the vitality and variance of the communities they represent. Similarly, the theories and concepts used to explore each film create a series of snapshots taken from the oeuvre of black diasporic thought and brings to the fore critical engagements with issues of racism, globalization, hybridity, transnationalism, and gender that can greatly benefit similar discussions taking place in western theory and beyond.

The first three chapters of this book explore different approaches and histories of slavery with the goal of providing some illumination regarding the still ongoing implications of slavery's legacy for black diasporic communities. Gilroy has charged that in the history and expressive cultures of the African diaspora, the practice of racial slavery and the narratives of imperial European conquest need to be drastically rethought (1993a, 42). For this reason, these chapters interrogate established and disputed facts that underlie the major debates on this complex subject and cover such topics as commodification of labor, the dispossession of culture and language, and the presence of African influence in current cultures, including the survival of orality, religions, and African world-sense.[2] Finally, the chapters provide differing perspectives on discourses of slavery in black diasporic cinema as both implicit and explicit narrative strategies that explicate diasporic identities, cultures, and survival strategies.

Chapter 1 explores the complicated relationship between the legacies of slavery and the desire to reconnect with an African origin. As Carole Boyce Davies argues, "Back to Africa" movements are emblematic of a desire to rewrite and recoup histories that have been obfuscated and denied through persistent and systemic racism (1994, 17). Given this context, the chapter begins with a general examination of the means by which slavery dehumanized and commodified black subjects as labor within a racist framework. In addition, it investigates some of the ways in which black diasporic theory has responded to the legacy of slavery through a discussion of "Back to Africa" movements. Focusing primarily on Molefi Kete Asante's concept of Afrocentricity, the chapter discusses the way in which Asante recenters the locus of black identity on African origin, thus challenging the Eurocentric precepts that continue to underpin racist beliefs (1987, 6). In addition, the chapter also considers some of the challenges brought to Afrocentrist discourses by theorists Kwame Anthony Appiah and Stephen Howe, who interrogate Asante's recoupment strategies. Taken together, these

INTRODUCTION

theorists raise intriguing questions concerning the nature of African diasporic identity in which the issues of center or periphery demonstrate the complexity of diasporic experience. Like Afrocentrism, Haile Gerima's *Sankofa* (United States/Ghana/Ethiopia, 1993), presents the reclamation of origin lost through slavery as a defining feature in diasporic identity construction. The film, set in a fictional landscape that offers a pan-African perspective of slavery, brings together a complex interaction between past and present that argues for African origin as the defining element of black diasporic identity. The film's focus on the primacy of Africa in diasporic experience has generated considerable debate, particularly in regard to questions of representation and Gerima's own position as a transnational subject. Taken together, these elements both challenge and problematize slavery as a process of cultural destruction and reemergence.

The Caribbean experience of the Middle Passage offers a set of paradigms that are quite distinct. Thus, chapter 2 examines some of the intellectual cornerstones that have influenced the process of conceiving and articulating Caribbean identities. Focusing on the French Caribbean, the chapter begins with a discussion of Aimé Césaire and the rise of the Négritude movement. This movement, which began in the 1930s by African and Caribbean students as a means of challenging the racism they faced in their daily lives, initiated a debate around the interrelationships among assimilation, slavery, colonization, and the need to "embody Negro African culture in twentieth-century realities" (Lilyan Kesteloot, quoted in Jules-Rosette 1998, 242). The emergence of Négritude provided the foundation for thinkers such as Glissant and Patrick Chamoiseau to go beyond its restrictions into evocations of Antillanité (Caribbeanness), Créolité (creoleness), and *métissage*, articulating the complicated landscape of French Caribbean realities. Hence, this chapter presents Négritude, Caribbeanness, and creoleness not as identities exclusive of one another but, rather, as alternative and complementary means of defining Caribbean history, identity, and nation. The discussion is furthered in the analysis of Euzhan Palcy's *Rue casesnègres/Sugar Cane Alley* (Martinique/France, 1983). Set in Martinique, the film looks at a variety of social clashes between French and Creole as languages, French culture and education versus African heritage and oral teachings, the devaluation of black Martinican culture, and the

INTRODUCTION

complex struggle between differing categories of race. Unlike *Sankofa*, which sees return to Africa as the only source of recoupment, *Sugar Cane Alley* searches for black Martinican identity among competing interests, a position that aligns it with the theories used to explore the film.

The third chapter presents a gender perspective on the legacies of slavery. From the beginning of slavery, black women have fought to bring their voices forward against the barriers of racial discrimination and, in some cases, gender prejudice. Hence, black women's discourses have historically sought to place black women's representations at the center of discourse through a variety of strategies addressing the complicated "locations" of "variable subject positions" generated by the multiplicity of positions occupied by black women in history, culture, and communities (Boyce Davies 1994, 8–9). These discourses also challenge white feminist constructions that have negated or ignored race as a constituent in women's experiences and, thus, return black women's concerns from the periphery of gender discourse to the center (Reid 1993, 112). Additionally, although black female subjectivity conjoins both feminism and pan-Africanism, the Eurocentricity of the former and the phallocentricity of the latter have marginalized issues specific to the struggles of black women to survive in inherently hostile territories (111–12).

Given the above, it is not surprising to find that black women frequently focus on the following goals: uncovering the roots of black women's traditions through examination and reintegration of women's experience into black history, debunking social myths in order to undermine the black woman's acceptance of sexist oppression, and envisioning methodologies for the simultaneous liberation of people from all oppression (Riggs 1994, 1–2). Thus, this chapter explores the writing of Jacqueline Bobo, bell hooks, Boyce Davies, and Gwendolyn Audrey Foster and considers how black feminism has been in the forefront of defining issues of black female representation. In addition, the chapter investigates Clenora Hudson-Weems's concept of Africana Womanism: forged as an alternative to black feminist constructions, it foregrounds race and the need to recoup African cultural contexts as the primary issues facing black women and their communities (1994, 22). Africana Womanism, with its focus on family as central to black

INTRODUCTION

female diasporic identity, is especially useful in exploring Julie Dash's extraordinary film, *Daughters of the Dust* (United States, 1991). The film explores the Gullah culture and the implications of retaining its roots in Africa and slavery versus accepting assimilation to white culture and religion. The film conducts this debate through the women of the Peazant family, a strategy that allows for the representation of a variety of conflicting perspectives on the subject. By doing so, the film demonstrates the strength and power of African American women to shape and act on behalf of their communities in times of change.

The next three chapters of the book move away from slavery to examine the maps and histories of the black diaspora from the perspective of migration and exile. Like the previous chapters, these evidence engagements with history and oppression, but the focus shifts from the Middle Passage to contemporary sociopolitical conflicts in Africa and the legacies of colonialism. In particular, the chapters consider how exile and migrancy's complicated interplay of origin, journey, arrival, and return formulate black identities dispersed by political conflict and economic necessity. Regardless of the original impulse, exile and migrancy produce unique dislocations as well as theoretical constructs that are distinct from those created by slavery, and thus they generate alternative ways of circumscribing black diasporic issues and experiences.

Chapter 4 focuses on notions of identity envisioned as transnational experiences. From this perspective, common struggles against racism and oppression create a commonality among dispersed black populations that supersede national boundaries and the constraints of ethnicity (Gilroy 1993a, 19). Beginning with an examination of the ideas of Gilroy and W. E. B. DuBois this chapter delves into what Gilroy has described as "the problem of weighing the claims of national identity against other contrasting varieties of subjectivity and identification" (30). Central to this discussion is an exploration of DuBois's concept of double-consciousness and its intersection with Gilroy's black Atlantic, affording consideration to the significant roles played by both in defining questions of black cultural subjectivity. In Gilroy's vision of a diasporic consciousness that reflects the "rhizomorphic, fractal structure of the transcultural," the commonalities of the journey shared by black diasporic peoples supersede locale and ethnicity to forge a shared place at the intersection of histories and cultures (4). Furthermore, by rereading DuBois's double-consciousness in a new configuration, Gilroy offers a means of describing the alienating effect of racism that extends DuBois's work from its original context in African American culture to a transnational landscape. The black Atlantic and double-consciousness are reflected in the worldsense of Med Hondo's *Soleil O/O Sun* (France/Mauritania, 1970). Normally considered within the auspices of African cinema, *Soleil O* is apropos to the discussion of black diasporic migration because it deals with the social, political, and economic implications of African migrants arriving in a postcolonial European space. In addition, the film adds to the discussion of the implications of assimilation begun in chapter 3 by demonstrating the pitfalls of valorizing Western culture by repudiating African origin. The film's vision of migrancy as a pan-African issue and its depiction of racism and its alienating effects make it ideal for exploring the black Atlantic and double-consciousness.

If arrival in exile is problematic, so is the notion of return to origin. Chapter 5 examines "the refractions and discontinuities of exile" in which transformation of identity, resulting from the pressures of exile, creates a state of disjunction from origin upon return (Said 1990, 361). By investigating arguments advanced by Avtar Brah, Edward Said, and Abdul R. JanMohamed, this chapter examines the dissociative effects of exile and the role of arrested memory in contributing to the impossibility of return. As Brah argues, the very concept of diaspora challenges the view of an idealized and unadulterated, fixed origin (1996, 180). Thus, chapter 5 investigates how political strife, borders, territory, and personal responsibility are internalized as facets of exile and how these combine to challenge concepts of idealized and unadulterated fixed origins (180). John Akomfrah's *Testament* (United Kingdom/Ghana, 1988) explores these very issues by positing return from exile as a conflicted act. The film, which examines the fall of Kwame Nkrumah's regime from an exilic perspective, considers how exile creates a gulf between past memories and present realities resulting in changes in both the exilic subject and her or his origin. Return to a pure origin becomes an unobtainable desire and is thus emblematic of the disjuncture that Brah, Said, and JanMohamed suggest is integral to exile as an experience.

INTRODUCTION

Chapter 6 provides an alternative view of the disjunction between origin and arrival. This chapter explores the works of Clifford and Chambers, emphasizing the importance of history as a factor in diasporic experience. From Clifford's perspective, although the outward journeys of diasporic cultures are often propelled by political and economic disparities, these do not prevent such cultures from establishing and sustaining "distinctive political communities and cultures of resistance" (1994, 319). For Clifford, the flow of individuals across borders in the black diaspora establishes transnational connections to origin that "maintain[s] structured travel circuits, linking members 'at home' and 'away'" (309). Similarly, Chambers recognizes that the multiple border crossings of exile construct identity and origin not as fixed and static concepts but, rather, as fluid interrogations of the myriad parameters demarking black diasporic cultures (1994, 4). Thus, both theorists see "slippage" as integral to the difficulties in assigning boundaries in an artistic practice that is inherently transnational (Clifford 1994, 302). Salem Mekuria's documentary, *Ye Wonz Maibel/Deluge* (Ethiopia/United States, 1997), embraces this interest in the polyphonic exchanges between origin and exile. Unlike *Testament*, which views the disjunction of exile and origin as negative, *Deluge* treats it as a site of slippage where the gaps between personal and national histories can act as stimuli for understanding and rapprochement.

The final three chapters of the book examine films of the diasporic experience with depictions that bend the boundaries of slavery, migrancy, and exile. Although they share with the previous three chapters commonalities such as experiences of slavery and exile, the way in which they explore the issues associated with their communities offers a relationship between map and history that is either unique in perspective or transnational in form. As such, the films and theorists associated with them attest to the impossibility of generalizing black diasporic experience in any meaningful way.

Chapter 7 demonstrates the adeptness of black diasporic filmmakers to question and critique the underpinnings of black diasporic discourse itself. Exploring the work of Frantz Fanon, and its pivotal role in placing issues of blackness on the international arena, the chapter probes Fanon's notion that a "colonial gaze" not only exists but also continues to symbolize the estrangement felt by those who were forcibly dispersed from Africa by slavery. Fanon's work challenges earlier concepts of Négritude and revolutionizes the way in which colonized subjects conceive of their relationship to the colonizer. Although controversial, to read this work is to experience, as Homi Bhabha suggests, "the emergence of a truly radical thought that never dawns without casting an uncertain dark" (1999, 181). In this context, the chapter relies upon a wide variety of perspectives on Fanon including those of Stuart Hall, Homi Bhabha, and Kobena Mercer, among others. Regardless of the debates, or perhaps because of them, the effect of Fanon's ideas is truly transnational, and he has been credited with influencing Black Power and Third World Liberation movements (180). It is at this point that Isaac Julien's stunning documentary, *Frantz Fanon: Black Skin, White Mask* (United Kingdom, 1996), takes over the discussion. Through a series of innovative recreations and interviews with family members and authorities on Fanon's work, the film reexamines Fanon's writing from a contemporary perspective by unearthing Fanon's homophobia and his pursuit of a perfect black masculinity. The inquiry, conducted from a black British point of view and spanning Martinique and Algeria, creates a transnational dialogue with Fanon's work that renews it even as it is critiqued.

Focusing on issues of locality, memory, and syncretism, chapter 8 explores Haiti's unique position as "the first Black Republic" (Dayan 1993b, 165). Although Haiti shares a history of slavery with other Caribbean nations, it was the site of the only fully successful slave rebellion, which began with an uprising in 1791 and ended with independence in 1804. This triumph not only affected the entire slave trade but also placed Haiti in a distinctive local context in terms of its political and social development. René Depestre's writings, considered integral to understanding the complexities of Haiti, provide the theoretical foundation of the chapter (Dayan 1993b, 156). Depestre underscores the importance of distinctive local contexts when he argues that the concrete conditions of history are more important to the development of nation in the Caribbean than "belonging to the same race . . . or the 'diaspora' which resulted from the slave trade" (1976, 65). For Depestre, Haitian identities are "the result of a long process of cultural 'mestizaje' (mixing up) and syncretism" in which history figures as a fundamental force (66). Raoul Peck's film, *L'homme sur les quais/The*

INTRODUCTION

Man by the Shore (Haiti/France/Canada, 1993), explores territory similar to that staked out by Depestre. Although the film does not directly address the issue of slavery, the complex interplay of politics and history central to the film depicts Haiti as a society that is torn apart by racial polarization originally instituted in slavery that pitted the *mulâtre* urban elite against the *noiriste*, or rural peasants. More important, the film's representation of factional violence in the Duvalier regime raises questions of social and individual responsibility in perpetuating such divisions.

Black Canadian discourses are the focus of chapter 9. Exploring black Canadian cultures within a transcultural framework, this chapter considers how the multiple histories of slavery, exile, and migrancy among black Canadians create identities at the crossroads of maps and locales that challenge the concept of a monolithic black community in Canada. Canada presents a particularly difficult national paradox in terms of its illusory commitment to multiculturalism and racial harmony and, as Joseph Mensah indicates, the reluctance of many Canadians to "admit that racial oppression and inferiorization persist in this country" (2002, 1). As he points out, "Historical records and contemporary comparative studies suggest that, when it comes to the maltreatment of racial minorities, Canada has a disreputable past and present" (2). As these comments suggest, there is an urgent need to reclaim black Canadian counterhistories in order to expose the distortions that have accumulated in dominant discourses of culture. Hence, chapter 9 concentrates on the work of Walcott, Cecil Foster, and George Elliott Clarke, who offer perspectives on black Canadian issues, assessing and confronting some of the varied influences, strengths, and weaknesses that result from a destabilized cultural context. As Foster (1996, 15) suggests, the experience of black Canadians goes beyond constructs of double-consciousness because black identities in Canada must negotiate "many more layers" of experience. This requires, as Walcott argues, the development of a confident African Canadianness that challenges the myth of Canadian tolerance by reinstituting black histories into Canada's national narrative (2000, 7). Clement Virgo's groundbreaking feature film, *Rude* (Canada, 1995), addresses this challenge by exploring the lives of three African Canadians in crisis over the course of an Easter weekend. Taking on issues such as homophobia, abortion, and drug dealing, the film creates a transnational diasporic space that underscores the multiplicity of African Canadian identities.

In a very real sense, the goal of this book is not to arrive at a definitive concept of the black diaspora or even to arrive at a resolution for the ongoing tension between maps and histories that differing concepts of black diaspora generate. Instead, the films, theories, and concepts explored here are intended to provoke debate and to bring to the table a variety of challenges to existing modes of Western thought and history. In many ways, this is the true strength of engagement with the black diaspora, because the very diversity of ideas serves to unseat and illuminate the ways in which racism and oppression are internalized in society. Finally, the black diasporic subject, forged in intersecting flows of histories, inscribes race as a salient element of transnational discourse in a way that expands how we conceive the interrelationship of history, power, and politics.

ONE

Africa and the Middle Passage
Recoupment of Origin in *Sankofa*

One of the most powerful metaphors of the black diaspora is that of the Middle Passage, a phrase coined to describe "the portage from Africa to the New World" on slave ships that signified the enslavement of Africans in the Americas (Wolff 1996, 24). As a milestone in black consciousness, the multiple histories of slavery have a powerful grip on both black and Western cultures, marking a schism based on race that still exists in contemporary times. The Middle Passage itself is emblematic of profound alienation because slaves, stripped of human status and valued in monetary terms as livestock, were managed with the sole purpose of ensuring maximum profitability to the white slave traders and the investors in their cargoes or trading companies (24). The journey thus serves to mark the transition between the Africans as human subjects and their transformation into commodity. Imported from the mid-fifteenth to the end of the nineteenth century in order to sustain labor-intensive plantation systems stretching across South America, the Caribbean, and North America, these African slaves laid the foundation for many contemporary black communities and movements that shaped the world politically, culturally, and economically (Thompson 1987, 1). Thus, the role played by the Middle Passage and slavery in delineating black experience is crucial to understanding black diasporic identity strategies.

Slavery and its legacies are highly contested, due in part to the unevenness of the historical record and the prevalence of historical imperatives that advanced Eurocentric concerns. As a focus of debate, the latter is of critical importance to black diasporic discourses as the need to reconfigure such imperatives is foundational to reclaiming a past that rendered black peoples as objects rather than subjects of the very histories they profoundly shaped. Paul Gilroy argues that in order to redress the one-sided Eurocentric view of modernity, it is vital to reconfigure this history from the perspective of the slaves. Gilroy views this move as not simply intended to reveal how plantations were built on the uneven power dynamics of economic models fundamentally reliant on oppression but, rather, to challenge the monolithic, universalist structure of that history which denies polyphonic slave cultures the right to voice their own histories (1993a, 55). Given this context, this chapter, in concert with others that follow, begins an exploration of several theoretical, historical, and filmic constructs of slavery offering a variety of strategies that decenter Western histories and precepts. Unlike subsequent chapters, which explore specific maps and histories of slavery, this chapter focuses on a broader context of slavery as a global and black diasporic phenomenon.

Slavery was a key component of what has been sometimes referred to as the Triangle Trade, composed of the movement of goods to Africa, slaves to the New World, and goods from the New World to Europe. From the 1440s to 1500, the primary destination for African slaves was Europe (Klein 1978, 4). Although the New World attracted many European settlers, however, they did not immigrate in large enough numbers to support the labor needs of mining or plantation agriculture (3). By 1650, with local aboriginal slave populations decimated by epidemics of European diseases, the high demand for plantation workers created by such labor-intensive crops as cotton, indigo, tobacco, rice, coffee, and—most desirable of all—sugar, resulted in the New World becoming the slave trade's lucrative focus (5, 9). Africans, with their adaptability and resistance to European diseases, became the laborers of choice.[1]

CHAPTER I

The role of Africa itself in the promulgation of slavery is a contentious one, primarily because slavery was an established facet of many African cultures. Slavery in Africa, however, differed greatly from the type of slavery that emerged in the New World. For example, Claire Robertson points out that slavery in an African context was malleable, ranging from chattel slavery to kin-based slavery, pawnship, and clientage (1996, 6–7).[2] Furthermore, African forms of slavery differed from the large-scale slavery in the Americas because even the most extreme forms of chattel slavery, usually referred to as "Islamic or market-based" slavery, offered the possibility of manumission to many of the enslaved (6). Thus, unlike New World slavery, in which slave status was passed on from parent to child, multigenerational slavery was uncommon in Africa (6).

Whatever the differences, the presence of this widespread tradition on the Atlantic coast of Africa was foundational to the advancement of European interests in obtaining cheap labor, especially as the infrastructure for slave trading was well established and the buying and selling of slaves played a legitimate role in accumulating wealth in many African cultures (Thornton 1992, 94, 95).[3] The convergence of Africa's willingness to supply slaves, along with the labor demand of the New World, created a powerful economic impetus that ultimately resulted in the forced displacement of ten million sub-Saharan Africans to the New World (Klein 1978, 243). Furthermore, the enormous range of Western European countries that engaged in the practice evidences slavery's role as an important driving factor in the New World economy. Although the major slave-trading nations were the Portuguese, Dutch, English, and French, minor participants also included Spain and the Scandinavian countries, among others (Patterson 1982, 160). Given the tremendous wealth created by this captive labor force, the stakes in maintaining the lowly status of African slaves was both an economic necessity as well as a function of established Western European racist attitudes already embedded in colonial imperialism.

As later chapters deal specifically with the effects of slavery in the Caribbean, the focus in this chapter is on delineating the broad strokes of slavery's rise in America. Here, the transition from chattel to pure commodity was an evolving process. For example, Winthrop Jordan notes that both black and white English slaves were sold to early settlers (1970, 107). This suggests that, at least initially, such servitude was not differentiated on the basis of race (Patterson 1982, 6–7). In both cases, masters possessed total control over every aspect of black or white slaves' lives, including administering corporal punishment by whip and selling them at will (7).

A new concept, however, very swiftly emerged: the term *Negro* set African slaves apart from their European counterparts on the basis of race, as evidenced by the earliest Virginia census that uses the word to distinguish black peoples from white (Jordan 1970, 107). In addition, the fact that *Negro* individuals were often recorded without benefit of a personal name signals a fundamental change in the status of African slaves and the commencement of the process of total deprivation of human rights (107). Uprooted from their place of origin, desocialized and depersonalized through a process of social negation by being separated as a distinct class of slave, African slaves made the final passage from human to commodity with the institution of what Orlando Patterson has termed *natal alienation,* or the "loss of ties of birth in both ascending and descending generations" (Patterson 1982, 38, 7). By 1640, records reveal that there had been a shift in the conception of black slavery with the emergence of an increasing tendency toward lifetime servitude and, along with it, a trend toward black children inheriting the slave status of their parents (Jordan 1970, 107). The institution of such hereditary lifetime service meant that slaves' ties to their communities and kinship were severed and that they no longer had power of any kind to pass on to their children. In effect, a master was able to claim ownership of slave children by asserting that the meager support provided to sustain the children of slaves actually amounted to the accumulation of a debt, making the children the master's property in payment (Patterson 1982, 9). Thus, slaves all over the New World became indistinguishable from other livestock commodities: not only could adult relationships be disrupted by sale, the fact that families were routinely split up as children entered the market meant that lineage and kinship ties were extremely difficult to maintain or even trace. This was a key factor in destabilizing cultural and social ties, resulting in a final and absolute severance from stable African identities located in specific maps and locales.

CHAPTER I

Another indicator of the racist basis for the nonperson status of black slaves is evident in "early distress concerning sexual union between the races" (Jordan 1970, 110). By the 1660s, as slavery was increasingly recognized as a statutory institution, colonial assemblies began constructing laws that forbade sexual congress between blacks and whites. For example, Virginia prohibited interracial relationships as early as 1691, describing the children issuing from such miscegenation as "abominable" (110–11). In addition, Virginia's decision to deny African slaves the right to bear arms, a privilege accorded to whites, further entrenched their inferior status (109). Clearly, such laws demonstrate a hierarchy of racial superiority that ranks whiteness above blackness: the argument was even rationalized on the basis of religion with the reasoning that the so-called heathen and uncivilized nature of the slaves' religious beliefs and cultural traditions made them unworthy of residing in the same community as civilized European Christians (Patterson 1982, 7). Yet it is extremely difficult to disconnect such prejudice from the desire of the white population to retain the wealth created by this degradation. Hence, slavery evolved along a continuum that saw increasingly restrictive and dehumanizing policies and racist rhetoric rise as the importance of African slaves as a labor force emerged. As C. L. R. James notes, masters strongly resisted any attempts to educate slaves, contending that this would only sow discontent among slave ranks by raising false expectations and making them less proficient at carrying out their agricultural duties (1977a, 245). This created a double barrier for African slaves: cut off from their own cultures by the denial of their birthrights, they were also barred from participating as citizens and equals in their New World context.

The institution of slavery also frequently used strategies that divided the slave communities into a hierarchical structure, reducing, in part, the likelihood of slave revolts. For example, overseers and domestic and skilled craft workers were often provided far better living conditions than fieldworkers, who were "treated as the capital stock of the plantation, on par with the animals, and maintained at bare subsistence level" (Bush 1996, 196). Ironically, this distinction supported the rise of slave cultures that maintained diverse elements of what Barbara Bush has described as "Africanisms," creating rich oral and other cultural practices that preserved links to cultures of origin (196). In contrast, domestic and skilled slave laborers were more likely to become acculturated to white religious and cultural values (196). In particular, slaves of mixed race were generally preferred for such positions, as their familiarity with plantation procedures and white culture made them "easier to train than African outsiders" (Geggus 1996, 263). These strategies splintered slave communities by creating competing factions within them dedicated to both ending and perpetuating the status quo.

Despite all these factors, African slaves brought to the New World succeeded in reconstituting their identities and cultures within a new context. James notes that, in the face of a contradictory situation in which Africans of many cultures were thrown together to survive, there "was no model to follow, only one to build" (1977a, 244). These strategies arose on slave ships and plantations as different African ethnic groups, united by a desperate drive to survive, created bridges across cultural gaps, thus encouraging resistance and sharing, which in turn gave rise to a new and distinctive amalgam of identity (Stuckey 1987, 3). In a very real sense, the slaves moved beyond the divisions of locale and language to an expression of identity that is representative of Africa as a continental concept (3). In this process, orality and memory became driving forces: as families used oral tales as a means of educating and entertaining their children and themselves, the stories became the property of the entire community, regardless of specific ethnic derivation (10). Such stories not only preserved links with African origin, they also became the basis for maintaining affirmative connections to communities and families, bridging the disruption caused by being sold. Hence, African cultural patterns were not only maintained but also transformed into a distinctive evocation of African diasporic consciousness.

Although it is not the sole defining sociohistorical factor of the black diaspora, the North Atlantic slave trade has provided a powerful impetus for shaping black identities outside of Africa. In particular, the circumstances of slavery that undermined and demeaned direct links to African origin and cultural specificity have led to the need to redefine and/or recoup this origin. As this relationship may be viewed many different ways within many different sociopolitical realities, it is often highly contested in theoretical debates about the nature of the diaspora itself. It is therefore most useful to think of these differing articulations not as competing definitions but as responses to myriad flows of maps, histories, and experiences within the black diaspora.

The historical fact of slavery, combined with colonization, has imposed what black diasporic thinker Molefi Kete Asante describes as the "collective subjectivity of European culture" that presumes to be "the measure by which the world marches" (1987, 3). As Tunde Adeleke argues, the "distinguishing character of Eurocentrism is its glamorization of its own historical heritage and experiences," thus reinforcing "cultural manipulation and domination" (1998, 505). From this perspective, black diasporic culture, rooted in the rhizomes of African origin, often faces the imposition of European cultural criteria that are not necessarily valid or of critical import within an African construct. The implications of this are both explicit and insidious in nature. For example, when Robert "King" Carter, a wealthy Virginia planter, purchased African slaves in 1727, he chose to assign them European names, an act of possession that signified their passage from subjects of African culture to objects of European dominance (Berlin 1999, 19). Many of the names reflected common English diminutives that invoked children's names or focused on physical attributes, exemplifying the African slaves' inferior status and reinforcing Carter's European ancestry by the simple fact he had the power to rename them in any way he chose (19). Some might argue this history is not reflected in present-day society, but such valuations are not merely contained within a discrete historical event: instead, the event acts as an epicenter, creating ripples that spread out over centuries and affect all institutions and levels of culture. Hence, the question of who has the right to evaluate black culture and history and by what criteria has its origins in a flawed presumption of Eurocentric mastery over "inferior" African cultures.

One of the ways in which this need is addressed is to place Africa at the center of black diasporic identity, in order to redress the devaluation of blackness that occurred under slavery. Such strategies foreground African cultural imperatives over Eurocentric valuations, advancing the argument that African diasporic slaves are fundamentally African in terms of social construction and should return to values drawn from these cultures rather than assimilating Eurocentric ideals. For example, "Back to Africa" movements have been active in the black diaspora from very early on. In the case of the United States, the prom-

Recoupment of Origin in *Sankofa*

inent black leader Martin R. Delany advocated a literal return to Africa in the years leading up to the American Civil War (Katz 1968, v). For Delany and others such as James Forten and Bishop Henry M. Turner, black separatism was a response to lives spent mired in systemic racism in which it seemed that there was no other solution to oppression and slavery's enduring legacy than to leave America entirely (v). A similar position was advocated by Jamaican-born Marcus Garvey, who immigrated to the United States in 1916 (vii). Shaped by the oppression of British colonialism in Jamaica, Garvey was highly critical of the "triple caste system" resulting from slavery that placed the white race first, light-skinned mixed-race blacks second, and dark-skinned blacks at the bottom of the social ladder (viii). Describing the plight of black Americans as composed of "lynching, peonage and dis-franchisement," Garvey called for the peoples from the Caribbean, America, and Africa to reclaim Africa from the degradation of colonial subjugation and establish a truly African nation that would have the power to protect and advance the interests of all dispersed Africans globally (Garvey 1968, 52). This could only be achieved by returning to Africa, as Garvey fervently believed that if blacks remained in the Western hemisphere, they would be doomed to the constant racism inherent in being a minority within a hostile majority (53). Confrontational and often religious in its fervor, the power of Garvey's work lies in his passionate belief in the value of an African heritage that is equal or superior to that of Western civilization. For example, Garvey takes the position that while Europe was in its uncivilized infancy, Africa had already generated complex and learned African societies that surpassed anything Europe would ever produce (77). By evoking such images, Garvey's work demonstrates the desire found in many "Back to Africa" movements to reclaim history, culture, and a common community as a means of restoring the losses inflicted by slavery and its enduring legacy.

Perhaps one of the most powerful and contentious discourses to arise out of the drive for such redress is that of Afrocentrism.[4] Proposed by Asante, who is still considered the movement's leading writer and theorist, Afrocentrism has had a profound and lasting impact on discussions of race within American and diasporic society (Howe 1999, 231).[5] Asante was born in Georgia in 1942 and lived through some of the most violent and intensely racially segregated conditions in recent history (230). As Stephen Howe suggests, these experiences were foundational in the formulation of Afrocentrism and led to Asante's perception of race relations in America as permanently rifted along racial lines. A leading scholar and publisher, Asante's role as a groundbreaking proponent of "Afrocentric school curricula throughout the USA" has made his work influential in shaping the politics of African American society, as well as contributing to diasporic discourse throughout the world (231).

Afrocentrism is defined as "placing African ideals at the center of any analysis that involves African culture and behavior" (Asante 1987, 6). Like Garvey, Asante proposes a "return to Africa" but in contrast to the literal return proposed by the former, Asante champions a psychological one that involves embracing African values and culture as a central driving force in black identity. From Asante's perspective, Afrocentrism is confrontational in its commitment to championing African culture and origin and restoring its proper status as a means of opposing the negation of African culture perpetuated by the West (170). Inspired by the slave narrative, Afrocentrism's primary goal is to create a new style of rhetoric that moves away from the oppressive, monolithic structures of Western histories that place primacy on singular narratives. Instead, Afrocentrism refuses the linear constructs of thought and history so prized by Eurocentric theory in favor of "a more circular system of thought" (171). Hence, Asante challenges the Eurocentric "bias of categorization" that "divides people into teachers and those taught, sinners and saved, black and white, superior and inferior, weak and strong" (184). Alternatively, he proposes aligning Afrocentrist approaches by dismantling the reliance on such binarisms and replacing them with holistic precepts drawn from traditional African cultures. Afrocentrism thus takes on three key elements that reflect a uniquely African worldsense, including "(1) human relations, (2) humans' relationship to the supernatural, and (3) humans' relationships to their own being" (168). From Asante's perspective, these elements define and place African subjectivity at the center of Afrocentric discourse, thus undermining, or more accurately negating, the dominance of Eurocentric criteria (168). Ultimately, Asante promulgates the rise of new social, political, and cultural paradigms that eliminate artificial reliance on standards determined outside of African experience.

Recoupment of Origin in *Sankofa*

One of the central elements in Asante's position is his concept of community and spirituality. For him, an Afrocentric sensibility recognizes the interrelationships among communities, technologies, environments, and ancestral worlds bound together through memory and orality (1987, 184, 186). Describing African Americans as "profoundly verbal," Asante contends that orality is a fundamental aspect of African, and hence Afrocentrist, expression (187). The innate need to communicate by words places a strong emphasis on community and is expressed in African American society by the "transpersonal" experience evident in great orators, including Martin Luther King Jr., among others (188). Community, therefore, is more than a sum of individuals: it is an expression of shared goals that can only be achieved when an individual strives in tandem with the community to achieve power (188). This signals a profound refusal of Eurocentrism's lionization of the individual in favor of a model that foregrounds collective interest.

Although intended to "bring blacks closer to Africa as they develop in knowledge of Africa," Afrocentrism's project of "re-education and re-socialization" in order to promote a "state of mental decolonization" by radically revising and reinterpreting African and black history has proven highly contentious (Adeleke 1998, 507, 509). In particular, Asante's emphasis on a collective African heritage that moved out from ancient Egypt, or Kemet, to become a universal foundation for all African cultures has been challenged on the grounds that it presumes the diverse cultures of Africa share a single monolithic worldview (Howe 1999, 231, 232). Such a position fails to accord cultural autonomy to Africa's many distinct cultures by rendering them subordinate to a single controlling source. It further suggests an estrangement between Africa as imagined by Afrocentrism and the contemporary realities faced by the continent (13). What arises is a state described by Howe as an imaginary Africa "without a real human history," based on "mythographies" of a heroic past that negates the often grim realities and ethnic divisions negotiated by contemporary African societies (13). This, Howe suggests, serves to estrange Africa from both its history and present struggles (13). From this perspective, it would seem that reinvention and reclamation supersede reality and history with Africa becoming a symbol, an ideal or utopic imaginary from which a new type of mythology arises.

CHAPTER I

In pursuit of an ideal Africa, Afrocentrism has also been charged with mirroring the very Eurocentric ideologies it seeks to dismantle (Appiah 1997, 730, 729). Appiah argues strongly that the Afrocentrist claim on Egypt reflects a shared bias with Europe because such claims minimize the contributions of ancient African cultures that do not possess writing (730). There is a certain irony to the emphasis on Egyptian literature and architecture in Afrocentrism, especially given the weight Asante accords to orality as a defining feature of African cultures. For Appiah, the desire to espouse a central universalizing core for African cultures corresponds to an earlier focus on a similar aspiration in Western cultures, and it is a strategy that makes Afrocentrism vulnerable to charges of cultural chauvinism (731). Hence, in centering on the "unicentricity, or one-centeredness" of African cultures, Afrocentrism assumes the same type of center-periphery discourse as Eurocentrism (Boyce Davies 1999). Considering this, it is reasonable to debate whether Afrocentrism has truly moved beyond Eurocentrism or simply replicated its constructs within an African context.

Selected for its strong reliance on oral tradition and Afrocentric symbolism, the film *Sankofa*, directed by Haile Gerima, is representative of a black diasporic imaginary that defines itself against a history of slavery and dislocation by a return to African roots. As the Akan word *sankofa* suggests, the characters in this film must "return to the past in order to go forward," demonstrating a rhetorical connection between concepts of past and present time that makes the film an ideal subject for probing the concept of Afrocentricity (Grayson 1998, 212n2). In addition, *Sankofa*'s representation of the Middle Passage offers an explicit articulation of the return-to-Africa trope that is influenced by Gerima's own transnational experience of Africanness. The film's focus on the primacy of Africa in disaporic experience has generated considerable debate, particularly in regard to questions of representation. Taken together, these elements both challenge and problematize slavery as a process of cultural destruction and reemergence.

Gerima is considered a major figure among African independent filmmakers working in the black diaspora. Born and raised in Ethiopia, Gerima came to America in 1967 to attend the Goodman School of Drama in Chicago with the intention of pursuing a career in theater.

Recoupment of Origin in *Sankofa*

Sankofa (Courtesy of Mypheduh Films, Washington, DC)

Later transferring to the theater department at the University of California, Los Angeles, Gerima was exposed to African and Latin American films that awakened his interest in the medium. By the completion of his education in 1976, Gerima was an accomplished filmmaker whose fiction feature *Mirt Sost Shi Amit/Harvest 3000 Years* (1976) won the Oscar Micheaux Award for Best Feature Film, Grand Prize at the Locarno International Film Festival, and the Georges Sadoul Prize at Cannes, among others. In addition to *Sankofa* (1993), his feature film works include *Adwa: An African Victory* (1999), *Ashes and Embers* (1982), and *Bush Mama* (1976).

As a filmmaker, Gerima is dedicated to innovative narrative and aesthetic approaches to his subjects, focusing on creative story structures that enable him to "tell the trillion untold stories of [his] people" in a counternarrative style that challenges mainstream cinematic forms (Gerima and Woolford 1994, 90). *Sankofa* thus offers a strong testament to Gerima's ability to infuse cinematic language with African oral tradition in order to recenter history and memory as a positive means of cultural expression.

CHAPTER I

Sankofa focuses on the personal journey of Mona, a young African American woman, who comes to the fortress of Elmina, a major departure point in the slave trade, in order to model for a fashion shoot.[6] There she is confronted by Sankofa, a mysterious African man who magically propels her on a journey back in time where she becomes Shola, a house slave on an Antebellum plantation. Through Shola's evolution from complicit victim to rebel, Mona comes to have a deeper understanding of her own history and innate African identity, which she embraces on her return to the present day. The film possesses a circular narrative that blends past and present in a conception of convergent time. As such, the film's structure eschews Eurocentric linear conventions of history and storytelling in favor of a narrative system that places Africa at the center of black experience. Described as "a new Afrocentric metanarrative," *Sankofa*'s treatment of slavery and valorization of the return-to-Africa myth as a means of reconnecting black cultures to a valued past makes it well positioned for an Afrocentrist analysis (Kandé 1998). In addition, the film's reliance on African-centered discourse has also made it controversial, and criticism of the film has focused on the way in which its perceived shortcomings mirror the limitations of Afrocentrism as a theoretical construct.[7] Given Gerima's stated intention of creating debate around the issues of slavery and the state of contemporary black experiences of oppression, however, the presence of such criticism suggests that the film was successful in achieving its goals (Gerima and Woolford 1994, 101).

In order to initiate this debate, the film establishes African origin as a central defining tenet of black diasporic experience early in the film. Beginning with a series of close-ups of an African carving depicting a woman and child, the images suggest an Afrocentrist context by founding the psychological and historical order of the film "on the concrete reality of African experience in the vortex of Western thinking" (Asante 1993, 46). As an art object in a neutral space, the carving evokes the Western preoccupation of collecting history without context. Yet, as the camera moves in a circular pan, it encourages the spectator to savor the loving relationship exhibited by the child leaning against the woman. This domestic familial image serves to humanize African experience and, given the later events of the film, symbolizes loss incurred with the destruction of family units and ties that are characteristic of

Recoupment of Origin in *Sankofa*

slavery. The sequence thus foregrounds "Africans as subjects rather than objects" by suggesting that the woman and child depicted in the carving maintain an "authentic relationship to the centrality" of their Africanness that cannot be stripped away by force of foreign history (46).

Later in the same sequence, a slow tilt up is used to explore a beautiful staff, revealing a carved vulture perched on its apex. As Sandra M. Grayson notes, the staff's vulture is a *sankofa*, a term and symbol that means "Se wo were fi na wosankofa a yenkyi," or "Return to the past in order to go forward" (1998, 213). Thus, the sankofa becomes a symbolic nexus, connecting past with present and black experience with past African contexts. As a sculpture of a slave replaces the sankofa, these multiple connections are emphasized by the soundscape of driving drumbeats and an African chant, coupled with voice-over narration that commands the spirits of long-dead African slaves to rise up and tell their story. Thus, the film suggests that victims of slavery are linked to an idealized African origin by virtue of an almost supernatural psychic bond that Eurocentric history cannot sunder or render inconsequential. By doing so, the film's ideological discourse is aligned with an Afrocentrist identity paradigm that presupposes retention of the "essential aspects" of Africanness in all black diasporic peoples (Adeleke 1998, 525). Furthermore, by positing such a mythical impulse, the film lays the groundwork for a specific version of a return-to-Africa archetype in which the restoration of an authentic black self is dependent on surrendering to the primacy of African origin.

This project is set in motion early in the film by its focus on the power of the dead to intervene in the course of contemporary lives. The drumming and chanting established in the opening become the points of contact between the past and present. In a montage of brief superimposed images, the ending of the film is foreshadowed by portraying characters that are yet to be revealed as they watch a ritual performed by a sacred drummer. Exhorted through voice-over narration that calls on the ancestors to rise up and "possess your bird of passage," the sacred drummer's performance is intercut with close-up images of a vulture, which, as a messenger of the ancestors, will accept the sacrifice of the individual who will be transported to the past. As the drumming progresses, Mona, the central character of the contemporary time line, is introduced as she participates in a fashion photo shoot on a beach near the fortress of Elmina. Wearing a revealing bathing suit, Mona's physical beauty is objectified in a progression of high-angle medium and close-up shots as she lies supine on the sand and responds to the white photographer's praise and calls for "more sex." The visual strategy is further emphasized by the high-angle medium reverse shot focused on the photographer as he controls her movements and the emotional tenor of her performance. By foregrounding a power relationship in which Mona is manipulated by white desire, the imagery posits Mona's physicality as a commodity for white consumption, thus subtly invoking a contemporary parallel with slavery.

Perhaps more importantly, Mona's acceptance of the photographer's right to commodify her physical body suggests what Asante has described as "a loss of terms" in which peoples of the black diaspora internalize "the other's attitudes, models, disciplines, and culture," thus displacing the validity of their own Africanness (1993, 48). As Asante argues, this "massive loss" of identity results in a profound alienation from history, psychological identity, and cultural tradition, which, in turn, perpetuates slavery's legacy in contemporary contexts (48). Mona, whose unquestioning acceptance of this dynamic indicates complicity with these forces, must therefore uncover, from an Afrocentrist perspective, a "world voice" within herself that reinstates "the rhythms" and "anthems" of truly African terms of identity (48).

The process of redefining Mona's terms of identity begins with the arrival of Sankofa, the self-proclaimed guardian of Elmina's sacred dead. First revealed in a medium shot by a slow tilt up from the sand that places him in context with the distant fortress behind him, Sankofa is an imposing elder dressed in white, carrying a wooden staff topped by a carved vulture. He silently communicates his disapproval of Mona's display by forcibly planting the staff in the sand in a gesture of disgust. Suddenly sensing his presence, Mona screams and leaps to her feet, taking refuge behind the photographer. Portrayed in an exchange of close-ups, Sankofa stares intently at Mona as she cowers behind the photographer, alternating between fear and embarrassed laughter. By placing the white photographer in the foreground, the film draws attention to the irony of Mona's denial of her African self by hiding behind a barrier of assimilation to white cultural ideals.

Recoupment of Origin in *Sankofa*

This proposition is further advanced in a later scene where Mona, now wearing traditional African dress, continues to pose for the photographer on one of Elmina's cannon parapets while a nearby tour guide lectures tourists on the area's history in the slave trade. Walking toward her, Sankofa directly confronts Mona with fierce intensity, causing her to back away. He orders her to return to her source, thus identifying her as an appropriate vessel for the sacrifice. He then turns to confront the photographer and the tourists, pounding his staff into the ground and demanding to know what they want from this sacred ground symbolic of African suffering. The question is significant: just as Mona is selling herself for white pleasure, so too are the tourists prostituting the history of the slave trade by engaging in it as an afternoon's entertainment. The culmination of the scene takes place in a long-take medium shot that begins with Mona on the right and Sankofa in the center of the frame. The camera pans with him as he turns away from Mona, confronting the camera in direct address, condemning the genocide of African slaves sent to America, Jamaica, and Trinidad. With this statement, the Afrocentric discourse of the film is bared, identifying the importance of African dispersal as the salient feature of slavery and uniting differing historical strands in the common, overarching experience of being forcibly torn from African origin.

Mona's return to the past begins as she assumes the role of a tourist, descending alone into the depths of Elmina to visit the dungeons that once held slaves awaiting transport to the new world. Her descent into the tunnels is portrayed by using a long take that begins in a medium long shot of Mona against a stone wall as she tentatively moves deeper into the recesses of the dungeon. The framing progressively tightens into a close-up, creating a sense of progressive entrapment as Mona is wedged visually against the wall. The shot is accompanied by the tour guide's off-screen lecture in which he describes the often-year-long confinement of the slaves in the dungeon while being held for transport. His comment that their despairing sounds and cries are still remembered up and down the coastline reinforces the notion of the fortress as a sacred conduit for the meeting of past and present.

The tourists disappear down a passageway, leaving Mona alone near the entrance to a slave pen. Her obvious apprehension indicates that the spirits pervading the fortress influence her psychologically, de-

CHAPTER I

spite her contemporary Western experience that should discount such supernatural forces as nonexistent. Her reaction supports an Afrocentric view that certain African traits are psychically encoded and cannot be eradicated by either distance in time and geography or exposure to Western histories. The power of this psychological link is demonstrated when the passageway goes dark and Mona, terrified but drawn against her will toward a flash of firelight, glances into the entrance of the slave pen. She sees a group of slaves: men, women, and children, each wearing heavy metal collars and shackles. Attempting to flee the apparitions by running through the labyrinth of passageways, she is confronted at each turn by another group of slaves. In general, these are medium to medium-long shots of long duration supported by pans that move across groups of slaves creating a sense of social space in which ethnic differentiation is obliterated by shared oppression: similarly shackled and reduced to rags, some of the slaves engage the spectator in direct address, forcing her to face the scope, context, and consequences of such massive cultural disjunction and oppression. The sequence of shots reinforces that, once slaves are captured and collared, the ethnic distinctions between them are rendered immaterial, and they are forced to embrace a new incarnation, one based on a generic concept of Africanness.

Mona experiences this dehumanizing process firsthand as she pounds on a door calling for help and it opens abruptly onto an exterior courtyard filled with white slave traders in nineteenth-century dress. They seize Mona and pull her back into the fortress while she screams that they are making a mistake because she is American, not African. Dragged down the passageway against her will, the slavers refuse to address her, their faces often obscured by camera angle or framing. This visual strategy emphasizes the inhumanity of the situation by making them part of a faceless, monolithic, and oppressive authority. In addition, her desperate struggle is punctuated with tightly framed close-ups of slaves who act as a silent restatement of her degradation, foregrounding slavery, not as an abstract historical event, but as a human tragedy that affected (and continues to affect) an entire race of people. Hence, Mona's "American" identity is subsumed by her African racial heritage, much in the same way that the ethnic differences between

Recoupment of Origin in *Sankofa*

Sankofa (Courtesy of Mypheduh Films, Washington, DC)

Africans were rendered immaterial when they were commodified in service of Eurocentric modernity.

This is certainly not an uncontested position. *Sankofa* has been criticized for its universalized portrayal of African cultures, which fails to distinguish between the different histories of those societies. This seemingly replicates the essentialism found in Eurocentric accounts of slavery despite the film's avowed intention to counteract such portrayals (Kandé 1998). In addition, the film's portrayal of a monolithic African identity also appears to reduce all African experience to a single mythical African culture. As Sylvie Kandé points out, such an Afrocentrist view "draws us, with its Hegelian grip, away from the West or from sites of the Diaspora and back towards Africa, away from the present and back to the past, away from liberalism and back to gerontocracy" (1998). Kandé's position certainly has merit: the right to judge the correctness of Mona's behavior is given to Sankofa, who imposes what may be described as an African standard of comportment on a woman raised in a more permissive context. Furthermore, Mona's character is so completely passive that she does not speak up in her own defense against Sankofa's disparagement of her behavior, nor does she utter a full sentence on her own behalf until she denies her Africanness in favor of her American citizenship.

Although these examples certainly support a discourse that privileges a male prerogative, there are aspects in addition to gender that are worth considering. First, *Sankofa* is a counternarrative, offering an idealized interpretation of both history and African realities intended to provoke debate on the nature and importance of African origin in contemporary diasporic identities. As such, the "composite African" foregrounded by the film is not intended to inscribe a monolithic, immutable African culture; rather, it seeks to evoke an Afrocentrist "unity that exists even with the specific cultures that exist in every African society" (Asante 1993, 106, 48). Ostensibly for Gerima, as well as Asante, "the African orientation to the cosmos" becomes the bridge that connects dispersed black peoples to natal identities despite all attempts to sever that connection (106). Second, both male and female characters share cultural authority in the film, certainly in terms of abilities to connect with and harness supernatural abilities, as further discussion in this chapter will substantiate. Hence, although Kandé's concerns are valid to a degree, the film's intended project and narrative structure are not focused on a singular presentation of gender. Ultimately, despite the inherent shortcomings involved in reversing the binarism of center/periphery discourse in favor of Africa, such Afrocentrist constructs have a role to play in subsuming Eurocentricity (Boyce Davies 1999).

As Mona is stripped and branded by the slavers, the last vestiges of her identity are removed and she is possessed by the spirit of Shola, a nineteenth-century house slave living on the fictional Lafayette plantation. The use of multiple time lines to create an environment where past and present coexist simultaneously not only is a reference to African cosmologies but also serves as a device to disrupt the primacy of linear histories. As Asante points out, the linearity of Eurocentric histories is not a coincidental arrangement as it facilitates the creation of a global discourse defending the right to colonize other cultures and territories (Asante 1993, 80). The role of categorization as a means of establishing the primacy of such a discourse is critical because hierarchical ranking of historical events facilitates and rationalizes dominance (79, 80). *Sankofa* challenges this hegemony by positing an alternative structure of time. Mona's journey from contemporary to past times, aided by mystical forces, decenters Eurocentric narratives of slavery by transforming her from an object/slave to a subject/human through an African cosmological viewpoint and an African sense of time. Furthermore, the strategy allows for the spectator to compare and contrast histories as they interact, providing an opportunity for active debate.

The connection between Shola's and Mona's psychological states is manifested during Shola's initial appearance. Shola is first introduced in a high-angle extreme close-up, and the tight claustrophobic framing of the shot indicates the entrapment of her situation, providing an ironic counterpoint to her voice-over narration as she asserts that being born a slave makes it easier to accept a slave's lot. The tension between Shola's visual depiction and her words suggests that she fails to appreciate the full implications of her unquestioning acceptance of her position in Western society. Her lack of self-awareness or, perhaps more accurately, her willful state of denial creates a parallel between Shola and Mona. Both are assimilated into societies that view their bodies as commodities to be exploited without their challenging that construct: although Shola is not in a position to aspire to American citizenship as a means of protecting herself, her passive acceptance of her position is also a refusal of African identity, as evidenced by her acceptance of the inevitable degradation of her race under slavery. Thus, like Mona's ordeal in the lower depths of Elmina, Shola must also undergo a process of education to reclaim a sense of her authentic identity and worth that transcends her enslavement.

The location of the Lafayette plantation and its exact historical context are ambiguous. As Kandé notes, "It is of some importance that nothing permits us to situate the [film's] plot in space or time," a stance she views as problematic because "geography and economics

CHAPTER I

in large measure governed the forms of resistance to slavery" (1998). Gerima's artistic intent, however, is to explore slavery as a worldwide phenomenon, a focus achieved in the film by an ahistorical setting that foregrounds slavery as a lived black experience (Gerima and Woolford 1994, 91). As James argues, although an African slave brought the language and practices of his historical culture with him, he faced a "contradictory situation" by being thrown in among others of different ethnic backgrounds in which new means of coping had to be established (1977a, 243–44). *Sankofa* offers a similar structure as Shola's fellow slaves come from a wide diversity of backgrounds: Shango, Shola's lover, is from the West Indies; Nunu is an Akan woman and slave leader whom Shola regards as a mother figure; Nunu's son, Joseph, is a mulatto; and Noble Ali is a head slave whose accent places him in the Antebellum South. Each of these characters represents a strand of slave experience, and by bringing them together in a single community, the film emphasizes that the effects of slavery cut across borders and nations. In effect, the composite slave identities created here parallel Asante's notion of composite African identities as the common struggles faced by the slaves demand a unity that supersedes nation (Asante 1993, 106). As a narrative construct, this tactic decenters Eurocentric strands of history and all their attendant biases in favor of a fictional history told from Shola's point of view as she recounts her own experiences and those of her fellow slaves.

As a house slave, Shola is estranged from the field slaves on the Lafayette plantation by virtue of her close relationship with whites. Like Mona, Shola's closeness to white society has resulted in a devaluation of her own African terms of reference. In addition, this association has also ingrained in her a certain set of values predicated on compliance and complicity with her own enslavement. This attitude, as Asante points out, is a direct result of a racist system designed to assure compliancy and servility by breaking down African values while simultaneously valorizing white culture. The result was a decentering of slave identity that forced slaves to accept the subordination of their cultures in order to survive (1993, 119). The film outlines the consequences of this process by exploring how Shola's isolation in the white milieu of the plantation house differentiates her from the field slaves who evidence a sense of pride in their Africanness, retained in part because they created a black culture defined by oppression and rebellion.

The contrast between Shola's status and that of the field slaves is evident in a scene where she wanders through the cane fields searching for Shango. Portrayed in a medium shot as she moves through the field slaves as they cut cane, Shola wears a sparkling white apron and clean Western housedress that contrasts with the soiled and ragged clothing worn by the others. She makes direct eye contact with a female field worker, and when the woman does not lower her eyes, Shola steps in close, staring at her in an act of intimidation. Such behavior suggests that Shola believes in her superiority over the field slaves, indicating a sense of hierarchy instilled by her white masters in order to undermine slave solidarity. Her isolation from the others is further established later in the scene as she gives Shango the food she has brought him. When Shango urges her to poison the Lafayettes' food, Shola refuses because she believes that killing is evil, no matter what her master has done to her. In addition, she refuses to kill the other house slaves who could not be warned to refuse the food, as they would reveal the plot to the Lafayettes. Shango dismisses this sentiment on the grounds that it is sometimes necessary to commit violence in order to attain freedom. Finally, when Shango argues that the nearer one gets to the white man, the more one is reduced to eating what is left, Shola points out he is among that number as the food he is eating comes from the Lafayettes' table. Shango spits the food out and throws the remainder away in a gesture of disgust. His refusal of the food, despite his obvious hunger, underscores the difference between his worldview and that of Shola's. For Shola, proximity to the Lafayettes and emotional ties with the other house slaves have broken down her ability to resist her oppression by breeding fear and a sense of helplessness in the face of an overwhelming authority that urged slaves "to be servile, and to contain anger, to control the bitterness they felt about enslavement" (Asante 1993, 119). In Shango's case, the violence and cruelty of his enslavement have created a deep-seated hatred of the same authority and those complicit with its power, compelling him to risk everything, including his own life, in order to resist it. These diverging views open a discursive space focusing on questions of complicity and resistance, framing Shola's eventual transformation from a passive to active participant in the course of her own future.

CHAPTER I

From *Sankofa*'s perspective, if slavery is an instrument of Eurocentric discourses of white racial superiority, then black resistance to these discourses is a marker of African resilience and heritage. The maintenance of black history in the face of an overwhelming and systemic oppressive authority is a testament to the power of oral tradition among slaves and the concept of time it both created and preserved. As Henry Louis Gates Jr. argues, "In antebellum America, it was the deprivation of time in the life of the slave that first signaled his or her status as a piece of property. Slavery's time was delineated by memory and memory alone" (1987, 100). As Gates suggests, such dependence creates a discontinuity in time because a slave's past did not extend beyond memory (101). Although this certainly contributed to the fundamental cultural dislocation suffered in slavery, memory was also preserved by African oral history in which stories of the past offer the opportunity to both preserve history and serve to educate others within a contemporary environment. Thus, far from being completely extinguished, cultural influences continued to be passed on through the transmission of memory encoded in oral storytelling. The film presents this persistence of African origin by positing *Sankofa* in part as an oral document: Mona experiences Shola's life through narrative recollections and direct interactions as her life events unfold, a relationship that places Shola in the role of griot as she weaves an oral retelling of her experiences.

In addition to Shola's role as griot,[8] oral tradition emerges as a major force in transmitting and sustaining African culture in the slave population. For example, in the scene that introduces the character of Nunu, a series of extreme long shots of the landscape is used, a method frequently repeated in the film to transition between plot episodes. These are coupled with Shola's voice-over narration as she describes Nunu as a woman of great strength, passion, and tenderness who, as an African, is still "living in her birthplace" in spirit. The use of narration against the backdrop of extreme long shots allows the spectator to focus primarily on Shola's words and her role in framing expositional information, thus foregrounding the oral form of the history she is relating and reliving. Later in the scene, a group of adult field slaves gather around a cooking pot, taking respite from their labors. Nunu rests against a tree, her eyes closed while a female field slave holds the group's rapt attention as she describes Nunu confronting the overseer by chanting in her "country talk." Describing Nunu's act as one of resistance, the field slave relates how her chant was echoed by the other slaves present at the time, who joined in without understanding the meaning of her Akan words. The field slave's words, "I don't know what got into him, whether it was God or the devil, but something sure enough got into him," and her description of his eyes rolling back into his head and his foaming mouth all suggest that his death was caused by a supernatural force emanating from Nunu. This is reinforced as the slave ends her story with the words, "Folks 'round here say it was her mother tongue. You know, where our people come from. Nunu is an Akan. She always talks about her peoples." It is significant that Nunu's power to kill is linked first to her "mother tongue" and later to her Akan heritage because it indicates that her act of resistance stems from her inherent sense of Africanness. Furthermore, the pride with which the field slave relates the incident emphasizes the vital importance of maintaining African identity as an affirmation of self-worth. By linking resistance directly to Afrocentric roots, *Sankofa* takes the position that only by valorizing such connections can contemporary black diasporic peoples restore what was initially disrupted by slavery and later further eroded by assimilation of Eurocentric values.

Shola's own reaction to the story further supports Gerima's intention. Hidden in underbrush, Shola takes in the oral history from the perimeter. This visual arrangement underscores ideological separation from the field slaves. Such status, however, comes with a very high cost: as the field slave nears the climax of her story, brief scenes of Shola being brutally raped by Lafayette are inserted. An indicator of her intense shame, the scenes present Shola as helpless in her own degradation, exposing as illusory any "status" gained as a house slave. Shola's rape is, in Gerima's view, an indication that "white men's relationship to black women was like an outright treatment of an animal," and hence the visual depiction of the rape focuses on Shola's suffering (Gerima and Woolford 1994, 95). She is first portrayed in a medium long shot as Lafayette drags her across a courtyard, and then in a tight close-up as she is raped from behind. By permitting only brief glimpses of his face, Lafayette is thus dehumanized as an aggressor, which places emphasis on the human costs of such brutality to Shola. In addition, this visual strategy allows Lafayette to symbolize systemic cruelty by re-

CHAPTER 1

fusing any rationalization of his act. As a result, Shola's powerlessness is contextualized within her perception of a master that has ultimate supremacy over her life and death. This contrasts with Nunu's act of resistance against the overseer, an equally powerful force. As the field slave's story ends, Shola is portrayed in a close-up, wracked with the memory of her rape and praying in voice-over narration for just a little of Nunu's power as a means to end her own degradation. Her admiration of Nunu's ability to kill an overseer by the supernatural force of her African heritage represents a type of generational gap. Such power is denied Shola because she is no longer directly connected to her own African roots, the memories of which have been obliterated by her birth into slavery. Nunu, as a first-generation slave, actively persists in maintaining her cultural connections. The narration at the end of the scene stresses the difference between the two women when Shola reveals that she grew up with Nunu's son, Joe, in the big house, and that they were baptized together on the same day. Such a revelation underscores Shola's assimilation of Eurocentric values and further indicates her suppression of, and estrangement from, her African self. Yet, Shola is instinctively attracted to Nunu's Africanness, as attested to by her admiration of Nunu's power, thus creating a tension between her desire to conform to her assimilated identity and her need to rekindle her African values. This suggests that she cannot stake out a space between these two binary opposites but, instead, must embrace her Africanness in order to resist her enslavement.

The interconnection of Mona, Shola, and Nunu places women at the center of *Sankofa*. Grayson argues that the focus on women as subjects and as active agents of change makes them "warriors in the fight against oppression," a narrative choice that links them with Asante cosmology and "disrupts the Eurocentric theory" that presumes women are passive (1998, 226).[9] Given that Mona and Shola are connected through magical transformation, Nunu emerges as a critical bearer of African culture as her example and teachings contribute to both women's realignment of their identities. As a leader and a warrior in action and in spirit, Nunu epitomizes "the women who founded the Asante clans, *ohemmaa*, and female chiefs, establishing a network among black women in the past, present, and future" thus underscoring their "essential place in world history" (227). Furthermore, Nunu's active role and decisive nature stand out in contrast to Mona's and Shola's passive demeanors: by taking risks and acting courageously in the best interests of the slave community, Nunu assumes a social stance that favors community over individual advancement. Providing a counterpoint to Shola's isolation and detachment from her community as a house slave, Nunu's Africanness is crucial to fostering and sustaining a sense of worth among the field slaves. Hence, Nunu is equal in power to Sankofa, the guardian of Elmina, as her supernatural power and leadership places Africa at the center of resistance, creating a counternarrative challenging Eurocentric oppression and exploitation.

An example of this role is evident during the scene in which several slaves are publicly whipped for trying to escape. Among these is Kutu, a pregnant woman who desired a life for her child free from slavery. Despite the advanced stage of her pregnancy, Kutu is lashed to a whipping post, in order to—as the white overseer exhorts the black headmen—draw some "nigger blood" for fun. Intended to demonstrate the barbarity of slavery, Kutu's whipping becomes a nexus for several strands of discourse on complicity and resistance. For example, Shango runs into the cane fields to find a machete in order to end the brutality. Desperate to stop him, Shola leaps on his back, screaming that the whipping is none of his business. Although motivated by love, Shola's attempt to stop Shango is a selfish act predicated on the narrow basis of her own personal interest. In contrast, Nunu defies her son, Joseph, as he tries to prevent her from approaching the hilltop on which the slaves are being punished. When he menaces her with the whip he carries, Nunu dares him to strike her. Pulled back from the confrontation by another field slave, she screams in Akan, "You are useless, should I have a walking stick longer than me?" The epithet underscores Joseph's complicity with the white slavers he serves and the deep shame Nunu feels at her son's impotence as he abandons his African sense of community through his active participation in Kutu's torture. As the whipping continues, Nunu, deeply moved by a horror she cannot alter, tells the field slaves that control of their physical bodies "is the only chain they have on us," and that if it were not for "this flesh," they would be free to fly back to Africa. This statement not only links true freedom with a return to Africa, it also emphasizes that the slaves must be prepared to risk death in order to achieve freedom, a foreshadowing of the slave rebellion to come.

In contrast to Shola's desire to protect her lover from harm, Nunu's attempts to intercede on Kutu's behalf are motivated by community solidarity, a concern that places her on equal ground with Shango. Breaking free from Shola, Shango races up the hill and attacks the white overseer who has taken over Kutu's whipping. As he is beaten and dragged away by the whites and head slaves, Nunu and another field slave rush up to release Kutu, who is lifeless. Discovering that Kutu is dead, Nunu picks up Shango's abandoned machete, raises it above her head, and calls out in Akan to the gods that it is time to go to the aid of a mother and child. As she cries out, "Warriors stand firmly behind me," the field slaves, who have passively witnessed the proceedings, are suddenly galvanized into action: they race up the hill and form a protective ring around her as she cuts the ropes from Kutu and lays her body on the ground. This act of solidarity is depicted in a medium dolly shot as the camera travels around the circle of slaves, as they face outward, holding their weapons at the ready. The sense of connected space produced by the camera movement portrays the act as communal resistance initiated by Nunu's appeal to shared African values. Her leadership and courage in defense of the most vulnerable of her society thus separates Nunu's worldview from Shola's own selfish goals and creates an oppositional discourse between the traditional African emphasis on community and the Eurocentric ideals of individualism. It is also significant that Mona is linked to this scene near its end. Nunu cuts Kutu's child from her dead body and raises the baby on high, thanking the gods and naming the child Kwame, which means *witness* in Akan. The film cuts to a flashback featuring a brief high-angle long shot of Mona as she is branded. By relating the agonizing circumstances of Kwame's birth to Mona's suffering, the film draws a parallel between past and contemporary resistance by black peoples, thus suggesting that the fight for freedom and equality is still ongoing and impossible to achieve without embracing Africa as a salient determinant of identity.

The correlation between African origin and resistance to slavery is further evidenced by Nunu's role in the dissemination of oral history,

Recoupment of Origin in *Sankofa*

a critical element in Shola's reeducation. Nunu is portrayed in several instances teaching the field slaves Akan culture through her stories of Efriye, whom she describes as a little porcupine girl. In one such scene, Shola is depicted in a medium shot as she listens with rapt attention to Nunu's description of Efriye's family, including a mother who is a great healer and a father who is a great warrior. As the camera dollies from Shola to Nunu, it pans across a group of children gathered at Nunu's feet. The emphasis on children signals the pedagogical function of Nunu's storytelling and demonstrates the importance of oral history as a means of sustaining African roots. As Nunu explains that Efriye's name means "special" and that the whole family loved and protected her, Shola is depicted in a close-up as she lowers her eyes and looks away, a framing that emphasizes her wistful expression. This indicates sorrow at the fact that she remains isolated from such a caring family, a subtext that is underscored by her physical position on the periphery of the group listening to Nunu's story. Furthermore, Nunu's portrayal of her mother's great skill as a healer and her father's power as a warrior valorizes African culture, imparting to Shola and the children a pride in their heritage. As an adult undergoing rape in a situation where she is powerless, however, Shola's pensive reaction to Nunu's teaching demonstrates a longing for all that was taken from them when they were first enslaved. This tactic accords spectators the opportunity to consider the profound disruption and human cost of slavery.

In parallel to Nunu's influence as an embodiment of African heritage, Shango's stubborn resistance to slavery also shapes Shola. In contrast to Nunu, whose actions she never directly questions out of respect for an elder, Shola's relationship with Shango allows for heated debate on the issue of complicity. This is demonstrated in a scene that takes place after Kutu's death. Shango, confined to stocks for his role in the disruption of the whipping, is brought food by Shola. As she strokes his forehead, Shola asks him why he "can't act right? It don't take that much." When he does not respond, she tries to feed him, but he turns his head away silently, once again refusing food that has come from the big house. In frustration, Shola berates him for not thinking of her and taking her away. This statement indicates that despite Nunu's teaching, she is still focused on her own needs, as if she is somehow separated from the slave community's interests. Shango retorts by asking,

CHAPTER 1

"Why can't you be like one of we? Eh? Why can't you crawl on your belly like a snake through the trees, through the grass. One of dem day the whole uh [us] we gwine eat frog. That is the only way we'll get our freedom." Shango's metaphor of slaves crawling like snakes indicates that the appearance of compliance with the master's rule should not be misread as complicity, given that they are waiting for the right moment to strike back. Shango's position echoes Nunu's earlier assertion that the only chains holding the slaves in their place are physical ones. In both instances, a premium is placed on maintaining resistance by preserving psychological freedom, an act that foregrounds the use of the mind as the primary means of resisting enslavement. Shango's condemnation of Shola's selfish individual desire reflects what Asante has described as Afrocentric culture's "distaste for individual achievement that is not related to collective advancement" (1987, 105). From Shango's perspective, until Shola is able to put her community's needs above her own, she will not truly embrace her African heritage and will remain estranged from her own people. Furthermore, as an individual acting in her own interests, she remains open to continued exploitation. Her statement that it does not take much to act right is highly ironic given Lafayette's continued raping of her: no matter how perfectly she conducts herself or how self-effacing she is, she has no defense against his brutality. Hence, the protection promised by obedience and complicity is completely illusionary.

Community solidarity as an African cultural trait is further demonstrated by the presence of a secret society among the slaves. Described in Shola's narration as an organization of field slaves from different plantations and escaped ex-slaves living in the hills, the secret society is dedicated to rebellion. As such, the society relies on African constructs of authority and spirituality as a means of promoting community solidarity. In the first scene depicting the society, Nunu, dressed in a grass skirt and wearing cowrie shells wrapped around her waist, accepts greetings from the visiting free hill people. Later, the chief of the free hill people faces Nunu as an equal, addressing his report on their community's progress to her. Both of these acts elevate Nunu to the status of an elder speaking and acting on behalf of her people. In a later scene, she oversees a ritual chanted in Akan that initiates slaves into the society, calling on the gods to aid them in whatever they undertake. By framing the slaves' resistance movement within an African context, each slave symbolically embraces that heritage as the locus of their struggle and self-definition. Thus, the initiated slaves transform themselves from mere property of the master to agents of destruction in a united community prepared to protect itself by going to war.

Although Shola is present at the ritual, she remains on the periphery, unable to bring herself to cross over and submit to it, frozen, as her narration explains, by "the years of the Church" in her. The ritual, however, has a psychological effect, compelling her to flee without food or plans toward the hills, an impulsive act of self-determination that initiates a sequence of events that transforms her passive complicity to open rebellion. Captured that night, Shola is disciplined by Lafayette in front of Joe and Father Raphael, the plantation's priest. Depicted in a medium shot in center frame, Shola is naked and on her knees, her hands lashed together by a heavy rope. Shola's entrapment is heightened by Lafayette towering over her on the right holding a knife and Father Raphael leaning in on the left with a bible and crucifix in his hands, symbolizing the societal pressures of slave owner and religion. Lafayette terrorizes Shola by cutting a piece of hair from her head, accusing her of mixing with "them heathen niggers." By relating Shola's rebellion causally to African spirituality, Gerima is arguing that slavery ensured compliance by stripping away African beliefs and replacing them with Christianity. This is reinforced later in the scene in a disturbing high angle close-up of Shola. Hung with her hands above her head, and a crucifix pressed brutally into her bare breasts, Shola is forced to repeat after Father Raphael that she is possessed and enslaved by God and will never again worship heathen African gods. Far from achieving the desired effect, however, the brutality and humiliation of Shola's discipline causes her to repudiate the white values that render her less than human. Later, as Shango tends to her wounds, Shola asks him if he is afraid of death. Shango relates how he was unable to understand the deaths of his father and sister because he could only see their bodies and not beyond. But when he awoke one morning to find his close friend Jake hanging from a tree, he realized that death was nothing to fear: it would only take him back to the ones who loved him. He gives Shola a hand-carved sankofa, a talisman passed down from his own father. As Shola's narration reveals, once Shango places the bird around her neck, she becomes

CHAPTER 1

a rebel, unafraid of flogging or death. The sankofa creates an interstitial relationship between her journey of self-discovery and the one undertaken by Mona. Both began the process enveloped in denial as they believed that their assimilation of Eurocentric values gave them status and protected them from harm as long as they passively accepted the commodification of their bodies. But as Mona is stripped and branded, and Shola flogged and humiliated, the suffering forces a reevaluation of their identities, illusory beliefs, and the Eurocentric history that underpins both.

One of the most controversial elements of the film is Gerima's treatment of Nunu's son, Joe. A mulatto child resulting from Nunu's rape at the hands of a slaver, Joe is *Sankofa*'s most conflicted character. Completely estranged from his mother because of his role as head slave and from the other slaves because of his mixed parentage, Joe is openly derided and belittled for his belief in Christianity. For example, as Noble Ali and Joe set up the whipping posts in preparation for the runaways' discipline, Noble Ali notices Joe gazing at Lucy, a young house slave who is in love with him. Calling Joe "Bible Boy" as other slaves watch and laugh, Noble Ali mocks him for reading the Bible rather than living life, joking that he should make his mind up about Lucy rather than "acting like some kind of animal." Depicted center frame in a medium three-shot with Lucy on the left and Noble Ali on the right, Joe is clearly torn between two competing forces. Finally, when Noble Ali alludes to Joe's mulatto status by taunting, "you think you're too pretty for her boy?" Joe takes a swing at him, which Noble Ali easily deflects by pinning his arms. As the camera dollies in to a tighter shot that makes Joe's torment apparent, Noble Ali conducts a mock marriage between Lucy and Joe, advising her, "this boy is as slippery as a snake, so just hold on tight to him." Showing off to his audience of laughing slaves as he forces a grinning Lucy and horrified Joe up against one another, Noble Ali adds, "boy changes colors faster than a chameleon, so just don't let him out your sight." Although Kandé argues that "Gerima's hasty Ethiopianist reading" posits Joe as a representative of Western colonialism because of his allegiance to the Church and his master, the same charge could easily be laid against Shola's character and does not adequately account for either Joe's profound estrangement from the other slaves or his obvious conflicted relationship with the religion he obsessively embraces (1998). Rather, Joe is caught in a barren space between cultures, repudiated on the one hand by a white society that does not acknowledge his connection and, on the other, by a black slave society that despises him for it. Certainly, Noble Ali's ridicule of Joe as someone who changes color indicates the strong level of derision Joe's mulatto status engenders in his own community.

The difficulty, as the film constructs it, is that Joe must either repudiate his white heritage to find community with the slaves or exorcize his African heritage to become a true Christian. Asante argues that the result of this process of forced assimilation is *menticide*, or an annihilation of the mind where profound self-hatred leads to violence (1993, 49, 120). Unable to find succor in either culture, Joe's intense disjunction thus serves as an illustration of what both Mona and Shola might become if they turn their backs on their African heritage. The dynamics of his crisis are revealed during a scene in the plantation chapel. As Joe confesses to Father Raphael, he is depicted in a tight close-up as he reveals a paranoid fear that Nunu will poison him for his belief in Christianity. The bars of the confessional screen obscuring his face add to the sense of claustrophobic isolation as Joe remarks, "Everybody knows that I'm different." The confessional scene is then crosscut with a flashback to Lucy seductively urging Joe to make a pretty brown baby with her. Returning to the scene in the church, Joe stares out of the confessional at a painting of the Madonna and child adorning the distant wall. Joe's subsequent question to Father Raphael, "Whose son am I?" indicates his irreconcilable paradox: the lust he feels for Lucy, and the black child that may arise from it, are in conflict with the unattainable ideal represented by the Madonna and child. Father Raphael's reply, "We all have one Father in the Almighty," demonstrates why Christianity holds such appeal for Joe: with its promise of salvation and peace for all those who follow its doctrines, it offers an illusory safe haven and a sense of identity for someone who belongs nowhere else. As the complex crosscutting between the scenes continues, Joe breaks off making love to Lucy when she touches the medallion of the Virgin Mary he wears around his neck. Thrown out of his quarters and called a heathen by Joe, Lucy lashes out by crying, "You ain't nothing, Joe. What's missing? Ain't I woman enough for you? Is it my breasts you need or that damned Virgin Mary herself?" Kandé describes Joe's

CHAPTER I

sexual impotence as an exploitation of "a stereotype in the discourse of racial classification that would have it that the mulatto, like the mule or any other 'unnatural' product of the mixture of races, is sterile" (1998). Joe's impotence, however, goes beyond sexual performance to reflect the struggle of a man at war with his essential being: rejected by a black slave community that devalues him and barred from joining the white community by racism and his status as a slave, Joe is unable to establish a psychological center for his own identity.

Joe's crisis culminates in his matricide of Nunu during a hallucinatory event induced by a love potion administered by Lucy in a desperate attempt to gain his affection. Disoriented, Joe stumbles into a stream in a frenzied search for water. Nunu, who has followed his disoriented flight through the forest, initially decides to abandon him to his death. Overcome by maternal feelings, however, she wades into the water and keeps him from drowning. In one striking sequence, they are depicted sitting in the middle of the stream while Nunu cradles Joe and sings a child's lullaby in Akan, a device that foregrounds their shared African heritage. The shot is poignant because it portrays the only moment of true mother-son closeness during the course of the narrative and allows the spectators emotional distance to consider the effects and roots of their estrangement. The opportunity for rapprochement is destroyed when Nunu rips the religious medal from Joe's neck and he, in his drugged state, drowns her, mistakenly assuming that she is trying to poison him. Kandé describes this act as a destruction of "Mother Africa" (1998), but the film's intent appears somewhat more complex and considerably more ambiguous. There are three circumstances that mitigate Joe's responsibility for his actions. First, he is in a hallucinatory state, having been administered drugs without his knowledge. Second, the confrontation between Nunu and Joe is crosscut with a reprise of the confessional scene in which Father Raphael informs him that the devil is trying to get to him through his mother. By adopting this construction, *Sankofa* places some of the responsibility for Nunu's death on the destructive force of Christianity. The third mitigating factor is introduced when Shola arrives at the stream and discovers Joe's actions. When Joe cries out that he had not meant to kill Nunu, Shola furiously informs him that he is the product of rape and, as such, has no future. Joe's anguish and disbelief makes it obvious that Nunu never shared the circumstances of his conception with him, allowing him to cling to an idealized paternal image. The tempering of Joe's actions is necessary to allow him to recognize that he has been betrayed by his beliefs. Kandé points out correctly that Joe is the only head slave "who will not redeem himself through the rebellion," but Gerima does position the character to return to an African center despite the tragic events (1998). Joe carries Nunu's body to the plantation church and lays it on the altar. Father Raphael orders him to remove "this heathen creature," adding that Joe, like "the rest of these niggers," has no soul. Instead of being intimidated by the priest's authority, Joe grabs him by the arm and asserts, "This woman that you call heathen is my mother and you're going to have to stop disrespecting her." By at last taking direct action and ownership of his African heritage, Joe initiates his own rebellion, which ends in the murder of Father Raphael.

Sankofa climaxes in a slave rebellion that brings the disparate time lines of the narrative together in screen space. When the rebellion begins, Shola, who has been demoted to a field slave as the result of her escape attempt, is cutting cane in a distant area of the field. Lafayette rides up and dismisses the headman who is supervising her work. As Lafayette stares at her, he is portrayed in a low angle close-up that accentuates his power. The reverse shot of Shola frames her from a low angle, but she meets his eyes defiantly, indicating her resolve not to be victimized again regardless of the personal cost. This sequence is followed by a montage of various lines of action. Brief flashbacks of Shola's rape are intercut with scenes of Shango and the other slaves preparing to kill the white overseer. The montage also includes extreme long shots of Elmina and flash-forward scenes of Mona, naked and staggering toward the exit from the slave pens as she emerges from her trance. Bound together by a reprise of the sacred drumming soundscape from the beginning of the film, the sequence reemphasizes a nonlinear African concept of time that refuses encapsulation in Eurocentric linear history. Shola attacks Lafayette, killing him with a machete and is then forced, along with the other slaves, to flee as a headman appears wielding a gun. Her death is revealed through narration over a series of long shots of the cane field and the sky. This sequence dissolves into an extreme aerial long shot traveling across the sea onto which a close-up of the sacred drummer is superimposed. The feeling of movement in these shots gives a sense of flight: Shola's narration lyrically describes her death as a feeling of lightness as a buzzard takes her up into the sky, away from "this miserable earth." The aerial shot culminates in the appearance of a monument closely resembling that of Abu Simbel in ancient Nubia (contemporary Egypt), indicating Shola's return to Africa.[10] This construct reaffirms the importance of the role of what Carole Boyce Davies describes as "the 'flying back' stories which originated in slavery" as a means of addressing the "need to re-connect and re-member" with a cultural past obliterated by forced movement through the Middle Passage (1994, 17).

The parallel between Shola and Mona's journeys is strengthened by the events that follow Mona's release from her experience in the slave pens. Now wrapped in a piece of cloth given to her by the kindness of an African woman who welcomes her back, Mona refuses further engagement with the white photographer by ignoring his demand that she return to work. Instead, she joins a group of black people watching the performance of the sacred drummer. As she watches the drummer, the camera pans across the group of fellow observers to reveal Africans, Caribbean blacks, and those from Western locales in the black diaspora. The pan, which unites these diverse people in a common social space, suggests that they are all experiencing a profound sense of connection with each other and with Africa as represented by the sacred drummer's performance. As Mona turns to look across the crowd, the camera pans and connects her gaze to that of Nunu, who smiles and nods at her. Dressed predominantly in white, Nunu's presence is ambiguous: is she an audience member who has shared in Mona's revelatory experience, or is she a supernatural presence drawn by the sacred drummer's power? Ultimately, the exact nature of the mystery is left up to the spectator to debate. More important, Nunu's gaze indicates that she is well satisfied with the outcome of Mona's return to Africa. Their unity, based as it is on shared experiences that surmount and flow through multiple borders, represents "Africa asserting itself intellectually and psychologically, breaking the bonds of Western domination in the mind" (Asante 1993, 46). Thus, by reclaiming Africa, Mona and Nunu achieve personal peace.

Shola's journey from compliant house slave to rebel is thus directly paralleled by Mona's journey from denial to acceptance of her Africanness. In both instances, the characters move from a suppressed view of their identities to a state in which they embrace their African origin regardless of consequences. Far from being a defeat, Shola's death is an uplifting act that reaffirms her selfhood. In a similar context, Mona's refusal to continue the commodification of her body is also a refusal of Eurocentric exploitation. It is significant that both these positions result from the experience of an oral history that preserves and maintains an African center as a defining aspect of their identities. As Gerima notes, "I think the only weapon the African race has is history. And history exorcises, history heals, the African people. I think memory and history heals [sic] everybody" (Gerima and Woolford 1994, 100). Thus, the Afrocentric structure of *Sankofa* presents a triumphant ideology that seems to suggest that, for diasporic identities, the schism created by slavery cannot be effectively healed without an African locus in which to anchor identity construction.

TWO

Collision of Cultures
Occulted Caribbean Histories in *Sugar Cane Alley*

The consequences of the Middle Passage, and the subsequent racist ideology that accompanied it, took some time to develop in the Caribbean. Initially, plantations relied on slave labor drawn from indigenous Carib Indians, African slaves captured from enemies during various wars, and Russians and Greeks from various European slave markets. As Gordon K. Lewis observes, it was only when earlier sources such as "native Indian[s], indentured servant[s], peasant emigrant[s], transshipped prisoner[s] and convict[s]" became unavailable or proved unsuitable that trade in African slaves became dominant (1983, 98). Although France participated in the Atlantic slave trade as early as the sixteenth century, its emergence as a major power did not take place until the late seventeenth century, when monopoly-trading companies emerged as driving forces (Klein 1978, 175). Third only to the British and Portuguese, and spurred on by the establishment of its own plantation economies, France's traffic in slaves eventually accounted for as much as one-fifth of all Africans transported to the Americas by the eighteenth century (175).

During the first half of the seventeenth century, France began accruing colonial possessions in the Lesser Antilles and, drawing on Dutch technology, successfully created a sugar-export economy in Guade-

Occulted Caribbean Histories in *Sugar Cane Alley*

loupe and Martinique (Klein 1978, 176). By the early eighteenth century, France had become a leader in the American French sugar zone when Saint-Domingue (Haiti) became the single most productive sugar and coffee plantation economy in all the West Indies (175–76). In addition to the increased need for labor caused by expansion of the sugar trade, the cruel conditions on the sugar cane plantations caused high mortality rates that, in turn, also increased the demand for new slaves: living in unhealthy conditions, slaves on sugar plantations were maintained at bare subsistence levels and performed excruciatingly hard labor for long hours (Bush 1996, 196).

Lewis suggests that there are three principles underpinning the emergence of racist ideology directed at African slaves: first, African slaves became identified with menial labor; second, they were viewed as heathen beyond redemption from a religious standpoint; and third, blackness itself is identified with evil (1983, 98). Perhaps more to the point, the racist ideology that emerges does so because of a need to justify the act of slavery by a new master class of slave owners dependent upon this strategy for economic and political prosperity (99). Beginning with the European-Indian confrontation in the Caribbean, and later transferred to African slaves in the plantation economy, the proslavery apologetic was underpinned by the racist assumptions that, owing to their religious and cultural superiority, white Europeans were entitled to colonize and dominate nonwhite peoples. In turn, the so-called deficiencies of the latter made it inevitable that they would serve European interests (103). From these assumptions flowed a series of racist premises that survived the end of slavery in the Caribbean and form the foundation of slavery's pervasive legacy. Hence, the assertion of Europe's natural right to rule over non-European peoples necessarily entrenched the degradation of the Africans that came to form the basis of the black Caribbean population.

This process was initiated early in the history of slavery in the Caribbean. For example, as early as 1685, Louis XIV proclaimed the Code Noir (Black Code), an edict that set out parameters for "The Discipline and the Commerce of Blacks and Slaves" in French Caribbean colonial lands (Dayan 1995, 285). Although resisted by the white population who ignored its precepts and gave precedence to more excessive local customs, the Black Code nevertheless offers insight into the development of a "philosophy of denaturalization" that underpinned the rationalization of systemic racism and dehumanization endured by African slaves (286). Under the administration of the Black Code, African slaves found their status reduced to that of livestock, which reinforced a power dynamic in which white European culture was viewed as economically, politically, and socially superior to theirs (287). Such polarities were later further accentuated in the French West Indies through France's *mission civilisatrice*, which imposed French language, culture, and history as the epitome of civilization in one of the most ambitious and destructive assimilation projects ever undertaken in colonial history.

As one of France's oldest colonies, Martinique has a history tied to slavery and sugar cane production (Britton 1999, 1). Martinique's profile, however, is unique in the Caribbean because, unlike many other Caribbean nations that sought independence, it remains intimately connected to France owing to its controversial status as a *département d'outre mer* (overseas region; Britton 1999, 1). Given its history as a French colony and slave center, and its continuing subordination to France, Martinique has been described as an object rather than a subject of history (Burton 1984, 302). The paradoxical tension between France and the many cultural forces at play in Martinique has led to the unfolding of several hotly contested major theoretical positions in the quest to forge unique cultural identities out of common histories of slavery and colonialism.

Prominent among these theorists is Aimé Césaire, a renowned Martinican poet and political activist, whose literary acumen and perceptiveness is credited with providing the foundation for the emergence of Caribbean literature (Claverie 1998, 89). Most important, Césaire's drive to recoup black Caribbean identity from its devaluation under French colonialism led to his involvement in the Négritude movement. Transnational in scope, the Négritude movement was founded by Césaire, Léopold Senghor (Senegal), and Léon-Gontron Damas (Guadeloupe) in Paris and focused on the valorization of blackness as a vibrant cultural force. Conceived as a means of resisting colonial oppression, Négritude predates the departmentalization of Martinique and sets the stage for later theoretical constructs of Caribbean identity, such as Antillanité and Créolité.

Occulted Caribbean Histories in *Sugar Cane Alley*

Négritude has its conceptual roots in the student newspaper, *L'étudiant noir*, established by Senghor, Damas, and Césaire in 1934. Although the lifespan of the newspaper was short, the essence of many of the student discussions it engendered had far-reaching impact. Thirty years later, Césaire would reminisce on these discussions, stating that the term *Négritude* was coined as a response to the derogatory word *nègre*, which was used to insult blacks. It was a necessary legitimizing move and a resistance to the systemic racism faced by the students in their daily lives because, as Michel Giraud points out, "in the language of traditional colour ideology in Martinique, white is from every point of view synonymous with everything that is good, and black with everything that is bad" (1995, 78). By turning the word on itself, Césaire, Senghor, and Damas affirmed that Africa had something valuable to contribute to world culture (Jules-Rosette 1998, 242–43). The coining of the term thus became, from Césaire's perspective, an act of reclaiming and validating blackness in the face of systemic alienation that made black Antilleans reluctant to accept race as a positive aspect of their identities (1972, 73).

It should be noted that Césaire's and Senghor's views of Négritude later diverged, and it can be argued that Césaire altered the fundamental concepts of the movement to suit Caribbean concerns. Although the movement began with a commitment to renewing pride in African origin, Senghor takes a narrow view of Négritude, restricting it to only the expression of black African cultural values, resulting in a somewhat essentialist discourse (Jules-Rosette 1998, 242–43). Césaire's definition is more fluid and argues that black Caribbeans, living in an atmosphere of assimilation and devaluation, need to arrive at "a concrete consciousness of what we are" (Césaire 1972, 76). To achieve this consciousness, he maintains, black Caribbeans should affirm their connection to Africa as a source of cultural legitimacy by emphasizing that they have a bona fide history and have made important contributions to humanity (76). Césaire, however, envisions Caribbean identity within a transnational conception of Négritude that includes recognition of a commonality with other black struggles and the need for black Caribbeans to acknowledge their shared stake in advancing black issues globally (77). Thus, it may be argued that Césaire's Négritude possesses a concept of

CHAPTER 2

black diaspora in which black Caribbean experience is linked to other black cultures by virtue of its connection to African origin.

Although Négritude offers a positive construction of black Caribbeanness, there is an internal tension in Césaire's construct that has engendered considerable controversy and debate. In seminal works such as *Discourse on Colonialism*, Césaire powerfully outlines how colonization functions by stressing how both the colonizer and colonized are destroyed by slavery through "relations of domination and submission which turn the colonizing man into a classroom monitor, an army sergeant, a prison guard, a slave driver, and the indigenous man into an instrument of production" (1972, 21). Thus, colonialism poisons all levels of society by undermining the social importance of racial tolerance and compassion in favor of advancing economic gains (Gill 2000, 380). This position, however, is problematized by Césaire's stance on the continuing role of France in Martinican society. For example, in regard to his use of French as his primary written language, Césaire championed the development of a form of French that possessed a distinct African Caribbean means of expression (1972, 67). Furthermore, the connection Césaire feels to France, however Caribbeanized, is also evident in his political actions. When DeGaulle offered Martinique full independence in the 1960s, Césaire led a successful campaign to maintain the island's status as an overseas department (Gill 2000, 380). Although motivated by his belief that an instantaneous move to independence would lead to the type of strife seen in newly independent African states, Césaire's actions led other important Caribbean thinkers such as Frantz Fanon to charge that Césaire failed to follow the logic of his own teachings when he valorized French language and culture over other potential African Caribbean cultural modes (380).

Perhaps even more importantly, Négritude's focus on a notion of a universal African cultural connection between all black peoples suggests that it may fail to take into account the multiple cultural influences that creolize Martinican and other Caribbean societies (Burton 1995, 142). To accommodate such multiplicities, the Martinican novelist, philosopher, and poet Edouard Glissant would go beyond Négritude to conceive of Caribbean identity as a "relation-identity" that focused on an "open, multidimensional, polyvalent conception of identity" (148). Based on his fundamental objection to Négritude's reliance

Occulted Caribbean Histories in *Sugar Cane Alley*

on a discourse of racial particularism that is rooted in African origins, Glissant's Antillanité, conceived at the end of the 1960s, de-emphasizes the notion of a universal black consciousness in favor of a sense of identity that is located in a specific geopolitical map. Burton has argued that Glissant is one of the first West Indian thinkers to envision Caribbean identity as a "free-floating, multiplicitous growth whose supreme image, in the Caribbean context, is the mangrove swamp" (1995, 148). This image underscores Glissant's conception of identity as a constant negotiation and renegotiation of competing imperatives across a multicultural landscape.

From Glissant's perspective, rigid historicism is of little value to Martinican experience as much of the island's history has been directly created by forces outside its own borders (J. M. Dash, introduction to Glissant 1989, xviii). Glissant places a higher value on the "synchronic relations within and across cultures" and thus rejects the idea of a universal black culture advanced by Négritude (xxviii, xliii). He draws a distinction between the experiences of exile, with its return or connections to a living culture, and the experiences of slavery (Glissant 1989, 14). The cultural disruption created by bringing together peoples of diverse cultures in circumstances that deprive them of cultural context and access to their own languages offers "the possibility of dealing with 'values' no longer in absolute terms but as active agents of synthesis" (16). As Glissant suggests, the notion of a universal African culture is undercut in the Caribbean by the unprecedented level of contact between slaves of diverse ethnic groups, which in turn led to the development of hybridities (16). Thus, identities created in slavery are subject to a process of constant transformation in which new experiences and cultural influences continuously contribute to the creolization of Caribbean identity.

In his groundbreaking work, *Caribbean Discourse*, Glissant proposes that both Antillanité (Caribbeanness) and a *poétique de la relation* (crosscultural poetics) are the principal foundations of Caribbean identity (Murdoch 1992, 3). Glissant himself, however, exposes a paradox or tension at the heart of Antillanité by suggesting that the very hybridity of Caribbean cultures prevents a coherent idea of nation from developing (Glissant 1989, 222). In effect, the plural nature of Caribbean histories, with differing colonial contexts and languages, actually bars the rise of a coherent Caribbean identity, even as it creates a multiplicity of them (222). Thus, although Antillanité is successful at revalorizing specific geopolitical Caribbean histories and accounting for the process of cross-cultural influences in Caribbean identity construction, it still remains more descriptive of its process of becoming than its arrival at an endpoint.

The next revolution in Caribbean identity discourse began in the mid-1970s when a number of academics and writers came together at the Centre Universitaire Antilles-Guyane to create the Groupe d'Etudes et de Recherches de la Créolophonie (GEREC) in order to provide new impetus to the central importance of the Creole language as a cultural force in Caribbean society (Burton 1995, 153). In many ways, the Creole language itself epitomizes Caribbean identity. Arising from the need to allow communication among African slaves from various cultures, Creole combines a "French-derived vocabulary married to a syntax and morphology of basically African origin" (137). Yet Creole cannot be viewed as a derivative of either: as a language of resistance first against slavery and then against the assimilationist project of the French colonizer throughout the French West Indies, Creole came to express a variety of unique Caribbean identities.

Spurred on by GEREC, the debate on cultural creolization came to have broad-based participation, including "teachers, educationalists, journalists, broadcasters and, not least, politicians and others involved in the unending debate on the status of the French West Indies" (Burton 1995, 153). This led to the emergence in 1989 of the literary and theoretical movement known as Créolité with the publication of its manifesto, *Éloge de la Créolité* (*In Praise of Creoleness*), a collaborative work based on the passionate commitment of Patrick Chamoiseau, Jean Bernabé, and Raphaël Confiant to the advancement of Creole language and heritage (Taylor 1997, 126). A social worker, essayist and journalist, Chamoiseau won the prestigious Goncourt Prize in 1992 for his third novel, *Texaco*. Bernabé is a poet, linguist, and dean of humanities at the Université des Antilles et de la Guyane, while Confiant is an activist, journalist, poet, and novelist in both French and Creole (126). Together, these three individuals represent a new generation of Martinican writers and thinkers determined to bridge the multiplicity of identities in the Caribbean through the valorization of Creole.

Occulted Caribbean Histories in *Sugar Cane Alley*

In some regards, it may be argued that Créolité takes the central tenets of Antillanité, expands, and radicalizes them. Like Glissant, Bernabé, Chamoiseau, and Confiant acknowledge that they are "forever Césaire's sons" because Négritude mounted the original challenge to the devaluation of black identities (1993, 80). Créolité, however, repudiates Négritude's racial particularism with a ferocity that goes well beyond Glissant's objections: Négritude, the Créolistes argue, is a trap that simply replaces the valorization of European culture with that of African culture, which suggests that Caribbean identities have not evolved beyond simplistic connections to points of origin (82–83). Rooted in more than African essentialism, this clash is also founded on Césaire's attitude to the Creole language itself, which he prefers to describe as a derivative of either pure French or, alternatively, a pure African language (Césaire, quoted in Burton 1995, 144). By subordinating Creole to distant outside origins, Césaire refuses Creole's distinct Caribbean particularity, thereby denying the very mechanism of identity that is so fundamental to Créolité (144).

On the surface, it may seem difficult to differentiate the basic tenets of Créolité from those of Antillanité, although the Créolistes distance themselves from Glissant's position by taking the stance that Antillanité is a geopolitical category and nothing more. Both, however, view Caribbean identity as a process, constantly in flux and responding to the many different influences that have contributed to the development of the geopolitical and cultural spaces that constitute the Caribbean region, including African, European, Asian, Amerindian, and Levantine cultures. One significant and controversial difference is that the Créolistes openly acknowledge the inherent Caribbeanness of white West Indians, a position repudiated by both Négritude and Antillanité (Burton 1995, 153). Such a position is strongly influenced by the fact that the Créolistes answer the question that Glissant did not: namely, that Caribbeanness is not rooted in race or culture but, rather, is determined by the speaking of Creole.

Créolité is by no means monolithic in its viewpoint or without internal tension. One site of tension focuses on the nature of Creole as a language that is complicated by a struggle between radical and moderate positions positing very different visions of what its essence should be. As Burton has pointed out, there are weaknesses in both radical and moderate conceptions of Creole. In the first, the radical insistence on phonetic Creole in order to create the greatest maximum distance from the French language threatens to create an awkward written and spoken language accessible to only an elite few. The moderate position, which favors closer linguistic ties with French in spoken and written Creole, opens the door to eventual assimilation of Creole by the French language (Burton 1995, 152–58). Chamoiseau has sought to bridge this gap by suggesting that basilectal Creole and standard French are linked by an intermediary language space where elements from both ends of the spectrum form and reform into what he describes as "natural Creole," represented by the various regional, or interlectal, expressions of the language (157). Thus, Chamoiseau considers all three conceptions of Creole as vital to maintaining unique West Indian identities (157).

The challenge to Créolité is not limited to interior disagreements within the discourse. Glissant, for example, disputes the assumption that Creole, with its roots in slavery and colonialism, could ever function as an uncontested mode of indigenous Caribbean expression: foundational to this is the fact that Creole maintains "a strategic relationship of resistance and subversion *to* the dominant language [that] is negotiated from the inside" (Britton 1999, 3). Thus, Creole is irrevocably linked to the French language and slavery, undermining the attempts of the Créolistes to posit it as an autonomous mode of expression. Accused by Glissant of wanting to create a Creole essence, Bernabé, Chamoiseau, and Confiant deny this charge by asserting that being Creole is not a response to a singular history but, rather, an existence created at the confluence of histories (Chamoiseau, quoted in Taylor 1997, 142). Although this position clearly echoes Glissant's own vision of Antillanité as a process of identity, it sidesteps the serious question of whether speaking Creole can be regarded as the defining feature of Creoleness in a system that, by the Créolistes' own admission, "remains permanently in motion, pushing us headlong in a movement of diversity, of change and exchange" (142). It would seem, then, that Créolité shares with Antillanité a certain indeterminacy of process that makes absolute certainties of Caribbean nation or identity difficult to substantiate.

Filmed in 1983, Euzhan Palcy's *Rue cases-nègres/Sugar Cane Alley* (Mar-

Occulted Caribbean Histories in *Sugar Cane Alley*

tinique/France) was created at a crossroads where Négritude, Antillanité, and Créolité discourses exist in contemporaneous contestation. The film offers an excellent opportunity to probe the influence of all three of these movements in advancing alternative views of black Caribbean identities. As Mbye Cham notes, *Sugar Cane Alley* was prominent among the limited number of films that emerged from the French Antilles during the 1980s (1992, 23). Along with such films as Benjamin Jules-Rosette's *Bourg la folie* (Martinique, 1982) and *Bon Dié Bon* (Martinique, 1986), as well as Guy Deslauriers's *Les oubliés de la liberté* (Martinique 1989), *Sugar Cane Alley* explores how contemporary Martinican identities are forged in the shifting transnational spaces between black Martinican experience and its conflicted relationship to the legacies of slavery and colonialism (Cham 1992, 23–25). What makes this film especially significant is the fact that Palcy, as the first Martinican woman to direct a feature film, created a work that struck a profound chord with its Martinican audiences as well as cultures beyond its original context. In particular, the film offers an implicit critique of the hierarchical and racially inflected social structure of Martinique that arose in response to inequities initiated by slavery.

Palcy was born in Martinique in 1955 and began her film career at FR3, the island's French national radio and television station. In 1975, she moved to Paris, where she studied at the Sorbonne and the Louis Lumière film school. *Sugar Cane Alley* is Palcy's first feature film, and she has continued to earn international acclaim with such pivotal feature fiction and documentary films as *Siméon* (1992), *Aimé Césaire: Une voix pour l'histoire* (1994), and *Ruby Bridges* (1997). Notably, she became the first black woman to direct a feature film in Hollywood with *A Dry White Season* (1989). She continues to make the issues of oppression, exploitation, and cultural identity the major concerns of her work.

When the film premiered, *Sugar Cane Alley* broke all box office records in Martinique and Guadeloupe (Herndon 1996, 265). One of the first feature films to depict black Martinican culture from within, the reception of the film illustrated both the high demand for such representations and Palcy's ability to strike a cultural chord with her primary audience. Based on Joseph Zobel's novel, *Rue cases-nègres* (*Black Shack Alley*),[1] the film explores education, assimilation, and the legacy of slavery as sources of power and oppression through the struggles of a young boy José and his grandmother M'man Tine in 1930s Martinique as they attempt to establish a future beyond the sugar cane fields. As José negotiates the complexities of Martinique's layered society, he must find his place between the rival influences of Médouze, an old man who imbues the boy with a sense of African heritage, and the French education so prized by his grandmother because it promises advancement and escape from the poverty of the sugar cane fields. As José discovers, however, through the experience of his mulatto friend, Léopold, who is the son of a white planter, assimilation to French culture not only involves cultural betrayal, it also is illusory in terms of establishing equality. Ultimately, with the death of his grandmother, who sacrificed so much for his education, José's black Caribbean identity is presented as a process of negotiating competing worldviews, thus offering an implicit critique of the hierarchical social structure that arose as a consequence of the inequities institutionalized by slavery and colonialism.

In order to place the film in full context, it is necessary to briefly consider the relationship between film and novel. As is the case with all film adaptations, Palcy faced the difficult task of maintaining the essence of the novel while condensing it in order to meet the time constraints of the film medium. Thus, there are necessary differences between Zobel's text and Palcy's: for example, the novel depicts José's life over a period of about ten years, whereas the film takes place over a much shorter duration. Furthermore, the film collapses the character of José's mother Délia into that of M'man Tine, intensifying the relationship between grandmother and grandson. Another important addition in the film is the development of a minor story element concerning a béké's failure to recognize his mulatto son into a major ideological examination of color politics in Martinican society.[2] Finally, and perhaps most significantly, the film contemporizes what some critics have referred to as Zobel's ideology of militant Négritude by infusing the film with a broader ideological approach reflecting elements of Antillanité and Créolité (Kandé and Gyasi 1994). Although it may be argued that these and other changes result in a simplification of Zobel's portrayal of black Martinican experience, they also serve to place *Sugar Cane Alley* in a context that encouraged Martinican audiences of the time to strongly identify with the issues and characters presented.

Occulted Caribbean Histories in *Sugar Cane Alley*

Sugar Cane Alley (Courtesy of New Yorker Films)

By the early 1980s, Martinique's status as an overseas department was credited with a continued downward spiral in terms of economic growth: during the mid 1940s when the sugar cane industry collapsed, Martinique's balance of trade shifted to a point where the island was flooded with French imports, transforming the economic situation in general from one of self-sufficiency to a growing dependence on France (Taylor 1997, 129). This underscores an interesting historical parallel between the context of the novel and that of the film: Zobel's novel was written four years after departmentalization, and the film was released two years after the controversial decision by Césaire to place a ten-year moratorium on the question of independence, thus perpetuating department status. Both works depict predepartmental Martinique from differing vantage points. Zobel's work explores the legacies of slavery and colonialism as a means of exposing the foundation of contemporary Martinican problems, focusing explicitly on the devaluation of black Caribbean culture and identity. The film's project is more complicated and implicit in nature in that it eschews the specific critique of colonialism in the novel in favor of a more fluid view

CHAPTER 2

of Caribbean identity construction by combining elements of Négritude with those of Antillanité and, to a lesser extent, elements of what would emerge as Créolité. Thus, the film's narrative locus becomes all the various societal and cultural influences—including education, assimilation, African heritage, and slavery's legacy—that José must mediate in the process of growing up Martinican.

In the opening of the film, an ideological position with strong overtones of Négritude is initially staked out: through a series of sepia postcards and photographs, the viewer is presented with life in 1930s Martinique, complete with images of black Martinicans in street scenes, in family portraits, and at work. In addition to setting the time period, the images signal an intention to valorize black Martinican experience by foregrounding that culture as central to the film's narrative. The most explicit statement aligning the sequence with Négritude is the film's dedication, which occurs over an image of a black man driving an ox cart. The words "Dedicated to the world's Black Shack Alleys" place the film in a pan-African context by linking the Caribbean experience to black Africa and the diaspora.

The valorization of African heritage is reinforced in the narrative strand that deals with José's relationship with Médouze, an elderly cane cutter. Serving as José's mentor, Médouze passes on traditional knowledge through oral teaching. Early in the film, the cutters and their families gather in Black Shack Alley for payday. As Médouze awaits his wages, he challenges José to answer a *titim*, or riddle. This action is depicted in a medium shot in which Médouze is positioned on the left side of the frame facing the camera and José is center frame, turned toward him. Around them, other cutters mingle conducting their own business. Although the shot focuses on Médouze and José, the presence of other community members places their conversation in a broader societal space, visually suggesting that the type of oral teaching Médouze conducts is part of everyday cultural life.

As an oral device, riddles in African cultures are often used as a form of wisdom literature encoding cultural information in symbolic meanings (Okpewho 1992, 101). For example, Médouze asks José to identify the following object: "Little black boy, dressed in white, in a green castle." As José considers his answer, Médouze's name is called. The camera pans with him as he picks up his wages from the paymaster and rejoins José, who is unable to answer the riddle. Médouze produces a custard apple from his pocket, revealing the solution. The riddle's metaphor relies on the structure of the green-skinned fruit itself, which has white flesh surrounding black seeds: like the custard apple, José must don the external trappings of white society by adopting a French education, but this does not negate the importance of his own black heritage which lies beneath this surface.[3] Taken within the overall context of the scene, in which the cane cutters are receiving their abysmal wages, the riddle assumes an ironic symbolic meaning, illustrating white control of black labor and the perpetuation of French colonialist economics.

In addition to riddles, Médouze passes healing lore on to José. In a scene beginning with an extreme long shot that places José and Médouze on a hillside within the context of nature, the elder quizzes the boy on the identification and properties of patagon grass. Médouze is seated on a tree stump on the left side of the frame, creating a difference in height between the old cutter and the boy seated at his feet. This accentuates Médouze's role as elder and locates his teaching in a place of respect, thus valorizing the African tradition of passing on oral knowledge. Furthermore, José's correct identification of the plant and his recitation of its healing properties indicate that Médouze's oral knowledge will be passed down through José's generation.

During the course of the scene, Médouze presents a philosophy of life and creation that challenges European precepts. For Médouze, speaking from the knowledge that has been passed down to him from his African legacy, the elements of creation such as fire, earth, and water possess their own secrets and should be regarded as complementary forces in the natural world rather than as enemies. He stresses to José that although man can take life, he does not possess the ability to create it or restore it once it is destroyed. Thus, he urges José to accept the workings of creation without weeping or sorrow. Although this may be regarded as a foreshadowing of Médouze's death, it can also be viewed as possessing a more symbolic meaning within the structure of the film: in the course of José's education—or perhaps, more accurately, his journey to black Caribbean identity—he will face a variety of forces that will all contribute to his sense of self.

CHAPTER 2

Although *Sugar Cane Alley* exhibits Négritude discourse, the film is also successful in questioning African origin as a sole index of black Martinican identity. This is reflected in a striking scene in which Médouze shares with José a story that his father told him, an act that simultaneously combines past, present, and future histories. The oral tale, which focuses on the capture of Médouze's father in Africa, and his subsequent enslavement in the sugar cane fields of Martinique, demonstrates that the knowledge Médouze passes on to José has both Martinican geopolitical roots and African specificity. The story begins with a call-and-response exchange of phrases *yi-cric* and *yi-crac* between José and Médouze.[4] Médouze relates how his father participated in the St. Pierre rebellion that ended slavery on the island, creating a counter-history that challenges French historical accounts by providing a specifically black Martinican perspective. Portrayed through an exchange of tight close-ups as Médouze speaks and José listens, the old man expresses his father's disillusionment when he finds that liberation from slavery has resulted in trading in a master for a boss: the persistence of the plantation economy after abolition resulted in the entrapment of slaves in a situation where their physical labor became their only commodity. Thus, as Médouze suggests, it became illegal to beat blacks but not illegal to pay them less than a living wage, perpetuating their dependency on the white landowners.

Another significant element in this scene is purely visual. As Médouze tells his story, he makes a talisman for José. Depicted in several extreme close-ups of Médouze's hands as he carves, the talisman comes to symbolize José's black Caribbeanness. Composed of a male figure on one side and a female on the other, the talisman is connected to the identity of a culture rather than to José personally. This is reinforced as José hangs the object on a wall in each of the homes he shares with M'man Tine throughout the course of the film, foregrounding it as a cultural touchstone for his identity as it connects him to Sugar Cane Alley wherever he goes.

The scene ends with a two-shot of José and Médouze positioned on opposite sides of the frame as the boy reveals that he would go to Africa with his mentor. Médouze glances toward the camera and replies that there is no one left for him there, implying that only his spirit will return when he dies. The exchange challenges the notion that African origin is the defining element of black Martinican experience, suggesting that black Martinicans have gone beyond that origin to become specifically Caribbean. This reflects Glissant's assertion that, although French Caribbean individuals must recognize the African part of their identities, they understand that the processes of history and multiple interconnections with other cultures have resulted in a hybridity that includes, but goes beyond, "pure" African origin (Glissant 1989, 8).

In addition to the importance of African origin as one element of black Caribbean identity, the film also presents Creole culture as a powerful force in José's education. Although the film was made six years before the initial publication of *Éloge de la Créolité* in 1989 (Bernabé, Chamoiseau, and Confiant 1993) and the formal emergence of Créolité as a movement, *Sugar Cane Alley* evidences the influence of the debate surrounding Creole as a language in its portrayal of the sugar cane cutters' community. This is achieved by presenting the Creole language as a means of resistance and cultural solidarity among the laborers. The very organization of Martinican society has been profoundly influenced by the legacies of both slavery and the sugar cane economy, instituting a polarized society in which the majority of power is invested in the minority white population versus a majority black population that occupies the opposite end of the power spectrum. A population of mixed heritage occupies a middle ground in this range, allowing access but not equality in terms of white societal power. The very language of race demonstrates just how complex such relations can be: the term *mulatto*, for example, refers to an individual of half-black and half-white heritage; *quadroon* denotes one black grandparent and three white ones; *béké* refers to an indigenous individual of all white heritage (Socolow 1996, 293n2; Herndon 1996, 262). This indicates very complicated relationships among the various strata of color in Martinican society, accentuated by the fact that individuals of mixed race often held positions involving the perpetuation of the white-power apparatus by disadvantaging black Caribbeans.

The film explores this complexity by illustrating both the oppression and resistance of the sugar cane workers as expressed through the use of Creole. In an early scene, the cane cutters are depicted working in the fields cutting cane, supervised by a manager and an overseer. The striated nature of color relations (edited for repetition) is demonstrated

CHAPTER 2

in the scene through a series of shots that expose the differing positions between varying degrees of blackness. In this case, the manager and overseer, both of mixed heritages, are depicted in a medium two-shot. The difference in their status is obvious: the manager wears a white colonial suit, helmet, and black tie, connecting him by dress to the white bosses. The overseer is clad less formally in a cream tropical suit, without tie. The manager's position on the left side of the frame, astride a horse, places him on higher ground than the overseer who is mounted on a donkey, giving the manager visual dominance. Most significantly, his use of French, as he berates the overseer for the poor quality of the cane bundles, indicates his superior social status. The overseer, in turn, barks in Creole at the crew boss, exhorting him to improve the quality of the work. Here, language becomes a marker of authority reinforcing a layered social structure in which black Caribbeans participate in exploiting each other.

A further layer is added to this discourse when the crew boss shouts at the cane cutter, Ti Coco, for taking time to relieve himself in the field. For this action, the overseer fines him fifteen cents. In response to this, Julien Twelve Toes, another cutter, begins improvising a song of resistance in Creole, which is joined by the other laborers. The opening words, "Whitey's in his easy chair. Black man burns in the sun," clearly express a bitter acknowledgment of their oppression, and the fact that it is openly sung in front of the manager, overseer, and crew boss, all of whom understand Creole, clearly identifies it as an act of defiance.

The portrayal of the Creole language as a foundation of black Caribbean culture and community evidences a position similar to that of the Créolistes, who state "the major aesthetic vector of our knowledge of ourselves and the world [is] Creoleness" (Bernabé, Chamoiseau, and Confiant 1993, 87). This suggests that the aesthetics of the language itself encode elements of black Caribbean identities and worldsense in its very expression. For example, after Médouze dies, the community gathers to mourn him. The scene begins with a long shot of the crowd gathered in the foreground outside Médouze's home with Médouze's body in the background visible through the opening of the shack. The cane cutter Saint Louis stands beside the body, and as the crowd calls out asking where he is, he appears and begins to perform the eulogy in Creole, using a call-and-response structure similar to that employed

Occulted Caribbean Histories in *Sugar Cane Alley*

by Médouze and José earlier in the film. This makes Médouze's eulogy interactive, placing the remembrance within the context of the larger community.

As Saint Louis performs the eulogy, he uses satire and symbolic imagery to decry the social and economic conditions under which Médouze lived and died. In African oral tradition, satire is viewed as a means of creating a social critique that is "meant to bring shame on the culprits and so discourage future misconduct" (Okpewho 1992, 118). In this Caribbean context, Saint Louis uses satire spoken in Creole to express a potentially dangerous sentiment in a coded fashion that permits his audience to empathize but also limits his exposure to retaliation by the bosses. For example, Saint Louis asserts, "The cane fields ate Mr. Médouze's life," thereby metaphorically portraying the cane fields as a colonial predator that destroys black Caribbeans. In another instance, Saint Louis is depicted in a medium shot as he satirizes Médouze's "vast estate" by commenting that Médouze "didn't want his old brothers to inherit his bantam, defeated in all its fights, or his barrels of gold and silver that Whitey gave him with a kick in the ass." This sequence, intercut with images of José sitting by Médouze's body in the shack, encourages the spectator to empathize with both the boy and his community and question the economic and political circumstances that continue to sustain such oppression. By once again presenting Creole as a means of resistance and the natural means of expressing the community's grief, Palcy links Creole affirmatively to black Caribbean identity. This establishes it as a vital cultural force, a position that reflects the social drive to establish Creole as a central tenet of Caribbean culture, which, in turn, culminates in the emergence of the Créolité movement.

One of the most significant differences between Zobel's novel and the film is their differing attitudes toward the role of French education in Martinique. The film has sustained considerable criticism for not reproducing the novel's critique of the French education process as the dominant force in stratifying Caribbean cultures (Kandé and Gyasi 1994). Kandé and Gyasi have described the film's portrayal of José's French education as anachronistic because José's experience seems libratory, rather than alienating. In addition, the film's critique, where it exists, is implied through subtext instead of being engaged in the explicit manner employed by Zobel in the novel (1994). This difference might be accounted for as an ideological shift from a point of view focused on Négritude to one foregrounding Antillanité. For example, in distinguishing his view of Caribbean experience from that of Négritude, Glissant rejects Négritude's colonizer/colonized binarism by suggesting that black Caribbeans are "no longer forced to reject strategically the European elements in [their] composition, although they continue to be a source of alienation" (1989, 8). This position is similar to the one taken by the film, where French education functions as one of many experiences that José must negotiate. Furthermore, the film challenges both the content and the means of achieving this education by presenting it as a double-edged sword, which simultaneously offers advancement and cultural estrangement.

Early in the film, while the adults are away in the cane fields, the unsupervised children of the village create mischief by getting drunk on rum and burning down the shack belonging to Julien Twelve Toes. Subsequently, they are sent to the fields to work, except José, who is forbidden to participate by M'man Tine. In a scene that opens in a series of medium and long shots of the children working beside the adults, José is shown watching from the edge of the fields. Depicted in a claustrophobic tight medium shot that accentuates his isolation from the working community, he appears miserable. This is followed by a loosely framed medium shot portraying the manager astride his horse in the foreground with the overseer on his donkey in the background. Addressing José, the manager scoffs sarcastically, "Lazybones. Your grandmother thinks that you'll get a government job!" This reference to M'man Tine's single-minded pursuit of French education as a means out of the cane field demonstrates the power of such education as a means of advancement. The sarcasm with which the comment is delivered, however, implicitly charges M'man Tine with having goals for José that are inappropriate to his social station as a black Caribbean. This suggests that the pursuit of French education can act as a divisive factor within the striated black Caribbean community, in which certain social strata may have a vested interest in preventing such advancement. Stung by the manager's sarcasm, José walks into the field to look for M'man Tine. He is intercepted by Tortilla, a female classmate, who taunts him, saying that he will not be among those getting paid on Sat-

Occulted Caribbean Histories in *Sugar Cane Alley*

urday. Tortilla's pride in her earning ability accentuates the economic value of the children's labor and further distances José from his own peer group.

When José finally confronts M'man Tine, he is depicted in a loosely framed medium shot that places him in the foreground with other adult and child cane cutters working in the background, placing José's challenge to M'man Tine's decision to forbid him from participating in the labor within a larger social context. Clearly, José's desire is simply to be at one with his larger community. The close-up reverse shot that follows locates M'man Tine on the far left of the screen in opposition to José on the far right as he faces her. She states emphatically that she refuses to allow José to end up in the cane fields, "like all blacks without pride who throw their kids into the same misery." The use of an extreme close-up of José's troubled reaction indicates that he does not fully understand her decision to maintain a position that clearly separates them from their community. The fact that the film does not fully resolve the conflict, however, opens a space for spectators to consider the implications of both M'man Tine's determination and the alienation that José continues to feel. Furthermore, such an approach presents José's experiences, not as oppositional binarisms, but as complicated facts of being black Caribbean that José must somehow mediate by using his best judgment as an individual.

Martinique's heavily striated racial topography is based on a hierarchical concept of color that "traditionally reaffirms the superiority of white over the black in such a way that the closer a category is to whiteness, the more it is esteemed" (Giraud 1995, 77). The film takes up the challenge of describing this from a cultural context that has moved beyond the binarisms of Négritude into a more complex environment informed by Antillanité's demand that the devalorization of Caribbean history and culture be countered by an awareness and pride in Caribbeanness itself (Murdoch 1992, 3). The film's depiction of race relations in Martinique shares with Glissant's position a sense of the complexity of Caribbean cultural realities that developed in response to, or perhaps out of, the fragmentation caused by European nations simultaneously devaluing such cultures (Glissant 1989, 235). Furthermore, although the film has a tendency to depict race relations without taking a firm

CHAPTER 2

ideological position, the ambiguity created generates a space in which the spectator can consider the roles of both black and white Caribbeans in perpetuating slavery-based cultural imperatives.

An example of this occurs in a scene later in the film, the function of which is to interrogate black Caribbean attitudes toward race. As José passes a cinema, a black Caribbean man attempts to enter without paying. Miss Flora, the black Caribbean cashier, is distraught and remarks to José that she really detests "that race." As he gently remonstrates Miss Flora for condemning her own race over such a triviality, José is depicted in a lyrically lit tight close-up shot that reinforces a certain childlike simplicity. Miss Flora's passionate response is also framed in a tight close-up, portraying her behind the mesh of the cashier's wicket as she declares her disgust and asserts that although she is black, her character is white. The dominance of the wire mesh in the composition reinforces Miss Flora's entrapment in a rigid hierarchical society that actively feeds her own self-loathing. The depth to which Martinican society is inculcated with discourse on skin color is illustrated when José states that Miss Flora would never marry anyone but a white man. Miss Flora concurs, remarking, "at least my kids would be light-skinned," thus linking upward social mobility to a whitening of the black race. Although José does not comment directly on the wisdom of such a desire, his final close-up, as he excuses himself to go meet M'man Tine, visually foregrounds his deep regret at this fact of Martinican life. Thus, by refusing to explicitly resolve Miss Flora's and José's positions, the film foregrounds the extent to which hierarchical racial structures have fragmented black Martinican culture, but it also allows the spectator space in which to draw his or her own conclusion on this complicated matter.

The film's greatest departure from Zobel's novel involves combining the character of José's childhood friend, Léopold, with a minor incident involving a béké man and his mulatto children in order to create a major story skein focused on béké culture and its relationship to black Caribbeanness (Haley and Warner 1997, 384–85). Léopold's introduction as a character immediately emphasizes his social distance from his black classmates. In a medium long shot of the children waiting to enter the classroom, his leather boots, pith helmet, and the fine material of his shirt starkly contrast with the other children's bare feet, clean but shabby clothing, and battered straw hats. As the other children discuss zombie myths, one boy suggests that the whites are really devils, prompting Léopold to call him a liar. As the boys begin to scuffle, Léopold shouts that they know nothing about whites. This comes to have an ironic tone in retrospect as it is later revealed that Léopold is the son of the béké Jacques de Thorail. This scene also demonstrates Léopold's conflicted position in Martinican society, which forces him to defend his whiteness against his blackness.

The first view of Léopold's home life illustrates the intricate nuances within which he is expected to develop a sense of identity. In a scene in which Léopold returns home from school, he is met by his mother, Honorine, on the steps of his father's elegant colonial home. As Jacques de Thorail's mistress and the mother of his child, Honorine clearly emulates European style in her fine Western clothing, jewelry, and excellent French. Ushering Léopold into the house, she reminds him that his father does not approve of him playing with the Black Shack Alley children. This evidences, as Gerise Herndon suggests, the profound rupture in the de Thorail household as Léopold is caught between loving his béké father and craving the company of other black children (1996, 263–64). Honorine's admonishment emphasizes the isolation created by Léopold's mulatto heritage and serves to separate him from a community he obviously values.

The importance of European culture in the de Thorail home is reemphasized later in the same scene when Honorine makes a point of playing Josephine Baker's "J'ai deux amours" on the Victrola. In response to Léopold's query, Honorine explains that it is the latest tune from France. The pride with which she makes this statement is accentuated in a medium close-up shot as she moves languidly to the music. Palcy's decision to use "J'ai deux amours" provides an ironic commentary on the obvious *monde béké* enjoyed by Léopold and his mother, underscoring the tension that arises between dualities. This is further advanced at the end of the scene when the film moves to a medium shot of M'man Tine outside her shack cooking over an open fire. M'man Tine's ragged clothing and the obvious poverty in which she lives creates a powerful contrast between the statuses of the two women.

CHAPTER 2

Despite fear of his father's disapproval, Léopold continues to pursue his friendship with José. This defiance eventually results in the unraveling of Léopold's comfortable existence when de Thorail catches him playing with José at the river. In a fury, de Thorail attempts to wrest the reins of Léopold's horse from José's control, resulting in his accidental trampling as the horse resists. Later, after being informed by the doctor that de Thorail's injury is fatal, Honorine and Léopold are depicted embracing in a medium close-up shot. Honorine's tearful face as she asks plaintively, "What will become of us?" demonstrates just how tenuous her status is: in the absence of de Thorail, she loses legitimacy and power despite her longtime committed relationship with him. Léopold's reassuring response, "I'm here, Mother" provides ironic foreshadowing of his own betrayal. In a later scene, he is depicted in a medium close-up peeking into his father's sick room as de Thorail tells Honorine that Léopold will inherit land specifically set aside for him. Framed in a medium close-up, de Thorail removes his family signet ring, giving it to Honorine for Léopold. Honorine's response is portrayed in a tight close-up as she pleads with him to recognize Léopold by giving him the de Thorail name. Shocked, de Thorail refuses, explaining that his name has been borne by generations of whites and is not for a mulatto. Completely devastated by what he overhears, Léopold runs away, and it is later revealed through José's voice-over narration that he does not attend the funeral or return to school. This exchange underscores what Giraud has described as the value of the "white phenotype" because of its ability to confer the highest social status in Martinican society (1995, 80). Thus, in refusing to dilute his European purity by claiming a mulatto son under his family name, de Thorail demonstrates the strict homogamy that perpetuates a devaluation of black Caribbean culture (80).

The valorization of French culture was not restricted to béké society but permeated virtually every aspect and institution of Martinican life, including education. Although the film does not explicitly deride French education, its values and impact on black Caribbean identities is probed through subtle critique. In an early sequence, the standard French educational environment is portrayed as a boxlike classroom with straight rows of desks dominated by a rigidly authoritarian teacher dressed entirely in white. This rigid structure provides a distinct contrast to the

Occulted Caribbean Histories in *Sugar Cane Alley*

Sugar Cane Alley (Courtesy of New Yorker Films)

natural space of Médouze's open-air "classroom." The male teacher is portrayed in a series of medium shots, carrying a pointer and towering over students confined to their desks. As he lectures them on the value of the school certificate to the "humblest of people," the visual composition stresses the distance between the status of the students and that of the instructor, emphasizing an environment in which learning is strictly controlled and structured. Furthermore, the teacher's portrayal of French education as the only way for the children to escape life in the cane fields for a "decent life" subtly devalues the validity of black Caribbean culture. Assimilation, therefore, into French culture is valorized, and the ability to move beyond the sugar cane industry is dependent on the degree to which a student conforms to the system.

It is significant that the first sentence the students record in their workbooks is "Learning is the key that opens the door to our second freedom," thus implying that the first door to freedom was liberation from slavery itself. This is an ironic assertion, given that liberation did not involve reparations or land reform and, in fact, entrenched a sugar cane plantation system as dependent on oppressed black Caribbean labor for profit as it was during slavery. In addition, the film also illustrates the absurdity of a French curriculum ill suited to Martinican experience. In a later sequence, Mr. Roc, the teacher, faces two lines of students outside the schoolroom as he instructs them to remember that he will quiz them on glaciers the next day. Depicted in a long shot that emphasizes the tropical architecture of the school, the reference to alpine glaciers seems almost comically misplaced. Finally, the film demonstrates that French education itself does not automatically assure advancement: when Tortilla and José are both selected to take the scholarship exam in Fort-de-France, Saint Louis regretfully refuses to allow his daughter to continue because the family needs the income she will generate working for the postmistress. Although this is some measure of escape from the cane fields, the poverty faced by her family means that Tortilla's labor is worth more to them than her eventual advancement. Thus, ultimately French education does not provide Tortilla with a means of escaping the cycle of poverty she was born into.

José's African and French education come together in a statement of black Caribbean identity through a story about Médouze that José writes as a course assignment while at school in Fort-de-France. The film uses medium and medium long shots to portray the teacher as he reads the conclusion of José's story to the class. This is intercut with a loosely framed high-angle medium shot of José listening with pride to the recitation. Written in French, the content of the story appropriates the colonizer's language to present a poignant indictment of the sugar cane industry and the oppressed black labor on which it depends from a point of view that is distinctly black Martinican. This suggests that, although José may be inculcated by French language and culture in a system that devalues his own culture and experience, he is capable of mediating that influence and transforming it into a means of expressing and valorizing the cultural underpinnings of his identity.

The devaluation of José's culture is made evident when the teacher accuses him of plagiarizing the story: the obvious inference is that a poor black Martinican child simply could not author work of that quality. Palcy's decision to have José's eventual exoneration lead to a full scholarship for his obvious talent seems, on the surface, to be a vindication of French education as a means of advancement for black Caribbeans. It certainly possesses an air of deus ex machina as the scholarship greatly relieves M'man Tine's ongoing struggle to make ends meet for herself and her grandson. The end of the film, however, undermines this position as it makes a clear statement that José's identity is a synthesis of his experiences rather than a product of a single influence.

Near the end of the film, José returns to the village in search of M'man Tine, who has failed to return to Fort-de-France from a visit to Black Shack Alley. He finds her seriously ill and being nursed by Tortilla. In an exchange of tight close-ups, M'man Tine tells José that while weeding around her shack the day before, she suffered a tremendous pain in her chest. In response to José's concerned expression, she tells him that she is feeling better and that old people are like machines because they keep on going "purely by routine." The tight close-ups of M'man Tine and José emphasize their close psychological bond and are used with calculation to draw the spectator into that intimate shared space.

As José helps M'man Tine light her pipe outside the shack, Tortilla's younger sister arrives with the news that Léopold has been arrested for stealing "Whitey's ledger," an act Tortilla describes as motivated by his desire to prove that the cane bosses have been cheating the workers. José leaves M'man Tine and goes to the factory where Léopold is being held, finding his friend being publicly humiliated as a crowd of cane cutters looks on. The scene begins with a medium shot of Léopold as an officer ties his hands in front of him with rope. The next shot depicts the crowd as they struggle against the fence, which is guarded by mulatto officers. As the crowd shouts, "Let him go . . . Whitey's niggers," the film cuts to a long shot of the mounted officers dragging Léopold behind on foot. In the following high-angle medium close-ups that accentuate his role as victim, Léopold's exhausted expression and ragged condition make his degradation seem oddly timeless, as if slavery had never ended. This, coupled with the complicity of the mulatto workers, stresses the film's ideological premise that as long as black Martinicans remain divided by gradations of color, they will not succeed in ending their own oppression.

Although the crowd cannot directly intervene, they are capable of expressing resistance and anger. This is illustrated in a series of medium shots of the crowd intercut with medium shots of Léopold's departure

CHAPTER 2

as they begin to sing a song in Creole that underscores that their misery is linked to a system that ensures their poverty and denies them justice. As the song progresses, the line "I crossed over the sea . . . to go and see . . . what was happening in Guadeloupe . . . their suffering is like ours," connects the situation in Martinique to a larger Caribbean perspective, thus linking the end of the film to the larger pan-Caribbean project first stated in the dedication at the beginning of the film. In addition, the intercutting of Léopold's departure while the crowd sings has implicit significance: Léopold, who has been separated from black Martinicans by virtue of being the child of a béké and forbidden to speak Creole or consort with those of darker skin, is now recouped into that community by virtue of his rebellious theft of the ledger. In effect, this links two acts of resistance, for Léopold has done what the mulatto workers have failed to do by choosing to stand with black Martinicans against their oppression. Finally, this is reinforced by José's last words to him. As Tortilla pushes through the crowd and whispers that José must return immediately, the film cuts to an extreme close-up of José's tortured face as he screams out to Léopold, "The people cry famine!" A close-up of Léopold's battered face pairs this shot as he looks back in recognition, almost smiling in response. Thus, the film suggests that although Léopold's sacrifice has been ineffective in the short term, his actions provide an impetus to further the struggle in the future.

José returns to the shack to find that M'man Tine has died. In a series of poignant close-ups, José washes the dirt of Black Shack Alley from his grandmother's hands and feet, symbolizing an end for himself as well as for M'man Tine. It is significant that the film intertwines the incidents of Léopold's arrest and M'man Tine's death in the narrative: both ultimately undercut the significance of his French education by underlining the sense that José's entire cultural context is the locus of his identity, rather than the product of any single element. This is visually illustrated by the closing shot of the film, a long shot that slowly pans across a hill reminiscent of the one he shared with Médouze. José's voice-over narration asserts that M'man Tine has returned to Médouze's Africa and that José himself will return to Fort-de-France, taking his Black Shack Alley with him. Thus, his identity comes to represent mediation between many layers of experience, including Médouze's traditional African teachings, the alienation and advantage of French education, the resistance and oppression of cane cutters in the sugar cane industry, as well as the striated race relations of his own people. Ultimately, the film portrays José's life as a process that continues to unfold.

By ending the film with José's exhortation, *Sugar Cane Alley* reclaims the ground staked out by the initial dedication of the film to all Black Shack Alleys around the world. This sense of belonging to an existence that goes beyond Martinican realities ultimately grounds the film in Antillanité. Glissant suggests that artistic vision "creates the possibility of cementing the bonds of unity in the future" in present-day Caribbean countries whose experiences are subjected to very different political, social, and economic factors (Glissant 1989, 235). In a sense, *Sugar Cane Alley* is a work that reflects a broad range of theoretical positions or, perhaps more accurately, acts as a bridge connecting Négritude, Antillanité, and Créolité in one continuous stream of Caribbean culture. As Herndon argues, the film successfully challenges the implicit belief that black Caribbean experience can only operate through imitation of Eurocentric culture by presenting José's experience as an affirmation of a complex Afro-Caribbean matrix (1996, 265). Ultimately, Palcy portrays the collision of histories that inform Martinican experience as positive and creative influences in the emergence of new Caribbean ways of being.

THREE

Reclaiming Africa
Black Women's Discourses in *Daughters of the Dust*

There is always a danger, when using categorizing terms such as *black women's discourses*, of creating intellectual ghettoes that reinforce margins and peripheries by assigning them convenient designations.[1] The term *blackness*, for example, is made relevant to discourses of racism and cultural difference because it carries encoded within it skin color, a history of oppression, and the racist concept of white superiority (Boyce Davies 1994, 7). Such a term demonstrates that language and terminology are politically loaded and carry with them whole histories and ideologies that may be obscured by familiarity or presumptions based on criteria that lurk beneath the surface. The exposure of such limiting factors is inherent to any discussion surrounding issues of representation and subjectivity for black women because "it is the convergence of multiple places and cultures that re-negotiates the terms of Black women's experience that in turn negotiates and re-negotiates their identities" (3). Hence, the very movement between differing subjectivities offers the potential for myriad ways of defining and interrogating black women's differences within an often-hostile terrain of cultural, racial, and gender imperatives aimed at delimiting that expression.[2]

Black Women's Discourses in *Daughters of the Dust*

In the quest for a means to adequately express black experience in the black diaspora, black writers and thinkers have always found it necessary to explode the barriers of Eurocentric frameworks that historically began with a racist belief in black inferiority. This is especially true in the area of women's studies, where feminism has generally been proscribed within the narrow circumference of universalist constructs that foreground white Western concerns and worldviews. For those black writers and thinkers who wish to explore black women's issues, these assumptions are at best flawed and at worst representative of the very systemic oppression they wish to critique. For example, Clenora Hudson-Weems describes the uneasy relationship with feminism when she states that some Africana women reluctantly turn to feminism because frameworks suitable for describing a black woman's experiences are not readily available or accepted in mainstream academic thought with the same fervor as feminism (1994, 18). This reflects a profound gap between the ideological foundations of Western feminism and its failure to adequately account for discourses of race. Based on the experience that "feminist terminology does not accurately reflect their reality or their struggle," some black thinkers have reassessed this troubled relationship with feminism and have developed new frameworks that directly address the very specific needs of black women (18). Such work has resulted in a lively and fruitful debate on the nature of black female experience and the ways in which it might be constituted in theoretical terms.

Discourses such as black feminism, for example, have moved issues of race and identity to the forefront of discussions on contemporary theory. As early as 1984, bell hooks argued that "white women who dominate feminist discourse, who for the most part make and articulate feminist theory, have little or no understanding of white supremacy as a racial politic" (1984, 4). Although this appears to suggest that the rise of black feminism, which has always existed in myriad forms, was a reaction to marginalization, it would be more accurate to argue that the gulf between white and black feminisms became insurmountable as the emphasis on women as a universalized category gained momentum.[3] The issue for hooks and other black feminists is that the negation of difference failed to account for the powerful force of "factors like class, race, religion, [and] sexual preference" on experiences of sexism in different women's lives (5). This made it imperative for black feminists to conceive and reconfigure new parameters better suited to their needs and desires (10). Far from being simply reactionary, black feminism is a complex response to the realities of black women's experiences as circumscribed within a "notion of fluidity, multiple identities, [and] repetition which must be multiply articulated" (Boyce Davies 1994, 48). Hence, as black feminism(s) grapple with the dynamic struggles resulting from the interplay between maps and histories, race and sexism, community and individual, one aspect that continually arises is the notion of demolishing boundaries that prevent the voices of black women from being heard in all their diversity. As hooks describes it, black feminism(s) are confrontational to all dominant practices because only by challenging both established and emerging theoretical constructions of black identity can new paradigms surface (hooks 1990, 145). If "borders are those places where different cultures, identities, sexualities, classes, geographies, races, genders and so on collide or interchange" then constructions "of Black female specificity and the critique of the multiple oppression of Black women" cannot ever assume a fixed position or singular point of view (Boyce Davies 1994, 16, 6). Within such terrain, a strict definition of what constitutes black feminisms remains necessarily elusive.

This is not to suggest that black feminisms are uncontested: other narratives of black women's subjectivities offer alternative constructs. One such stance is evidenced by *Africana Womanism*, a concept first defined by Hudson-Weems in 1987 (1994, 22). As a sociopolitical strategy, Africana Womanism places the agenda of language and criteria at the center of the grounds of contest (22).[4] Hudson-Weems's choice of terminology effectively distances her theoretical perspective from that of both white and black feminisms by explicitly asserting a distinctive experience of womanhood: as she argues, "*Africana* . . . identifies the ethnicity of the woman being considered, and this reference to her ethnicity, establishing her cultural identity, relates directly to her ancestry and land base—Africa" (22–23). The selection of the term *Womanism* creates a link to past struggles for recognition by referencing Sojourner Truth's confrontation of white racism in the 1851 landmark speech, "Ar'n't I a Woman," where she claimed equal rights with men from the perspec-

Black Women's Discourses in *Daughters of the Dust*

tive of being a black woman and an ex-slave (23).[5] Most critically, however, Africana Womanism is clearly distinct from both white and black feminisms because it eschews the binary opposition of patriarchal male versus oppressed female based on the position that "Africana men have never had the same institutionalized power to oppress Africana women as White men have had to oppress White women" (25). This is a critical distinction: although black feminism shares common ground with black men, the struggle of black women to achieve subjectivity is perceived as being different from that of black men, based, in part, on gender politics (hooks 1992, 46). In contrast, Africana Womanists refuse the position that gender issues are forefront in their lives, embracing instead a more inclusive approach that involves both men and women by prioritizing their culture's struggle for equality and advancement within an African framework (Hudson-Weems 1994, 25–29). In addition, among the eighteen prerequisites envisioned by Hudson-Weems as the foundation for an Africana Womanist theoretical practice, there is an emphasis on being "family-centered," a position that rejects the idea of personal victimization when the entirety of the community is endangered by racism and inequality (58–59).[6] The notion of a family-centered theoretical practice, therefore, replaces gender oppression issues with a concept of social agency that views women as integral in advancing community-based problem-solving approaches to social needs. Another distinguishing factor for Africana Womanism is that of the role played by spirituality, which, for Hudson-Weems, involves embracing an "African cosmology" in which "the physical and spiritual world co-exist" (70). By stressing the importance of reclaiming an African-inflected spirituality, Hudson-Weems reinforces the defining role of African tradition as a locus for black women's identities.

This chapter focuses on Julie Dash's groundbreaking feature film, *Daughters of the Dust* (United States, 1991), which is set in the Sea Islands just off the coast of South Carolina. Bordering productive coastal lowlands, the Sea Islands played a major role in the American slave trade both as a point for unloading slaves and as a lush plantation area (Washington Creel 1990, 69). Imported for plantation labor, the slaves in this region were involved "in the cultivation of indigo, then rice, and finally Sea Island cotton" (Pollitzer 1998, 54). The slave population of the Sea Islands came from a limited number of African ethic groups be-

CHAPTER 3

cause of the preferences of planters who were selective on the basis of geography and cultural origins of the slaves (Washington Creel 1990, 69). It is likely that the first slaves brought to the region were of Gold Coast origins: highly desirable in the Carolinas, approximately a thousand slaves from this area were imported by planters from the West Indies who settled in the vicinity (69). The second most sought after ethic group came from the Kongo Kingdom in Angola, but importation of these slaves was banned for a decade after the Stono Rebellion in 1739 (69). The gap was then filled by African slaves taken from the areas of Sierra Leone and Liberia (69). In addition, Africans from Senegambia and Ibos from the Bight of Biafra also contributed to the makeup of this population (Pollitzer 1998, 58). As a result of this selection process, Africans enslaved in the area were able to retain more cultural identity and continuity (Washington Creel 1990, 69) than others. Given that many of the slaves in this region came from West African cultures, "cultural similitude was coupled with relative isolation and resulted in a tendentious process of African provenance, American acculturation, and intergroup socialization" (69). Over time, this resulted in the emergence of the Gullah culture.[7]

The Gullah are an extremely important group in the history of resistance to American slavery. Defiant in the face of attempts to assimilate them to white culture, the Gullah were in the forefront of rebellion against slavery (Kly 1998, 20). Their impact is exemplified by their involvement in the "Gullah War," waged during a series of violent encounters across "the South Carolina/Georgia/Florida region between 1739 (the Stono Rebellion) and 1858 (the ending of the 'third Seminole War')" (19).[8] The role of the Gullah in this conflict was considered such a serious challenge to the institution of slavery that, in battlefield reports, any reference to African race was omitted or encoded to prevent any chance that the rebellion would spread to other slaves (28). This has resulted in an obfuscation of their role in this conflict, but it nevertheless stands as a testimony to the Gullah's deep commitment to securing their freedom and equality.

Gullah culture in the Sea Islands maintained much closer ties to African origin than many other African American cultural groups, in part because the islands themselves are isolated. As a result, "an African world view, an African theory of being, and some African cus-

Black Women's Discourses in *Daughters of the Dust*

toms were significant in Gullah religious tendencies and communal existence" (Washington Creel 1990, 71). For example, African basket-weaving techniques survive in the baskets made by Gullah women and quilt making often draws on textile designs found in various West African cultures (Pollitzer 1998, 65). The products of other crafts, such as "wood carving, ironwork, clay pottery and residential architecture-like graveyard decorations" also draw on similar artistic traditions (65). As William Pollitzer notes, the tendency to retain such influences as well as infuse them with New World experiences suggests that the hybrid nature of Gullah culture brings together a variety of influences that interact, intersect, and transform each other through contact (65).

A significant feature of Gullah culture is the survival of African spiritual practices. At the center of these beliefs is a concept that "spirituality affected one's whole system of being, embracing the consciousness, social interactions and attitudes, fears and dispositions of the community at large" (Washington Creel 1990, 72). Within such a construct, the wellness of the community is the locus of concern, reducing the emphasis on individualism (72). Furthermore, the Gullah's strong "belief in afterlife" was intimately linked to an African concept of existence that foregrounded "the perpetuity of life through time, space, and circumstance" (81). The power of these beliefs is such that they often exist in tandem with Christianity and other religious practices (Pollitzer 1998, 63). Hence, as Margaret Washington Creel suggests, the unique pollination between myriad African cultural influences has resulted in the emergence of Gullah culture as a culturally distinct African American community (1990, 69).

Becoming a filmmaker was not among Julie Dash's goals as she grew up in the Queensbridge Housing Projects in Long Island City, New York, because none of the African American images she was exposed to, especially those of women, suggested that this was possible (Dash 1992, 1–2). At seventeen, however, Dash joined a cinematography workshop at the Studio Museum in Harlem and became a member of a group of young African Americans discovering the power of making and redefining African American screen images (2). After graduating with a degree in film production, Dash moved to Los Angeles with the goal of enrolling at the University of California, Los Angeles, film

CHAPTER 3

school, hoping to emulate Charles Burnett, Haile Gerima, and Larry Clark, who were making narrative films (2–3). Although this opportunity never materialized, Dash subsequently received a fellowship to attend the American Film Institute. This led to a Guggenheim grant to research and write a series of films on black women, resulting in the short film *Illusions* (1982), about an African American woman studio executive who passes for white during World War II. During this time, she began intensive research for *Daughters of the Dust*, her first feature-length film (5). The success of this film gave Dash a place of note among "a radical group of black directors who came together at the UCLA film school in the 1970s and later came to be known as the L.A. Underground" (Ellis and Wexman 2002, 465). Creating such landmark works as Billy Woodbury's *Bless Their Little Hearts* (United States, 1984), Charles Burnett's *To Sleep with Anger* (United States, 1990), and Dash's own *Daughters of the Dust,* these filmmakers contributed to the redefinition of black representation in cinema (465).

As a filmmaker, Dash is well grounded in African American culture, and she perceives it both within, and as an extension of, explorations of culture. Dash's contribution as the first African American woman filmmaker to direct a feature film is especially significant because of her frank depiction of the power exercised by African American women in shaping their society. *Daughters of the Dust* is focused on the Peazant family on the eve of its migration from the Sea Islands off South Carolina to the mainland in 1902. The film examines Gullah culture and the aftermath of slavery, and Dash's depiction of the competing discourses of exploitation, spirituality, African origin, and contemporary assimilation that separate and unite the women in the Peazant family reveals the dynamicism and diversity of black female subjectivity. Finally, the film's use of orality as a rhetorical and historical device demonstrates the survival of African culture in an African American framework.

Daughters of the Dust draws on Dash's own family stories concerning the family's migration to the north from South Carolina (Dash 1992, 5). In addition, she was inspired by a series of photographs of African American women, taken at the turn of the century, by black Harlem photographer, James Van Der Zee (4). The film has been screened in a number of venues worldwide and has garnered numerous awards. Most important, the film examines a broad range of African American women's experiences within a discursive framework that invites engagement with, and scrutiny of, the many ways in which history, family, and race collide. The film presents spectators with "nothing less than a re-presentation of the process of envisioning, in its relationship to identity, community, family, and history" (Erhart 1996, 118). Highly innovative in its recombinant use of history, narrative structure, and aesthetic codes, the film seeks to reconfigure "formal, visual conventions" and reclaim specific African American histories that reveal community strategies for survival (118). The film's narrative adopts an oral structure based on the storytelling traditions of African griots, an approach that lends itself to a broad episodic structure of vignettes (Dash, quoted in Baker 1992, 151). Framed within Dash's extensive research on the Sea Islands and her own family's Gullah culture, the film presents "a nonchronological representation of history in which historical 'facts' are selected for representation according to whether they effectively reveal something about the 'essence' of a culture or a historical period, rather than according to 'objective,' historical demands for chronological accuracy" (Brøndum 1999, 155).[9] By taking such an approach, the film fashions a speculative history challenging existing Western constructs, thereby creating an environment that places black diasporic sensibilities at the center of the film's discourse (154).

One of the reasons why *Daughters of the Dust* is a film suitable for an Africana Womanist reading is its strong focus on the roles played by women as sources of leadership in the preservation of families. The family is headed by Nana Peazant, a powerful matriarch who began life as a slave and who now faces the extraordinarily difficult task of ensuring family cultural continuity as her children and grandchildren prepare to scatter in search of more prosperous lives. As the narrative unfolds and the women of the extended family debate their futures, a variety of female perspectives are presented for consideration: Viola represents the power of Christianity and the conformity it demands; Yellow Mary, a prostitute, offers an example of femaleness that is both independent and exploited by racism; Eula, raped by a white man and now pregnant, must find a way to heal her relationship with her husband, Eli, through the assistance of her mystical Unborn Child; and Haagar valorizes assimilation to white culture as she single-mindedly pursues the education and economic prosperity promised by migration

Daughters of the Dust (Courtesy of Kino International)

Black Women's Discourses in *Daughters of the Dust*

to the mainland. Over the course of the film, each of these viewpoints presents a challenge to Nana Peazant's determination to preserve the black cultural roots of the family, and each woman finds either succor or alienation within the context of the family as a whole.

More specifically, *Daughters of the Dust* shares with Africana Womanism the precept that, although women's oppression is an urgent social problem generally, for African American women, "the problem of liberating an entire people—exploited, repressed, and oppressed solely on the basis of their race—is an even greater one" (Hudson-Weems 1994, 58). Thus, the film shares with Africana Womanism an affirmation of African American communities as a whole. In this respect, the debate at the heart of the film is not focused on gender oppression as a sole concern, although in the cases of Eula and Yellow Mary, it is obviously a strand of contention: instead, Dash moves the discussion beyond these borders to frame these concerns within the need to persist and survive when faced with a society systemically programmed legally, economically, and ethically to dehumanize black families. Most important, Dash portrays these women as agents of change within a vibrant black culture capable of transcending the racist barriers raised to impede progress.

The family-centered debate of *Daughters of the Dust* is not sufficient on its own to sustain an Africana Womanist reading. As Hudson-Weems argues, Africana Womanism "has a definite slant toward Afrocentricity in its truest meaning/sense" (1994, 47). Hence, like *Sankofa*, *Daughters of the Dust* must evidence "an African-centered perspective of Africana women's lives" (47). One of the ways Dash achieves this involves employing the island culture as one of the principal characters in the film. For example, in the intertitles at the beginning of the film, "the Sea Island Gullah" are described as a "distinct, imaginative and original African American culture," that "remembered and recollected much of what their ancestors brought with them from Africa." This view, with its affirmative link to African origin, suggests that the isolation of the locale permits the perpetuation of an "authentic" culture that has not yet succumbed to assimilation by white American society.

As is the case with *Sankofa*'s Afrocentric narrative, *Daughters of the Dust* accords a primary position to African-based spirituality as a means of quantifying an authentic black identity. For example, the first

CHAPTER 3

dreamlike images of the film, which include a close-up of a woman's rough hands filled with red clay soil that is blown away by the wind, a long shot of Nana Peazant bathing fully clothed in a river and a slow pan of the bedroom interior of the shanty, are meant to evoke a place and culture where magic functions as an integral part of experience. The effect is heightened by voice-over narration, in which a woman's voice intones, "I am the first and the last. I am the honored one and the scorned one. I am the whore and the holy one. I am the wife and a virgin. I am the barren one and many are my daughters." The combination of images and narration creates a kind of narrative suspense by introducing apparently spiritual practices but delaying their explanation in order to raise spectators' curiosity. Furthermore, the images and the narration also serve to identify Nana Peazant as an individual who is in close contact with the African-inflected spiritualism of her ancestors, another aspect of her character that makes her suitable for an Africana Womanist reading (Hudson-Weems 1994, 70). Her position, both literally as the center of the narrative and metaphorically in context of the landscape as she bathes in the water, signals that Nana Peazant represents an immediate and living African origin. Thus, ancestral connection to African origin is maintained despite the disjunctive effects of slavery and cultural translation in a foreign environment.

The film depicts this interconnection between a mystical African origin and an American context through the use of dissolves as transition devices between the shots, a visual strategy that develops its own intrinsic meaning by repetition throughout the film. Dash describes this technique as "layered dissolves," which are intended to created a sense of interconnected images whose impact are accumulative rather than separational (Bobo 1995, 134). This parallels the use of multiple layers of discourse and histories in the film and creates a dense, sensual effect that foregrounds the physical, almost mystic, beauty of the environment. In addition, landscape shots are used to create bridges between narrative episodes to similar effect: for example, long shots of the beach and of the sun in the sky, along with sweeping aerial shots of the island, are frequently used to create a powerful sense of the Peazant family as an organic part of the landscape rather than an outside force dominating it.[10] As transitions, these shots provide discursive space enabling spectators to muse on what has been revealed in the narrative episodes that precede them.

Dash draws her inspiration for the narrative structure from two sources. First, she describes the film as created from "the scraps of memories, that these women [of the Peazant family] carry around in tin cans and little private boxes" (Dash, quoted in Foster 1997, 66). Second, she acknowledges the influence of the early black thinker W. E. B. DuBois, who wrote passionately about the disjunctive effects of slavery that effectively erased both lineage and personal histories (Dash, quoted in Foster 1997, 67). Both these impulses are signified by the box in which Nana Peazant, the family's matriarch, safeguards the significant artifacts of her family. The scraps of memory contained within the box, which preserve the family's African origin and history, symbolize how memory functions as a system "of resistance" based "within African ways of knowing" (Langley 2001, 153). In addition, the photographs taken of the family over the course of the day that serve as transitional devices between narrative episodes are symbolic of the creation and collection of memories. This gives the film an almost "kaleidoscopic" quality as history collides with fiction, encouraging the audience to view slavery and its legacies from a fresh perspective (Brouwer 1995, 5).

The film challenges Western cinematic codes by rejecting Hollywood's binary notions of conflict that focus on a central protagonist and antagonist. Instead, the narrative features a collective of characters whose actions change according to narrative need. The women of the Peazant family, including the characters of Viola, Yellow Mary, Nana, Eula, and Haagar, all express strong opinions, create conflict, and resolve differences according to their own specific worldsense. Furthermore, as the tension between return and departure exposes the striations among the women, the very notion of family is interrogated as a site of competing discourse. By excavating suppressed histories from the past, the film evokes Gullah culture through visual symbols and family rituals (Foster 1997, 49). Foster argues, the visual and narrative approach "strongly evokes an Afrocentric visual memory making" (65). As a result, the film creates a multilayered discourse as each of the Peazant women seeks empowerment for her race and family, debating questions of identity, cultural values, and self-worth.

CHAPTER 3

The significance of conflicting points of view is demonstrated early in the film with the introduction of Yellow Mary and Viola. In a scene near the beginning, Viola is presented as a committed Baptist missionary who returns from the mainland, with Mr. Snead, a photographer, in order to document the family's migration north. Dash describes Viola as someone who hides her fears, lack of self-esteem, and womanhood within "the cloak of the Christian missionary," and thus she represents the acculturating effects of Christianity, a religion often imposed on slaves in an effort to break their connection with their African roots (1992, 37). This separation is visually suggested by the low-angle long shot that introduces Viola and Mr. Snead as they wait at the edge of the water for the arrival of a boat. The shot scale immediately emphasizes the incongruity of their stylish but restrained formal clothing, which clashes with the wild profusion of the forest surrounding them. Furthermore, the prim way in which Viola is seated with Mr. Snead standing immediately next to her has the feeling of a formal portrait that is at odds with the untamed environment. Such composition foregrounds their urban lifestyles and identifies them as proponents of progress linked with mainland culture. In contrast, the high-angle reverse long shot that shows the approach of the boat raises mystery. Seated in the center are two elaborately dressed women, one of whom is completely obscured by a large hat and white veil. Although both of these women are clearly urban as well, their ostentatious costumes speak more of the bedroom than the church hall. This assessment is validated by a close-up of Viola as she experiences a flash of recognition and identifies one of the women as her cousin, Yellow Mary. Significantly, the shot allows the spectator to weigh the gap between Viola's polite words and her sarcastic nonverbal reaction, which definitely implies that Mary is not a respectable woman and her arrival is unexpected.

The visual strategy of the film advances this conflict through a series of shots that set the tone of the adversarial relationship between the women. Viola and Snead sit facing Yellow Mary and her lover, Trula, as if battle lines have been drawn between Christian and sinner. Depicted in a medium two-shot, sitting fastidiously next to Mr. Snead, whose cheerful expression indicates he is oblivious to the subtext of the situation, Viola's distaste is evident in her lowered eyes that refuse direct engagement and sardonic tone of voice that states "this has turned out

Black Women's Discourses in *Daughters of the Dust*

to be a very special day for the Peazant family indeed." Yellow Mary's reaction is framed in a close-up as she raises her veil and hesitates pointedly before acknowledging Viola's "welcome." The shot, which gives the first real glimpse of Yellow Mary, reveals a woman wearing lipstick and eye makeup, giving further evidence of her racy lifestyle. Thus, it is significant that the challenge between the two women is conducted through the exchange of character looks rather than explicit verbal repartee: by contrasting Viola's disapproving gaze with Yellow Mary's lazy, sensual manner, a space of ambiguity is opened allowing the spectator to actively interrogate the implications of both women's behavior.

As the scene progresses, Viola explains that she views the occasion as significant because it marks the family's first steps toward progress. Describing the impending move to the mainland as "an engraved invitation, you might say, to the culture, education and the wealth of the mainland," Viola valorizes Western cultural precepts, thus implying a repudiation of the cultural elements that make her people culturally distinct. Later, when Viola provocatively asks if Yellow Mary agrees with her, Yellow Mary and Trula exchange knowing looks and laugh mockingly. This act accentuates Viola's romanticized view of the benefits of becoming "pseudowhite," creating a contrast with Yellow Mary's more worldly, and more realistic, view of a potentially corrupt society. hooks suggests that Viola is a character capable of stripping away past memory and replacing it "with markers of what she takes to be a new civilization," a position that foregrounds Christianity as a powerful but concealed agent of acculturation (hooks, quoted in Dash 1992, 37). Given this context, Viola exists in a state of in-betweenness: neither fully accepted by white culture nor fully accepting of the validity of her own roots.

As narrative constructs, the women of *Daughters of the Dust* represent three strands of time that are continually interwoven with each other. Nana Peazant represents the past and a direct link to Africa as the matriarch of the Peazant clan and old enough to have lived through slavery. In contrast, her daughters and granddaughters are very much of the present, while the character of Eula's daughter, the Unborn Child, invokes the family's future. Although there are male characters in the film, most notably Nana Peazant's great-grandson Eli, Bilal Muhammed, and Mr. Snead, the film is primarily focused on the way that

CHAPTER 3

black women interact and communicate within a family setting. By placing women at the center of the narrative, the film is aligned with the Africana Womanist project of "creating an historical and cultural matrix from which women may claim autonomy and independence over their own lives" (Hudson-Weems 2001). This makes the film open to an Africana Womanist reading, particularly since the male characters in the film are portrayed as supportive, thus shifting the locus of the narrative from an oppositional gender construction to one that foregrounds race. When male oppression is present in the film, it is a product of white racism.[11] Yet it may be legitimately questioned whether this type of construct is the province of Africana Womanism alone: in describing black feminism as a "praxis" of different theoretical positions "in which each of the circles intersect, collide, bump against each other, relate, re-energize, separate and reorder themselves," Boyce Davies argues for a more fluid vision of what black feminism might be (1994, 55–56). From this perspective, the complex interplay among the women of the Peazant family may be considered in a larger cultural context: as representatives of different modes of experience, the Peazant women as a group challenge the notion of a monolithic, immutable black female identity. This suggests that the film is deliberately structured to invite multiple readings from different subject positions rather than offering a single, fixed point of view. Thus, although an Africana Womanist reading is possible, it does not exclude the possibility of a black feminist reading.

One of the ways in which the film achieves this is through the use of the Unborn Child. As a narrative strategy, the Unborn Child has two functions: first, she signals that this is an oral document in which past, present, and future coexist, interconnected both with words and the space between words. The second function of the Unborn Child is to connect the physical world of the island with the psychic world of spirituality. Introduced during a montage of images of the shanty in which the family lives, the Unborn Child's narration works to disseminate expositional information: for example, during a medium shot in which Eli turns away as Eula leans toward him in bed, the Unborn Child's narration identifies them as her parents, introducing the issue of Eula's rape by a white man as her parents' "problem." By placing the Unborn Child in the position of narrator, and providing her access to

Black Women's Discourses in *Daughters of the Dust*

information that may be unknown to the film's characters, the Unborn Child is posited as an omniscient figure, connected to all living events by virtue of her otherworldly existence. Later in the same scene, the Unborn Child openly acknowledges this existence when she relates that she traveled from the spirit world in answer to the call of Nana Peazant. As she does so, the camera tilts down a wall filled with children's drawings mixed with older, iconic images of animals and other figures that evoke a past time and culture. This reinforces a sense of seamlessness between the land and the spirit of the culture, between old times and new. In effect, the iconic imagery on the wall suggests that, although their exact meanings are lost or obscured by time and experience, they continue to exist in the imagination of the Peazant family as a kind of persistence of vision in memory, simply waiting to be transformed by rediscovery. Hence, the Unborn Child is innately linked to African sensibilities that have survived slavery and continue to influence the way in which the Peazant family interacts with the world.

In addition to the character of the Unborn Child, the centrality of African spirituality is demonstrated by the deep commitment of Nana Peazant to the preservation of these values. This is emphasized in a scene that takes place between Nana Peazant and Eli in the family graveyard as she tends her husband's grave. In a shot that begins in a close-up of Eli, Dash pans across the gravestone to Nana Peazant as the latter remarks, "I visit with old Peazant every day since the day him die. It's up to the living to keep in touch with the dead, Eli. Man's power don't end with death. We just move on to another place. A place where we go on watching over our living family." The camera movement underscores the importance of connectedness to one's center or ancestry by visually emphasizing the notion of an invisible familial link flowing from Eli, as representative of the present, to Nana Peazant as representative of the past or, perhaps more correctly, the source. This position is reaffirmed later in the scene when Nana Peazant implores him to accept the child Eula is carrying because "the ancestor and the womb are one in the same." Eli expresses his anger at Eula's rape when he asks Nana Peazant why her powers—and, by implication, her gods—failed to protect the family from violation by a white man. By placing the responsibility for that failure on Nana Peazant's shoulders, Eli is questioning the continued relevance of the old ways as a means of defining black selfhood. As Nana Peazant entreats him to remember that he is bonded through memory with all those who came before him, the film cuts to a montage of shots of the Peazant children dancing ecstatically on the beach. Shot in slow motion, the dreamlike images are layered with Nana's voice-over exhortation, "Let them old souls [African ancestors] come into your heart, Eli. Let them touch you with the hand of time. Let them feed your head with wisdom that ain't from this day and time. 'Cause when you leave this island, Eli Peazant, you ain't going to no land of milk and honey." The sequence valorizes African ancestry as a means of maintaining self-respect and a sense of place in the face of white oppression. Furthermore, the depiction of the girls as they dance emphasizes the omnipresence of an unbroken lineage of Africanity that transcends history and geography. Taken together, Nana Peazant's response echoes an Africana Womanist concern that "problems must not be resolved using an alien framework" but, rather, must be "addressed within the context of African culture" (Hudson-Weems 2000, 214). Hence, Nana Peazant's insistence that Eli actively center his identity on an ancestral praxis and seek the answer to his problem within that frame offers a resistance against the dehumanization both he and his wife have suffered through white violence against their persons.

Although there is certainly merit to arguing for the presence of an Africana Womanist perspective in *Daughters of the Dust*, the film does not present black women's selfhood as purely monolithic: instead, by fostering a conflicted space in which different ways of being jostle with one another, the narrative becomes a means of exploring myriad black female identities. The engagement of the Peazants with the positive and negative consequences of moving to the mainland from their varied perspectives shares with Africana Womanism a view of African American women as proactive in negotiating the social risks faced by their families (Hudson-Weems 2000, 213). For example, the character of Haagar might agree with Viola's commitment to modernity and Christianity, but she does so from the more material aspect of her family's economic advancement. For Viola, who may disagree with the ungodliness of Nana Peazant's "saltwater Negro" beliefs, there remains a deep respect for her elder's wisdom and strength. In contrast, Haagar not only repudiates these beliefs but also disparages them as a

Black Women's Discourses in *Daughters of the Dust*

Daughters of the Dust
(Courtesy of Kino
International)

sign of primitivism. This is indicated during a scene in which the Unborn Child runs through the woods near the Peazant shanty. Haagar is depicted in a long shot, standing near a tree festooned with bottles that is intended by Nana Peazant to ward off evil.[12] The Unborn Child runs up to her and touches her skirt, indicating a desire to embrace her aunt's spirit. Haagar, however, remains completely oblivious to the spirit child, signifying a total estrangement from her African center. The long shot, which presents Haagar within the Peazant family's social space, emphasizes this distance. Later, Dash uses a medium shot of Haagar, standing with her hands on her hips and her face raised to the sky as she shouts, "As God is my witness, when I leave this place,

CHAPTER 3

I'm never again going to live in your land." The shot accentuates the passion with which Haagar rejects the old ways by allowing the spectator to dwell on her defiant physical posture, while allowing sufficient distance to ponder the source of the anger that lies beneath Haagar's words.

To a degree, Haagar is marginalized within the hierarchy of the Peazant women. This is due in part to an outspokenness that is eschewed by the other women in deference to Nana Peazant's status as the family elder. Dash uses this character quality to initiate a debate between the centrality of Africanity in the lives of these women and the impulse to assimilate white values in pursuit of achieving equality with white society. Although Haagar is certainly a counterforce in the film's "unabashedly Afrocentric thesis," she also represents the right of black women to forcefully transgress and raise dissenting voices, a right the character asserts when pressured by her peers to remain silent (Cade Bambara 1993, 129). In a scene where the Peazant women are gathered on the beach preparing a meal for the gathering, Haagar expresses annoyance that Nana Peazant will not join them on the beach. Instead, Nana Peazant has elected to sit some distance apart from her female relatives in order to go through the "scraps of memories" she keeps in her tin box. The physical separation between the women and the matriarch is symbolic of Nana Peazant's decision not to accompany the family on their migration north, indicating a generational disjunction between the women.

The notion of conflicting generations is further developed by intercutting images of Nana Peazant with the conversation of the women on the beach. As she listens to their distant conversation, she examines the contents of her box. In a close-up of the box that focuses on the reverence with which she handles these small mementoes, the filmmaker reinforces the sense of intimate contact she has with the family's history. Nana Peazant's cherishing of the family history acts as a counternarrative to Haagar's eagerness to rewrite her identity and that of her family within the context of the prosperity and progress seemingly promised by migration to the north. This positions Haagar in an oppositional relation that allows for interrogation of the worth of Nana Peazant's worldsense to her family's future. In addition, Haagar's desire to "become confluent" with what might be described as the "White privileged-class phenomenon" by embracing white material values as the only means of achieving prosperity indicates that such assimilation often creates cultural disjunction: in order to achieve "whiteness," Haagar necessarily rejects her own Africanness (Hudson-Weems 1994, 31).

As the scene progresses, Haagar openly mocks Nana Peazant's attachment to these articles of the past, stating, "sometimes I think that old woman ain't got her right mind." Viola, appalled at the lack of respect, chastises Haagar for her behavior, pointing out that, "just like Eula, you married into this family." The comment demonstrates Haagar's outsider status in the family, a position that is visually reinforced through a long shot in which all the other Peazant women, including Viola, are clustered together on the left of the frame while Haagar is isolated on the right. When one of the women argues that Nana Peazant should go north with them instead of staying behind, "like somebody who ain't got no people," Haagar dares to transgress on family solidarity by expressing the opinion that Nana Peazant should stay behind if she wants to because, "we're moving into a new day. She too much a part of the past." For Haagar, who expresses frustration at having worked all her life without anything to show for it, the move to the mainland is an opportunity to better her family's way of life. Haagar, however, and perhaps more importantly, also views the journey as a means of cutting the ties to African traditions, thus leaving the legacy of slavery behind. Describing herself as an educated person, Haagar disparages "watching her [Nana Peazant] make those root potions . . . and that hoodoo she talks about. Washing up in the river with her clothes on, just like those old 'Salt Water' folks used to do." It is significant that Haagar describes herself as educated because this indicates exposure to institutionalized valorizing of white cultural values. Hence, although it is possible to regard Haagar's litany of criticism as simply reflective of her commitment to "seeing her daughters grow up to be decent somebodies," it also points to a devaluation of African American culture internalized through contact with a racist white culture. Furthermore, by framing Haagar's refusal of an affirmative connection to her African ancestry as a "denial of the primal memory," the film invites the spectator to consider the complicity of African Americans in the process of acculturation (hooks, quoted in Dash 1992, 37). In this way,

CHAPTER 3

Haagar epitomizes what Nana Peazant fears most: a rejection of self-respect based on pride of cultural roots in favor of an illusory mask of whiteness.

Like Haagar, Yellow Mary's status as an outsider allows her to bring to the fore issues that remain unspoken by other Peazant women. Described by a young family member as "a new kind of woman," Yellow Mary provocatively transgresses the boundaries of polite society, evidencing a type of rebellion that is denied both Haagar and Viola. For example, in a scene in which Yellow Mary and Trula lounge in the boughs of a huge tree, they engage in conversation with Eula, who stands below, looking up at them. Eula attempts to indirectly raise the subject of her rape by confessing to using magic in order to invoke her dead mother's spirit and seek her advice. Yellow Mary gently mocks Eula's reliance on folk beliefs by calling her "a real back water Geechee girl [Gullah girl]" and claiming that Daughter Island (one of the Sea Islands) must be "the most desolate place on earth." The comment appears to indicate that Yellow Mary sees herself as disconnected from her own roots. Later in the conversation, Yellow Mary openly acknowledges the true nature of Eula's situation by saying, "the rape of a colored woman is as common as fish in the sea." It is significant that she is the only one among the Peazant women to use the word *rape* in connection with Eula's pregnancy. Furthermore, her insistence that Eula not disclose to Eli who committed the crime must be understood within the confines of the historical period. In 1902, the Civil War and slavery still existed within living memory, and African American legal recourse against white transgression was unheard of. Hence, Yellow Mary's admonishment is not based on a desire to conceal the crime but, rather, reflects a real concern for Eli's safety, as any retaliatory action taken by him might well result in his own lynching. In a later vignette, the character of Yellow Mary is used to illustrate the long history of such criminal acts against black women by white men. Portrayed in a close-up, Yellow Mary is positioned in profile on the right side of the frame as she reveals that she herself was "ruint" while employed by a wealthy white family. This revelation is delivered with her face in profile, avoiding eye contact with either Trula or Eula, indicating that she is still deeply shamed by the event. The choice of framing provides Yellow Mary's story with a kind of visual irony, given her open defiance of social norms and flaunting of her sexuality. It raises the question of whether Yellow Mary is truly a "new woman" by hinting that her defiance of social norms is a defense mechanism borne of her own trauma and pain.

The power of myth and magic as a force for recentering black identity is one of the fundamental tenets of the film. For example, Eula and Eli's estrangement is healed during a sequence in which Nana Peazant's magic brings them together at Ibo Landing. At the beginning of the scene, Eula is standing on the bank of the landing, facing the water. In a crane shot, the camera moves from the ground up along Eula's body and above her to focus on the sky, giving a visual sense of her possession by the spirits of the landing. Eula begins to tell a story of resistance in voice-over narration concerning the arrival of a group of Ibo slaves on Daughter Island. The film then cuts to a long shot of Eula now speaking the words of the story aloud, creating an ambiguity that signifies a magical event. Eli appears as Eula relates how the slaves stepped onto the land, looked around, and "saw things that you and I don't have the power to see," including slavery, the Civil War, and the presence of herself and Eli at Ibo Landing.[13] Eli walks out beyond the shoreline and onto the water toward a half-submerged ship's figurehead of an African man wearing an iron slave collar. He kneels beside it and then, with tenderness, sets it free to float away, creating a parallel with Eula's myth as she describes how the Ibo refused slavery by walking across the ocean and back to Africa.[14] The scene ends as Eli returns to shore, falls to his knees and embraces Eula, his face pressed against the child she is carrying. This spiritual episode, which rewrites the historical event in which the Ibo walked into the water and drowned rather than face enslavement, signals Eli's acceptance of the Unborn Child as an act of resistance to the white oppression forced on Eula by her rape (Dash 1992, 29).

The culmination of the film underscores Dash's refusal to provide a simple solution to the divisions that exist among the Peazant women. As the gathering draws to a close, Nana Peazant presents the departing family members with a charm shaped like a hand and tied to a Bible. The combination of African and Christian symbolism offers the potential of mediation between those who embrace the old ways and those who embrace Christianity by suggesting that the persistence of the former is not incompatible with the existence of the latter. Announcing that "we've taken the old gods and given them new names," Nana Peazant exhorts her family to come and "kiss this hand full of me." Viola, on the one hand, is deeply torn between her Christian reluctance to participate in this "idolatry" and her desire to respect Nana Peazant's wishes. Haagar, on the other hand, is furious at this "Hoodoo mess" and strikes out at her daughters when they try to participate. She leaves the family gathering in disgust, an act that signals her final break with the family. The significance of this act is visually underscored by a long shot that emphasizes the physical and spiritual isolation she has willingly condemned herself to. In contrast, Viola overcomes her own resistance to the old ways and, in a gesture of respect and reconciliation, kisses the Bible first and then the charm. Viola's capitulation holds out the possibility for a hybrid position that combines new influences with an African core. The recoupment of Viola, Eula, and Yellow Mary into the African center of the family despite their varied positions is an expression of what Hudson-Weems has described as *genuine sisterhood*, in which the affirmative bonds between Africana women engender "a tremendous sense of responsibility for each other by looking out for one another" (1994, 65). Haagar's rigid position, in contrast, estranges her from this sisterhood, her family, and her culture. Dash's screen directions in the script state it most succinctly: "Haagar turns inward, perhaps to remain unenlightened and disenfranchised forever" (1992, 161). This commentary levels a negative value judgment against Haagar's right to dissent, suggesting that, although Dash recognizes other voices of black women's subjectivity, she ultimately upholds a model more closely aligned to Africana Womanism than black feminism.

    The ending of the film also reaffirms the need for a constructive African American identity rooted in an African context. Narrative closure is provided by the Unborn Child's narration, which informs the spectator that Eli and Eula elect to remain on the island with Nana Peazant and Yellow Mary. In the final shot of the film, Eula, Yellow Mary, and Nana Peazant are depicted in a long take strolling leisurely along the beach, as the Unborn Child's narration reveals that her birth occurs before Nana Peazant passes on. As the women clear the frame, the Unborn Child sprints across the beach following behind, visually signifying that she is the continuation and perpetuation of the "mythic memory" that is foundational to sustaining her culture (Dash 1992, 30). This action signals the recuperative power of returning to an African center, as Eula and Yellow Mary, both victims of racism, find the means to restore themselves by choosing to remain close to the source. In addition, the focus on black women at the end of the film is emblematic of Dash's desire to decenter the Eurocentric white gaze, enabling the spectator to see African American realities, histories, and struggles in new ways (40). By achieving this goal, *Daughters of the Dust* opens a new cinematic space that challenges past stereotypes and misrepresentations by foregrounding black women as complex subjects.

FOUR

Disjunction from Self
The Politics of Arrival in *Soleil O*

One of the most striking aspects of black diasporic theories is the way in which concepts circulate across boundaries, nations, and histories. Inherently nomadic, black diasporic theories that arise in one specific map in response to particular historical, political, and economic impulses can often find new life and new articulations as they move through time and space.[1] As a result, this chapter begins with just such a cross-pollination of ideas through a discussion of two seminal concepts, W. E. B. DuBois's notion of *double-consciousness* and Paul Gilroy's theoretical construct of *the black Atlantic* (DuBois 1994, 2; Gilroy 1993a, 16). From Gilroy's perspective, DuBois and other black theorists continue to speak to the contemporary black diaspora primarily because "memories of coerced crossing experiences like slavery and migration" are responses to global flows of histories that collide and affect one another (Gilroy 1996, 21, 20). In this model of the black diaspora, the continuous crisscrossing movements of black peoples as they engage in a variety of political, emancipatory, and economic contestations provide impetuses for exploring how journey, nation, identity, memory, and origin are central to black diasporic histories (Gilroy 1993a, 16). In this sense, the black Atlantic is composed of spaces where similarities outweigh or create links across differences: for example, although DuBois's work may have arisen in the complex history of African American experience, the alienation and racism he describes creates a commonality between diverse black peoples, thus bridging cultural differences and making his concepts applicable in a globalized context.

In exploring the possibilities of this paradigm, Gilroy advances the concept of a black Atlantic "as a supplement to existing formulations of the diaspora idea" that "provides an invitation to move into the contested spaces between the local and the global in ways that do not privilege the modern nation state and its institutional order over the sub-national and supra-national networks and patterns of power" (1996, 22). In doing so, Gilroy seeks to disrupt the historically inflected center-periphery dynamics of colonizer and colonized by de-emphasizing historical fixations of place in favor of a more fluid construction focusing on the circumlocutions of shared histories and issues that connect African peoples settled across distant borders (22). From this perspective, similarity and difference in diverse black diasporic cultures resist linear constrictions of histories imposed on them by outside forces in favor of "a non-linear system in which complexity is itself a powerful factor in fixing the limits of possibility" (22). Thus, as a theoretical construct, the black Atlantic challenges the constraints of ethnicity and the nation-state, which, as Gilroy argues, are concepts that have always proven too static to respond adequately to the challenges faced by black diasporic communities (1993a, 19). In the tension between roots and routes, Gilroy proposes that the experiences of black peoples should not be viewed exclusively through the very different types of traveling undergone by refugees, migrants, exiles, and slaves; the unifying similarities these journeys produce should also be taken into consideration (133). Given this, historical dispersals such as slavery, exile, or migration become the evidence of the many forms of geographical and cultural dislocation experienced in the black Atlantic. Ultimately, this position supports a pan-diasporic consciousness in which the black diaspora is defined less by the historical impetus of journey and more by the politics and complexities of arrival, generating shared experiences that supersede or undercut nation and difference as central determinants of diasporic identity.

This is not to suggest that Gilroy refuses to acknowledge the importance of cultural and historical difference between the movements and dispersals that populate the black Atlantic. His position reflects a desire to establish the black diaspora as a means of specifying black identities in a way that de-emphasizes or eliminates binary oppositions by opening the debate to more fluid ways of limning myriad black experiences (120). Viewing the interaction of black diasporic cultures as recombinant, Gilroy argues that it is the movement between ideas, identities, and geographical locales that keeps the black diaspora from being rigidly fixed in Eurocentric spaces (1996, 23). Furthermore, the black Atlantic seeks to valorize "something more than a protracted condition of mourning over the ruptures of exile, loss, brutality, stress and forced separation" shared by individuals in the black diaspora (22). Arising from a situation in which colliding social imperatives have affected the transformation of their cultures, individuals in the black diaspora must inevitably face the realization that, as a fixed configuration of identity, unadulterated origin is illusory at best (22). Cast within this light, Gilroy's emphasis on commonality offers an alternative method of challenging established Eurocentric precepts by foregrounding "new understandings of self, sameness and community" while at the same time refusing a reductive, monolithic imagining of black diasporic experience (22). Most critically, Gilroy's black Atlantic is a space that encourages the flow of ideas and identities across the barriers of nation and history as a means of improving the lives of all dispersed black peoples.

As a site of recombinant exchange, the black diaspora offers an opportunity to explore how such flows function as catalysts for the evolution or extension of theory. As Edward Said notes, theory arises as a response to specific historical impulses but does not necessarily remain contained within them (1983, 230). What are the consequences, then, when such theory is recycled within the context of different parameters and perhaps employed with different motivations? In such circumstances, it is necessary to ask what this process "can tell us about theory itself—its limits, its possibilities, its inherent problems" and how these factors reflect "the relationship between theory and criticism, on the one hand, and society and culture on the other" (230). For example, if one considers the multiplicity of conceptions of the black diaspora to

The Politics of Arrival in *Soleil O*

be rooted in myriad histories of migration, exile, and slavery, then it is possible to consider that the movement of theory is an expression of the complex crisscrossing of such journeys. Thus, one way of viewing diasporic theory is to consider that it is not only contained by historical specificities but also shaped and altered by the process of travel itself.

Gilroy embraces an approach to diasporic thought that considers the interstitial relations of theories created by the historical imperatives of slavery, migration, and exile as a transforming impulse that undercuts unidirectional notions of dispersal from a fixed origin instead favoring a more complex, fluid interchange (1996, 22). One of the strategies he uses to illustrate the importance of this exchange is represented by his exploration of the works of the African American writer W. E. B. DuBois and their importance to the construction of "an intercultural and anti-ethnocentric account of modern black history and political culture" (1993a, 115). DuBois's seminal publication, *The Souls of Black Folk,* originally published in 1903, is considered to be a highly influential early work on African American social identity. Chronicling DuBois's journeys through the American South at the turn of the century, the book explores the state of African American lives within the larger issues of slavery's racist legacy and emancipation's failure to deliver equality. As Gilroy suggests, much of DuBois's work in *The Souls of Black Folk* reflects the perspective of a writer in exile: as a black man teaching in a poor black school in Tennessee, he brings a northerner's perspective to the problems of southern black societies, allowing for the development of "a more relativist understanding of culture and ethnicity that could challenge the logic of racial eugenics" (1993a, 128, 130). This perspective, however, also makes DuBois a controversial figure whose conclusions are open to challenge given his cultural distance from the realities of southern social conditions and the institution of slavery (116). Despite this shortcoming, or perhaps more accurately because of it, DuBois took on the issues of racialized ontologies and "the tension between being and becoming black" as central tenets in his exploration of racism and its implications for African Americans (116). Framed in this way, it is possible to view DuBois's journey as a metaphor for his desire to reconfigure his regional blackness within a larger national context that blurred the artificial boundaries between north and south.

CHAPTER 4

It is worthwhile noting that at the time of the publication of *The Souls of Black Folk*, the American Civil War, which ended in 1865, was well within living memory. Consequently, DuBois's reevaluation of slavery and emancipation focuses on the contradictory relationship between these two historical events and how the promise of the second is ultimately denied by the persistence of the racism that fueled the first. Citing the ability of American votes to make war, emancipate millions, and enfranchise freedmen, DuBois's searching question, "Was anything impossible to a power that had done all this?" reflects the betrayal African Americans felt at the hands of a white society that had seen fit to tap black bodies for death in the fight for the Union but had failed to deliver on the promise of a real and tangible equality for all (1994, 4, 14). The perpetuation of such systemic racism leads to a profound alienation and discontinuity of identity that is described by DuBois as a state of double-consciousness in which "one ever feels his two-ness,—an American, a Negro; two souls, two thoughts, two unreconciled strivings; two warring ideals in one dark body, whose dogged strength alone keeps it from being torn asunder" (2). Thus, African American consciousness remains in a state of irresolvable war, fighting to assert its equality in a societal context that continues to refuse its validity.

Perhaps more to the point is the fact that *The Souls of Black Folk* had an impact that went well beyond its American locale. As Playthell Benjamin argues, DuBois's work spoke to such luminaries as C. L. R. James and Léopold Sedar Senghor. among many others, making his ideas a driving force in ending segregation in the United States and colonial control in Africa (2002, 6, 157).[2] The global scope of his influence is demonstrated by the fact that he was a key organizer of "a series of Pan-African conferences" that laid the groundwork for several of the early independence movements in Africa, arguably making him the most important intellectual influence in black liberation movements of his time and beyond (158). Given this context, Gilroy contends that the application of DuBois's vision of double-consciousness can be extended beyond its confines in African American history to include other black diasporic cultures that take account of slavery experiences (1993a, 126). By expanding it beyond its original parameters, Gilroy argues that the same basic experiences underscoring African American identity can be seen at work in other maps, histories, and locales where black identities have been formed in response to hostile dominant cultures. From Gilroy's perspective, double-consciousness takes on a new form, emerging from "the unhappy symbiosis between three modes of thinking, being, and seeing. The first is racially particularistic, the second nationalistic in that it derives from the nation state in which the ex-slaves but not-yet-citizens find themselves, rather than from their aspiration towards a nation state of their own. The third is diasporic or hemispheric, sometimes global and occasionally universalist" (127). Under this reconfiguration, double-consciousness takes on a wider definition in which the shared effects of alienation and racism create bridges between differing perambulations of histories. Hence, in order to provide the flexibility necessary to cope with a multiplicity of potential black identity constructions, double-consciousness comes to signify a broad concept of dislocation caused when black diasporic identities are formed in resistance to, or in defiance of, continued systemic oppression of mainstream dominant cultures.

The film examined in this chapter is *Soleil O / O Sun* (1970), directed by the Mauritanian filmmaker Med Hondo. The film explores the experiences of an African immigrant arriving in Paris during the 1960s in search of a new economic future. Within a metropolitan space composed of conflicting flows of histories, the black migrant finds himself in "the dangerous position of *speaking for* a native population *to* or *from* the metropolis," a situation shared by many African immigrants (Kanneh 1998, 31). Given that immigration always takes place within broader contexts of nation and that the experiences of migration are affected by the intersection between histories and cultures, it is worthwhile contextualizing the historical frame of colonialism and postcolonialism that informs the film's ideological discourse (Silverman 1991, 2).

As a term, colonialism refers to the occupation, usually by force, of a nation by an outside power. Its definition, however, goes beyond occupation to encompass the exploitation of peoples and resources for the sole economic gain of the outside power. Although not directly analogous, the devaluation of indigenous cultures and the commodification of their labor produce a parallel system to that of slavery, as many of the same struggles for equality and cultural autonomy are

CHAPTER 4

Soleil O (Courtesy of M. H. Films)

shared.³ In particular, the use of racial difference as a means of dehumanizing colonized peoples and the fact that the legacy of colonization has persisted beyond the historical event itself leads to a similar sense of alienation and dislocation as that produced by slavery.

As discussed in earlier chapters, France has a long history of imperialism that, by 1914, spanned "an empire twenty times its size, expanding into Africa, Asia, and the Pacific" (Sherzer 1996, 3). The economic importance of these colonies can be illustrated by the development of infrastructure, such as ports and railroads, created to exploit these distant lands as "a source of profit [that] contributed to the strength and power of the metropolis" (3). In addition to this, France legitimated colonization by reinforcing the disparagement of indigenous cultures through a cultural mission that enforced colonial control by creating allegiances with a variety of individuals in economic, political, administrative, and military positions of power who sought to profit from the colonial presence and could assist in entrenching and valorizing French culture (Jones 1991, 57). As it did in Martinique and other West Indian colonies, France also heralded the concept of *mission civilisa-*

The Politics of Arrival in *Soleil O*

trice in Africa, whereby acquiring French language, culture, and education became essential for advancement. This set up a contradiction for many colonized Africans since achieving power in their own nation was predicated on rejecting their own identities, and the requirement to speak and educate their children in French greatly advanced the fragmentation of indigenous societies.

With the advent of independence movements, the empire building of France came to an end in Africa. Elements of colonization, however, continued to persist in what has been described as the postcolonial period as economic disparities and exploitation continued to persist between France and its ex-colonies. Once the initial boom of independence had begun to fade, many Africans recognized that the dream of Africa fending for itself could not be realized immediately, and thus Africans left to seek their fortunes in the cities of ex-colonial nations such as France (Gourévitch 2000, 119). In this context, it seems possible that the contemporary metropolis provides the ideal locus for debates on the nature of *postcolonialism*.[4] Critics such as Iain Chambers and Alessandro Triulzi have postulated that the city, with its diverse cultural, local, and global influences, offers a space in which to engage in discussions of the symbolic production of the postcolonial (Chambers 1994, 92; Triulzi 1996, 79). For African migrants who have traveled to the cities of their former colonizers in search of new opportunities, however, the notion of a postcolonial space seems illusory when faced with systemic racism and continued economic exploitation. Rooted in power dynamics based on the advancement of white superiority and the entrenchment of black inferiority, such urban environments continue to play out center-periphery dichotomies established during colonialism (Laforest 1996, 115). Hence, the relationship of Africans to the metropolitan capitals of their colonizers is a complex and conflicted one. Held up in the past as bastions of wealth, culture, and liberty, these cities possess a mythological promise of prosperity and equality. Reinforced by colonial policies that undermined African culture, education systems and state bureaucracies reified the acquisition of French language and culture as the only expression of civilization and advancement. In effect, a paradox was created where the colonizer's metropolis came to be something simultaneously desired and loathed, a site and symbol of fractured modernity that both destroyed indigenous culture and promised an illusory relief from desperate economic inequities exacerbated by the colonial legacy still in force after independence.

France has a long history of depending of immigrant labor, and in the three decades following World War II there was a tremendous expansion of this labor force in response to a rising need for inexpensive manpower to fuel a period of rapid industrial expansion (Blatt 1997, 41). Up to this time, the majority of immigrant labor came from northern and southern Europe, but by the 1950s and 1960s, the increasing unavailability of European workers resulted in a wave of Third World laborers, including Africans from many former French colonies (41). Many of these migrants came from a lower socioeconomic scale and rural areas with little education, resulting in a stereotypical view that such individuals were illiterate and suited only for "executing menial tasks in industrial and other sectors which are unattractive to the majority population" (Hargreaves and McKinney 1997, 8). The widespread prevalence of this stereotype, however, also indicated that there were other forces acting on French culture, including the continuation of systemic racism rooted in attitudes formed in colonialism and perpetuated in a contemporary postcolonial environment (Jones 1991, 55). Thus, in France, as in other ex-colonial nations, "the living evidence of repressed histories and dead empires is not so easily consigned to oblivion" (Chambers 1994, 109). African immigrants arriving in France not only faced the inevitable struggle of establishing themselves in a new and alien environment but also carried the burden and preconceptions of a colonial system that devalued their cultures and regarded their labor as a commodity to be exploited.

Ironically, the triumphant ideology of equality for all remains a potent symbol in French culture. As Simon Njami observes, however, "the myth of the French Revolution of 1789 and the myth of a country [France] without prejudice should, however, have by then been disqualified by the facts" evident in the historical record of slavery and colonialism (Njami, foreword in Jules-Rosette 1998, x). In addition, the principles of an immigrant's equality established by the French Revolution were undercut by the Napoleonic code, which held that an immigrant is deprived of civil and civic rights (Gourévitch 2000, 103). In the initial stages of male immigration, the immigrants were "concentrated in the private sector, in slum tenements and 'bidonvilles'" (McMaster

The Politics of Arrival in *Soleil O*

1991, 17). The single male migrants were rendered largely invisible because the restrictions prevented them from competing with other citizens for choice housing, and thus they raised minimal concern in the local populace, especially since they were a source of considerable profit for French landlords (18). When immigrants, however, began to create permanent homes with their families in the 1960s, the metropolis could no longer ignore the rising costs of infrastructure to the city through increased housing and medical, educational, and social services (16). From this point on, the economic boon driven by immigrant labor began to have a significant price tag, eroding "the enormous global profits made by the French economy from migrant labour" (16). Thus, increasing immigration brought strong pressure to bear on public housing, triggering the increased use of a policy known as *seuil de tolérance* as a means of controlling where and how such immigrants could settle (17–18).

Seuil de tolérance is a "scientific" theory asserting that "when the percentage of foreign or immigrant people reaches a certain threshold within a given locality or institution (a housing estate, a 'quartier', a school or hospital) there follows an almost automatic process of hostile rejection by the indigenous population" (McMaster 1991, 14). It has proven a successful strategy by French authorities for establishing quotas and thus excluding settlement in specific areas by restricting immigrant access to collective consumption of housing, schools, and other similar social institutions (14, 17). In short, if an immigrant is denied access to housing in a certain area because of racial quotas, he is also barred access to other social services, resulting in a restriction of freedom and a devaluation of the immigrant's race, culture, and quality of life. Furthermore, by basing such a policy on a pseudoscientific principle, the resulting social discourse entrenches a second-class status for immigrant citizens. Africans coming into such a system that exploits their labor as a commodity while denigrating their cultures would most certainly recognize that the ex-colonial city perpetuates the same center-periphery relations that prevailed in Africa during colonialism. As Kathryn Trees poignantly asks, for whom is postcolonial "post" (1993)?

Born in the village of Ain Ouled Mathar, Mauritania, Med Hondo (Mo-

113

CHAPTER 4

hamed Abid Hondo) is one of Africa's leading filmmakers (Ukadike 2002, 57). He came to filmmaking through a circuitous route that began with his training as a chef in Morocco, which led him to immigrate to France to continue working in that field (57). Once in France he discovered that, because he was African immigrant, his education was discounted, and he was forced to earn his living through several menial jobs, including dockworker and fruit picker (Pfaff 1988, 157). Disillusioned with his experiences in French society, Hondo began studying drama under the well-known stage actor, Françoise Rosay. Creating his own theater company, Shango, with African and Caribbean friends, Hondo concentrated on the performance of works by Aimé Césaire, Amiri Baraka, Guy Menga, and others (Signaté 1994, 18–19). Cast in a number of film and television projects, Hondo developed an avid interest in cinema, which he adopted as a means of artistic expression (Pfaff 1988, 158).

Soleil O is Hondo's first feature film. Although this film is frequently included in the corpus of pioneering African cinema, *Soleil O*, with its focus on the experience of black migration to France in the 1960s, explores the specificities of an African immigrant's arrival in the hostile environment of France. Taken in context with Ousmane Sembène's *La noire de . . ./Black Girl* (Senegal, 1966) and Sydney Sokhona's *Nationalité immigré/Nationality: Immigrant* (Mauritania, 1975), *Soleil O* is emblematic of "a significant segment of the African and Third World cinema 'movement'" (Cham 2004, 64) that seeks to uncover the specificities of black experience in the face of complex flows of history and culture across postcolonial realities (Cottenet-Hage 2004, 107). As such, *Soleil O* achieved much acclaim when it first debuted. Invited to screen during the International Critics Week at Cannes 1970, the film won awards at the Locarno Film Festival 1970 and Fespaco (Panafrican Film Festival of Ouagadougou) 1971. Since then, Hondo has directed many award-winning features, including *Les Bicots-nègres, vos voisins/Niggers and Arabs, Your Neighbors* (1974), *Sarraounia* (1986), *Lumière noire/Black Light* (1994), *Watani* (1997), and *Fatima, L'Algérienne de Dakar* (2004).

Soleil O probes questions of assimilation, disjunction from origin, and the rise of identities that supersede boundaries and cultures. The film's unusual narrative, which combines an episodic structure with the internal monologue of its central character, chronicles the development

The Politics of Arrival in *Soleil O*

of double-consciousness generated in a diasporic environment, making it an excellent vehicle for discussing the work of Gilroy and DuBois. Furthermore, the film's sense of interconnection between articulations of black experiences proffers a view of the black diaspora as a global phenomenon. The film focuses on the migration of Africans to France during the 1950s and 1960s, a period sardonically referred to in the film as the "black invasion," and it offers an appropriate subject for a discussion on the development of the black diaspora because Hondo maps out an experiential space in which an African identity enters into, and is shaped by, a diasporic context. The film depicts the struggles of a black African migrant who has assimilated the culture of French colonizers, adopting their language and religion, and has come to Paris expecting to reap the benefits of full and equal French citizenship. The black migrant, however, is denied work befitting his education and adequate housing based on his race. In addition, he is denigrated by French social institutions and faces barriers created by racist stereotypes. Rejected by corrupt, postcolonial Africa and driven to despair in a space between clashing cultures, the black migrant suffers psychological alienation that eventually leads him to the revelation that, if he wants equality, he will have to fight for it.

Soleil O's depiction of the black migrant as persona non grata in both France and Africa creates a dislocation that allows the film to advocate the evolution of revolutionary ideology and its potential role in transforming the situation for black migrants in Paris. This process is initiated by interrogating the colonizer's metropolis as an illusory construct of cultural superiority, modernity, and equality. For example, *Soleil O* opens with "a schematic picture of African history" that documents the effects of colonization on Africa using "techniques that draw upon Brecht, guerrilla theater, and symbolic realism" (Cottenet-Hage 1996, 180). The film's vision of Africa as origin is not one of unadulterated indigenous source but is already transnational by virtue of colonization and acculturation. The opening scene of the film's prologue documents the breakdown of individual African nations by the repudiation of language, religion, and culture. Depicted through the visual metaphor of a Christian baptism conducted by a white priest, the film presents Africa as a continent in crisis through a culturally diverse group of African men. As each man approaches the priest, he asks in French to be forgiven for speaking his indigenous language: Peul, Bambara, Lingala, Creole and others. In effect, all of these individual cultures are reduced to one by the acceptance of the colonizer's language and the rejection of their own. Thus, as the priest exhorts the spirit of evil to "leave these Children," the African men become dislocated from a multiplicity of indigenous origins and begin a process of assimilation that falsely promises to lead them to cultural union with the colonizer. Perhaps more to the point, the citing of these cultures signals a challenge to Eurocentric notions of cultural purity as the black Atlantic becomes a reality through their dispersal (Gilroy 1996, 22). Thus, as a film, *Soleil O* is cast in a black diasporic milieu, in which "recombinant, ceaselessly reprocessed" struggles for equality and social subjectivity create points of intersection between global flows of black peoples (23).

Soleil O combines ideological montage with realist elements in a way that makes this film visually distinct. The prologue, in particular, makes use of close-ups as a device to forge an ideologically charged atmosphere. These are not psychologized close-ups in the Western sense, as the use of camera angle does not conform to standard emotive Western cinematic grammar. Rather, these close-ups are used to resist the homogenizing gaze of the colonizer by emphasizing each man as a member of an individual culture. For example, in the baptism sequence, the men are arranged in a semicircle around an altar and physically divided from the priest at the center in order to create separate planes of power. At first, this mise-en-scène suggests that the many African nations included here face the colonizer as a united continental force. The eventual fragmentation of this unity, however, is demonstrated when each man steps forward and accepts his baptismal name in an isolated space depicted in a close-up. The effect implies that Africa, as a continent, is divided by colonialism and therefore appears conquered. Although the men adopt the colonizer's language and names, it is not without overt defiance: each man spits as he turns to leave, suggesting that resentment and the potential for resistance exists just below the surface of assimilation. This act foreshadows eventual rebellion and undermines the outward air of acceptance by indicating that the colonizer cannot entirely subsume African identities despite concerted efforts to do so. It is also a sign of dislocation as the individuals recognize their displacement from origin through the acceptance of

The Politics of Arrival in *Soleil O*

an alien culture. This is underscored at the end of the sequence when the priest bids them to go in peace and the men turn crisply, marching out of frame in European military style, implying that colonization has now transformed origin, creating a transnational state in which *francisation* appears to have subsumed Africa, however imperfectly.[5]

The last scene of the prologue focuses on a theatrical presentation that portrays the role of the military in maintaining colonial power by breaking down black cultures. As the African converts march in a procession carrying crosses, they are portrayed in a long shot that emphasizes their shared histories of oppression within social space. As the men come to a stop, they are harangued by orders shouted at them in French and English. The men march in response to the commands, turning their crosses into swords. They separate into two columns of soldiers, an act symbolically linked to the forced conscription of Africans into colonial armies. The two columns of men line up in front of a white French corporal who not only stands apart from the struggle but is also raised on a platform looking down at them. At his command, the two columns of African men fight, signifying the colonial strategy of exploiting internal conflicts to divide and conquer Africans. On the corporal's right are a series of effigies intended to represent the distant colonial power. The effigies on his left represent those African leaders who became puppets of the colonial regime. The fact that they are lifeless, mute witnesses emphasizes their passive complicity with colonial oppression. In addition, irony is used to underscore the duplicitous nature of colonial rule. After the column of men "die" fighting each other, all that is left are the two Africans who stand to the right and left of the corporal, acting as his honor guard. Using money as incentive, the corporal entices the men to fight. He rewards the last victorious soldier by placing the money into his pocket, only to remove it again as the soldier collapses. Thus, the sequence makes a clear statement that only the colonizer profits from colonization.

The discourse on colonialism in Africa sets the stage for the film's larger concern of black migrancy in ex-colonial metropolises. This is reflected in *Soleil O* through an interrogation of the metropolis of Paris as a contradictory and ultimately treacherous terrain, promising freedom and prosperity in a new spirit of equality but delivering instead a continuation of colonial disparity. The sequence that marks the

CHAPTER 4

black migrant's arrival in France underscores this paradox. An interesting character construction, the black migrant is an unnamed Everyman who nevertheless personalizes the struggle of African migrants through his individual experience. The vulnerability of his situation is illustrated at the beginning of the sequence with a long silhouette shot. Positioned on the slope of a hill on the extreme right of the frame, the black migrant seems diminished by his surroundings. As the sequence moves through a series of close-ups that depict him from front and back, right and left perspectives, he comments in voice-over narration: "One day I began to study your graphics, read your thoughts, talk Shakespeare and Molière and spout Rousseau." The contrast between citing the European canon and the cinematic grammar, which reinforces the migrant's Africanness, creates a sense of irony. This is underscored as the series of shots progresses and the migrant narrates that, although he has been whitewashed by European culture, he is still as black as he was when he was born. It is possible to view this affirmative declaration of Africanness as evidence of an uneven power differential between France as center and Africa as periphery, where the latter culture is demeaned in comparison with the former (Jules-Rosette 1998, 240).

Within this context, it is possible to argue that *Soleil O* depicts the colonizer's metropolis as a space in which identity becomes fragmented and alienated in a contradictory environment where equality is promised but never delivered. For example, as the black migrant steps off the train into the city, he wanders down the platform, clearly energized by what he sees. His narration, which evokes his happiness to tread the soil of the colonizer's first city, claims the metropolis as his own capital as well. Furthermore, this declaration takes place over a close-up of his suitcase which is plastered with stickers representing many African countries, suggesting that his is a transnational claim. Hence, the black migrant is in a position paralleling that of African Americans, for whom "emancipation was the key to a promised land" (DuBois 1994, 4). Similarly, the black migrant's statement that "sweet France" will be his second home indicates that he expects to find an Eldorado based on equality and economic prosperity in a metropolitan space that is truly "post," or beyond, coloniality (Signaté 1994, 12). It also reflects the overwhelming desire that some migrants feel toward acculturating with their host nation in order to achieve equality within the new social milieu (JanMohamed 1992, 101). Thus, the black immigrant arrives in France open to the need to accommodate the culture he is entering, with the full intention of making positive social and economic contributions.

It is here that DuBois's double-consciousness becomes a useful means of describing the black migrant's paradoxical situation. Desiring to "better" himself, the black migrant has clearly adopted the qualities valued by the colonizer, but in doing so, he has stepped into "a world which yields him no true self-consciousness" because his race prevents him from being completely validated within a Eurocentric context that values whiteness (DuBois 1994, 2). Unable to fully reconfigure his race, the black migrant is clearly suspended in a no-man's-land between his Africanness and his adopted French culture. As DuBois argues, "This waste of double aims, this seeking to satisfy two unreconciled ideals" initiates a war within that often sends black subjects "wooing false gods and invoking false means of salvation" (3). Thus, like black subjects formed by the failure of emancipation to deliver true equality, the black migrant is placed in a position of anticipating full liberation, only to have it denied by systemic prejudices embedded in a system that refuses him human status.

Hondo initiates the black migrant's experience of double-consciousness through a series of scenes in which he is refused accounting jobs on the basis of his skin color, despite the fact that he is qualified for them. This occurs over a series of three short scenes interspersed throughout the film. In the first, the black migrant tries to enter a construction site to apply for a position. The encounter is depicted in a medium long shot, as the black migrant is confronted by a white worker who prevents him from entering the job site. The worker informs him that he has no business entering the premises, despite the black migrant's protests that he is only answering the job advertisement posted outside the site. Finally he is turned away, denied access because of the worker's racist belief that all Africans are thieves. In the second scene, he faces the covert hostility expressed by a garage owner whom he approaches for work. When he asks the owner if the job is taken, the owner replies, "No," which has the double meaning that the job is still available but there is no way the owner is going to hire him. In addition, the fact that the garage owner barely glances at him underscores his refusal to engage the black immigrant as an equal. This motivates the migrant to ask ironically in voice-over narration, "Isn't this the land of liberty? I'm at home here. Aren't you and I equals?" The statement, which signals the entrenchment of double-consciousness in the black migrant, echoes what DuBois describes as a "longing to attain self-conscious manhood, to merge his double self into a better and truer self" (2). Instead, the black migrant finds himself in conflict with his own subjectivity, which, despite his best efforts to internalize the values of French culture, is still pejoratively measured by the external darkness of his race (DuBois 1994, 2). Furthermore, reference to liberty also evokes the political myth of France as a land of equality, founded on the principles of the French Revolution, and indicates the depth of alienation experienced by the black migrant at the betrayal of his expectations (Wihtol de Wenden 1991, 98).[6]

In the final scene, he arrives in a courtyard on his way to apply for a job and is confronted by an angry white concièrge who is appalled to find him in her space. She expresses the most blatant racism when she utters, "We have enough niggers as it is." The black migrant, framed in a handheld medium shot, advances toward her as he asks in frustration, "Can you please tell me where I came from?" The concièrge, also framed in a handheld medium shot, retreats in fear inside the building where she locks herself in as the black migrant leaves. The black migrant's question reflects the profound disruption experienced by African migrants in the colonizer's metropolitan space: promised access to modernity and economic prosperity by assimilation, they find themselves stranded in a diasporic space between Africa and the metropolis where positive identity is difficult to sustain. Although this may be argued to be a postcolonial space, such an assertion is undercut by the presence of a polarized center-periphery differential between colonizer and colonized that has clearly survived, unchanged by independence. Furthermore, the betrayal evidenced by the black migrant's narration, evokes a state of double-consciousness in which he is forced to address the racism by interiorizing it because overt confrontation would challenge his ability to survive economically. Thus, the black migrant's emotional outburst echoes DuBois's argument that facing "so vast a prejudice could not but bring the inevitable self-questioning, self-disparagement, and lowering of ideals which ever accompany repression and breed in an atmosphere of contempt and hate" (1994, 6). It also indicates a rift in the black migrant's concept of identity as he finds he cannot be both black African and French in a postcolonial context.

One of the most compelling visual aspects of the film is the way in which Hondo uses the streets and architecture of the ex-colonial metropolis to create ideological debate. After he is forced to leave the construction site, the black migrant wanders down the street, eating a meager lunch of bread and looking at shop windows. In one sequence, he is framed in a medium shot with his back to the camera, staring at a huge display of jewelry and other fine goods. In another, he looks longingly at a luxury car displayed behind huge plate-glass windows. The poignancy of these sequences, and similar ones dispersed throughout the film, arises from the fact that although the black migrant is close enough to touch these consumer goods, he is also separated from them by a transparent barrier, a metaphor for the racism that keeps him from advancing in French society: he can see his dream all around him but cannot possess it.

The colonizer's metropolis is portrayed as an active agent in cultural disjunction through a number of avant-garde narrative and aesthetic strategies that reinforce the physicality of the metropolitan space as symbolic of colonial oppression. For example, the black migrant is sent by the employment office to speak to a French businessman. The interview, which is interspersed throughout the film in short sequences, takes place in an upscale office. As the black migrant enters, he is suavely greeted by the white businessman who pours him a drink and instructs him to sit in the chair opposite him. The long shot that portrays this "civilized" exchange presents a subtle ironic commentary on the insidiousness of racism as the black migrant's chair is lower than the businessman's, subordinating the former while the latter visually dominates the shot. Narrative ambiguity is created when the black immigrant begins to interview the white businessman about his firm's use of aptitude testing on African immigrants, thus altering the context of the scene from one of a job interview to a direct confrontation of French paternalism toward ex-colonial subjects. In a striking low-angle medium shot, the camera slowly zooms in to an extreme close-up of the white businessman as he explains that "it is indispensable to select

CHAPTER 4

individuals capable of seeing as we do . . . thinking as we do . . . retaining . . . absorbing, yes absorbing words as we do and above all, giving them the same meaning." The zoom accentuates the gap between the controlled, almost professorial tone of the businessman's reply and the clear racist implications of his words that emphasize a center-periphery dichotomy, thus implying that many African immigrants do not meet these French "standards." This position is further advanced as the black migrant's reply, "There'll soon be millions of white-thinking blacks," is portrayed in a blurred close-up that is slowly brought into full focus. This is contrasted by a repeat of the shot construction using an extreme close-up of the businessman as he responds, "That may not be the best meaning, but it is ours, and the *only* one compatible with our technology." Thus, the cinematic grammar visually strips away the veneer of civility by metaphorically bringing the competing agendas into direct focus.

In a later sequence, close-ups are employed to create a visual counterpoint to the ideological exchange between the two men. As the black migrant argues cogently that African immigrants must be present in France for such aptitude testing, the content of his voice-over is paired with a close-up of the businessman who drops his eyes and concentrates on the cigarette he is smoking. His refusal to engage directly through the gaze indicates his true position on the black migrant's question as the latter asks directly for the businessman's opinion on allowing free immigration of Africans into Europe. This is later borne out by the businessman's response, posed as voice-over narration over a close-up of the black migrant's face as he suggests that he cannot see how immigration can be stopped. A zoom into an extreme close-up of the businessman's shifting eyes adds emphasis as he states that this black migration should be weighed "against the interests of [white] Europe as a whole." The contrast between the black migrant's steady gaze and the businessman's shifting eyes exposes the hypocrisy of the image of France as a nation founded on equality and demonstrates the subtlety of racist rhetoric masquerading as good business or French national interests. This is further illustrated in another scene, in which the businessman's assertion that the dullest and most unpleasant jobs fall to black immigrants because French citizens have abandoned them, suggests a gross inequality and a devaluation of the contribution of the labor of these migrants to the advancement of French society. Thus, taken as a whole, these sequences illustrate the role of lingering colonial attitudes in creating the environment in which double-consciousness arises in the black diaspora.

The nonlinear narrative structure typified by the dispersal of these scenes throughout the film illustrates the film's narrative strategy of suspending sequences without contextualized beginnings or endings to indicate the externality, marginalization, and rejection faced on a daily basis by individuals sharing the black migrant's experiences (Cottenet-Hage 1996, 178). For example, the narrative is disrupted by a variety of street interviews of French citizens and intellectuals as they comment on their attitudes to the Africans in their midst. In one such instance, the interview begins with a long shot of a classical statue. The use of the statue, arguably a common sight in the city of Paris, provides a concrete symbol of the perceived superiority of European classical history. Thus, the fact that the Parisian is speaking with all this imperialist culture behind him gives his words clearly racist implications despite the pleasantness of his tone. The choice of this mise-en-scène challenges the spectator to critically consider whether this metropolitan space has progressed beyond colonialism at all. As the shot progresses, the camera then tilts down and zooms into a medium shot of a Parisian man walking a dog. He faces the camera in direct address and cheerfully asserts that the black migrants in Paris have begun to think "white." His interview is returned to in a later sequence when he charges ironically, "You're holding a glass of champagne." This scene transitions to a series of extreme high-angle long shots of the black migrant symbolically "tarred and feathered" with the colonizer's money. As the soundtrack emits sounds of war and anguish, the black migrant tears franc notes from his body and burns them in the fire. The sequence then returns to the Parisian with the dog as he comments, "What's to keep you from throwing it in my face?" The man's statements imply that black immigrants are not suitably grateful for the small economic foothold they are allowed in France. The fact that this scene ends with liquid violently flung in the Parisian's face, symbolizes a growing sense of rage in the black migrant at his oppression.

Although the black migrant remains connected to his African origin, *Soleil O* also suggests that his experiences in France ultimately transform his identity into a transnational concept of self forged in response to a black Atlantic space. Furthermore, shared histories of racism, poor housing, and economic exploitation among the immigrants initiate the translation of "dividing borders into a diaspora community," thus bringing together a diverse black Atlantic society whose similarities outweigh differences in culture (Busia 1997, 195). The creation of black diasporic consciousness is explored through the highly contentious issue of housing by using social space as a visual frame for critiquing France's policy of *seuil de tolérance*. In one sequence, the black migrant's voice-over narration is used to offer an illustration of French landlords making large profits by housing as many as eighty African immigrants in a single, ramshackle house. This rhetoric is paired with a medium shot of a broken-down iron gate, and, as the black migrant lays out his case in cold facts, the camera slowly tilts down and pans left to right, revealing a line of somber African immigrants standing against a crumbling brick wall. As they gaze into the camera in direct address, the pan accentuates their connected space and, hence, their shared plight, emphasizing the human costs of such exploitation. Furthermore, the brick wall functions as a metaphor for their entrapment in a corrupt system, an injustice that is heightened as the shot ends on a close-up of the black migrant at the end of the line.

Africa's role in this crisis, however, is not exempted from scrutiny. In a later scene, a group of immigrants gather in the black migrant's room to discuss an announcement concerning the housing issue. The arrival of some of the immigrants is depicted in a medium long shot that underscores the tiny size of the living space tightly packed with meeting goers. As the camera pans left over the crowd of participants, the shared space signifies a diasporic environment composed of individuals of different cultures and skin colors, united in a common concern. As the black migrant explains that the French authorities are locating and purchasing old but inhabitable buildings that will be reconverted into small, six-foot square dormitories to be occupied by six or eight men, cynical laughter breaks out in the group, indicating the inadequacy of the proposal. Through a series of medium shots that frame the debate within social space, the critique of neocolonial African regimes and their failure to intercede on behalf of the immigrants is situated within diasporic social space that foregrounds the solidarity of the participants. As the immigrants contemplate the possibility of contacting their embassies for return to Africa, they decry the fact that their ambassadors in France "only defend governments" and that their presidents have "sold out" to neocolonial interests. The failure to defend the immigrants' welfare in France by their nations of origin makes it apparent that this connection is somehow abrogated once they have left their homeland. Thus, black diasporic space is formed in a rift between origin and "otherness" that suggests the need for a new formulation of identity. Such a rift also offers solidarity based on a common oppression as a potential power base for black diasporic communities.

The mere existence of potential solidarity is not, however, enough for Hondo. Solidarity must be coupled with direct action. Since the most grievous transgression is to accept disenfranchisement within diasporic space and become "good whites," direct action begins with a refusal of victimization and complicit survival strategies. In other words, Hondo poses a rejection of double-consciousness as an acceptable state, arguing instead for a validation of black culture that challenges such a state. For example, in a sequence portrayed predominantly by high-angle shots, the black migrant destroys his tiny room, a violent rejection of the French system oppressing him. Hunched up in a corner, he is visually trapped by diagonal lines and narratively trapped by his own complicity. The narration, which functions as a choral element voicing the unspeakable, accuses those who accept their place within the system without challenging it as being accomplices to all the crimes on earth: slavery, murder, and genocide go on unhindered, and victims and persecutors are chosen according to their skin color. His bitter comment that those who accept the system as it is are "good whites now" signifies the impossibility of the choice facing the black migrant. He must either become complicit with a system that degrades him or reject it outright: both choices lead to alienation and marginalization. The statement also signals the death of the black migrant's aspirations as they collapse under the repression of systemic racism. This irresolvable dichotomy culminates during a sequence in which the black migrant races against the flow of a crowded street, charging in voice-over that any aid is an investment and that any gift is a future profit. The assertion that truth is a commodity further underscores the intense disillusionment and dissolution of identity experienced by the black migrant as he cries out for Africa.

CHAPTER 4

In a series of scenes culminating in the climax of the film, the black migrant's profound psychological disjunction is framed within the transnational context of the black Atlantic. In one incident, the black migrant careens blindly through the forest, stumbling to a stop at the edge of a river. As he stares at the rushing water, anguished screams are heard. Black men are flung into the waves and swept away by the torrent of water, drowning in the process. By choosing this image construction, the black migrant's alienation is aligned with the commodification and exploitation experienced by African slaves. In a later sequence, the black migrant huddles on the forest floor as a drum beat pounds and screaming sounds in his mind. Cowering as photographic images of iconic revolutionary leaders such as Malcolm X, Che Guevara, Mehdi Ben Barka, and Patrice Lumumba flash subliminally across the screen, the black migrant is unable to control his anguish and screams out in fury and defiance.

The film's climax completes the black migrant's transformation as he symbolically "vomits" all that he has ingested since his arrival in France (Cottenet-Hage 1996, 182). He continues his disoriented journey through the forest, eventually collapsing against the exposed roots of an uprooted tree. Beginning in a claustrophobic close-up, the camera zooms out to reveal the black migrant surrounded by some of the photographs of black leaders first seen in the forest scene. In the montage that follows, the photographs are reprised individually with flames superimposed on each image. Visually, these images are indicative of the rise of revolutionary consciousness in the black migrant, and by placing that consciousness within a global perspective, the film signals that the black migrant must move on to a new conception of identity that (re)inscribes origin within diasporic experience. This position is further enhanced by Hondo's decision to end the film with the words, "to be continued," suggesting that the black migrant's rejection of double-consciousness is the beginning of a longer process of reification. Thus, by ending the film on a revolutionary note, the black diaspora is portrayed as a space "in which natal alienation and cultural estrangement are capable of conferring insight as well as precipitating anxiety" (Gilroy 1996, 22). In the end, the final words suggest that the black migrant has initiated a process to reclaim his own subjectivity and redefine his black experience within evolving contexts.

FIVE

Arrested Memory
The Problematics of Return in *Testament*

As previous chapters have outlined, the black diaspora is a highly contested space in which dispersals, motivated by diverse impetuses such as slavery, migrancy, and exile, exist side by side in both peace and tension. Avtar Brah conceives of diasporic space as "the intersectionality of diaspora, border, and dis/location as a point of confluence of economic, political, cultural and psychic processes" that interrogate and challenge monolithic concepts of black identity (1996, 181). In this conceptual model, movement across borders and cultures is located at the center of diaspora as a theoretical construct. Individual experiences of diaspora, however, involve explicit journeys that must be placed within a specific historical context that answers the question of who is traveling *"when, how, and under what circumstances?"* (italics in original; 182). Hence, diaspora must be considered within the trajectories of cultural, economic, and political forces that shape them and underwrite their very rationale for existing in the first place (182). Viewed in this light, the black diaspora ceases to be a monolithic construct and, instead, becomes a composite formation composed of the warp and weft of multiple strands of historical and personal narratives that may act in synergy or conflict with one another (183). This creates a paradoxical image of a black diaspora united by African heritage but divided by geography, culture, and politics, which poses the following theoretical problem: how can the black diaspora, as a concept, effectively cope with competing maps and histories and still remain or present a unified front? Is it still, as Brah insists, a "pan-*ic* concept" or simply a series of unrelated fractures with the common racial identifier of black skin (196)?

Given these parameters, it is worthwhile considering the black diaspora as a "field of identifications," the power of which lies in its ability to explain or account for the "specific problematics associated with transnational movements of people, capital, commodities and cultural iconographies" (Brah 1996, 196). Successfully adopting this position, however, requires that the notion of the black diaspora transit from an idealized ideological model of the black Atlantic to one that actively embraces geography and borders as central defining features. Brah makes this distinction when she argues that the category of *diaspora space* (as opposed to that of diaspora) includes the entanglement of genealogies of dispersion with those of origin, a position that brings into focus the often strained interstitial relationship between point of departure from the original cultural space and arrival in the new (181). To disperse, therefore, involves parting from origin and moving through journey to arrival in a way that transforms not only the individuals undertaking movement but the origin itself. This implies an estrangement in histories in which the individual in movement maintains a view of origin arrested at the point of departure, creating a disjuncture with the continuous evolution of origin experienced by those remaining behind.

Brah's construct provides a discursive platform for the examination of exile as a form of diasporic consciousness. As a lived experience, exile poses a different set of parameters and conditions that make it distinct from migrancy: although both exiles and migrants cross borders, many exiles are in their new circumstances out of necessity rather than desire and are thus less amenable to their new culture than those who migrate by choice (JanMohamed 1992, 101). Edward Said offers a similar construct when he argues that exile "is the unhealable rift forced between a human being and a native place, between the self and its true home," thus indicating that the circumstances of leaving origin are as vital to the development of black diasporic identity as the conditions of arrival (1990, 357). In addition, John Durham Peters suggests that exile

The Problematics of Return in *Testament*

is usually associated with some form of political turmoil that makes remaining at point of origin impossible, a position that reflects Said's by accentuating displacement as a locus of exilic experience (1999, 19). These stances demonstrate a perceived difference between migrancy and exile in which the former is motivated by free choice to seek a new life in a different culture and the latter is compelled to abandon origin after a harrowing event such as war or political upheaval. In turn, this locates exile as an experience that occurs at the crossroads of history and violence, where journey is intended to be temporary and return becomes a contested object of desire. As Said asserts, "The achievements of exile are permanently undermined by the loss of something left behind for ever" (1990, 357). Hence, exile is a shifting state in which the individual resists the point of arrival by desiring to be elsewhere but is, at the same time, creating an idealized vision of origin based on the loss endured by forcible removal from origin.

Said makes the point that contemporary histories of exile differ from those of the past because modern warfare, imperialism, and totalitarianism create an impersonal setting in which the sheer scale of exile prevents it from being understood on a personal level by the public, making this the age of the refugee and the displaced person (1990, 357). In presenting a vision of exile as "unbearably historical" and a "discontinuous state of being," Said underscores the critical role played by conflicting notions of history and memory in exilic identities that destabilize the relationship between individuals and nations of origin (358, 360). Such tension suggests that return to origin for exiles is fraught with conflicted impulses of mourning, fueling the illusion that what has been lost in terms of culture and nation can be returned to its pristine preexilic condition (Peters 1999, 19). These longings, however, are ultimately unfulfilled, as exiles' desire to focus on the restoration of a history arrested by departure fails to adequately account for the continuous evolution of origin in their absence. Thus, return becomes an impossible objective because it requires reinstatement of events already passed.

John Akomfrah's film, *Testament* (Ghana/United Kingdom, 1988), offers an example of exilic experience and the problematics of return. Although he left for Britain as a young child, Akomfrah is "very attached to Ghana's history" and in particular to the political events of

CHAPTER 5

1966 that forced his family's flight (Ofori 1990, 625). This period in Ghanaian history marked the downfall of Kwame Nkrumah, the controversial leader whose commitment to the independence of Ghana drove the nation to become the first African state to achieve independence from colonial rule.[1] Plagued by corruption, Nkrumah's government was overthrown by a military coup in February 1966, resulting in the displacement of his supporters, a number of whom relocated to the United Kingdom. More to the point, Akomfrah's film characters are each intimately involved with, and affected by, the cult of personality that characterized the rise and fall of Nkrumah's regime. Thus, Akomfrah uses this context as a frame within which to explore issues of political exile and capture the complex "ideas" of Ghana held by such refugees, making it well worthwhile exploring Nkrumah's impact on the nation and the black diaspora as a whole (625).

Given the charisma of his leadership, it is not surprising that many facts surrounding Kwame Nkrumah are in dispute. Born in Ghana in 1909 to the senior wife of a goldsmith, he was a member of the Nzima cultural group.[2] Completing his early education in a time when black Ghanaian students faced considerable barriers in accessing education, Nkrumah began his professional life as a teacher in 1926 (Davidson 1973, 20–23). Inspired by the visit of Nigerian nationalist Nnamdi Azikiwe, who energized the young intellectuals of Ghana by urging them to explore the United States as a source of revolutionary spirit, Nkrumah chose to pursue further education at Lincoln University in Pennsylvania (29–32).

Nkrumah's educational journey makes him an interesting figure because his revolutionary consciousness was strongly influenced by a large breadth of black diasporic thinking, giving him a transnational perspective. While completing masters' degrees in education and theology in the United States, Nkrumah was exposed to key black theorists of the time and was highly influenced by Marcus Garvey and W. E. B. DuBois (Davidson 1973, 36). This resulted in the development of his deep devotion to pan-Africanism, which would come to occupy a major place in all his future political ideas. Nkrumah also studied American and labor union politics and the way in which they employed pressure tactics and campaign methods to achieve their goals (Omari 1970, 36). Most important, Nkrumah met C. L. R. James, whose dedication to

The Problematics of Return in *Testament*

Marxism would steer Nkrumah toward socialism as a means of ending the political and economic stranglehold of colonialism (Davidson 1973, 37–39).

When Nkrumah decided to travel to England to "re-Africanize" himself and pursue a law degree, James provided him with a letter of introduction to George Padmore, a Trinidadian intellectual who was highly influential in the struggle to free African nations from colonialism (Davidson 1973, 43, 39). Joining Padmore in 1945, Nkrumah entered an organization that was composed primarily of West Indian intellectuals living in England with inside experience of revolutionary politics (James 1977b, 76–77). Shaped by an active role in the West African National Secretariat and the Coloured Workers' Association of Great Britain, Nkrumah received an invaluable education in leftist political organization and labor politics that would stand him in good stead on his return to Ghana (77).

Receiving repeated invitations to join the United Gold Coast Convention (U.G.C.C.), a fledgling organization dedicated to establishing self-government, Nkrumah arrived in Ghana in 1947 after twelve years of absence to find a country that was wracked with social and economic unrest (Davidson 1973, 52–55). The staid members of the U.G.C.C., which was composed primarily of chiefs and educated elite inextricably bound by their colonial formation to perpetuate some form of self-rule relationship with Britain, expected Nkrumah to broaden the support base for the party (50–61). What they got instead was a revolutionary prepared to use his contemporary political organizational skills to broker nothing less than total independence (59–61). Most important, although he remained a pragmatist who realized that the divisions of culture and language would make this a long and difficult struggle, Nkrumah, inspired by the black diasporic thinkers, understood that African peoples empower themselves by recognizing that their shared interests outweigh their differences (41).

Nkrumah proposed a three-pronged approach to the U.G.C.C. The first stage involved expanding active recruitment and mass political education to the Ashanti and the Northern territories, as well as trade unions and co-operatives and farmers', ex-servicemen, and women's associations (Davidson 1973, 61). The second stage required political demonstrations throughout the country to test organization strength,

CHAPTER 5

and the third would use full-blown organized demonstrations, boycotts, and strikes as pressure tactics to force self-rule according to a constitution the U.G.C.C. would eventually create (61). The political fervor that came from enactment of Nkrumah's approach crested in a series of confrontations between the people and the colonial authorities, including a successful boycott of European shops and an incident in which police opened fire on a peaceful demonstration of ex-servicemen at Christiansborg Castle, resulting in one casualty and many injured protestors (62–65). The incident set off a period of rioting that spread to other towns, ultimately resulting in the arrest of Nkrumah and five other prominent leaders of the U.G.C.C. on charges of launching a communist conspiracy (64). Although a later commission failed to establish the existence of a communist plot and the leaders were released, the U.G.C.C. was suddenly confronted by Nkrumah's growing power and decided to distance themselves from him by finding grounds for his dismissal (65–67). They finally dismissed Nkrumah on a variety of charges ranging from exceeding his authority to using the subversive term "comrade" in some of his personal correspondence (66–67).

If their intention was to stem the tide of Nkrumah's rise, they had badly misunderstood the seat of his power. The Committee on Youth Organization (C.Y.O.), established by Nkrumah for the U.G.C.C., was composed of young people who were taking an active role in politics and were considerably more radical than those in the parent organization (Davidson 1973, 66–67). Demanding immediate self-government, this organization would break with the U.G.C.C. and, under Nkrumah's leadership, become the Convention People's Party (C.P.P.), which would ultimately sweep him to power (69–71). In 1950, solidly in control of the C.P.P., Nkrumah launched *Positive Action*, the third stage in his drive for independence: this ignited a general strike to which the colonial authorities responded with increasing oppression, setting off a round of sometimes violent confrontations with demonstrators that finally ended with the arrest of key leaders, including Nkrumah (74–76). This action, however, only resulted in an illusion of calm. When the elections were finally held, the C.P.P. won in a landslide, including a victory for Nkrumah, who had entered the race from his jail cell (75–80). When Nkrumah was released from incarceration, he began the nego-

The Problematics of Return in *Testament*

tiations that would eventually lead to Ghana's installation as the first independent African black state in 1957 (119).

To a certain degree, the compromises and strategizing necessary for Nkrumah to realize his goal of achieving independence "by sheer political and moral force without the use of arms" set in motion the very forces that would ultimately fragment his leadership in the coup in 1966 (James 1977b, 86). For example, Nkrumah was faced with making economic concessions that perpetuated colonial inequities and trade imbalances. Ghana was economically dependent on cocoa production, the bulk of which was sold to European companies whose primary goal was to purchase it as inexpensively as possible, resulting in a situation that "transferred wealth out of the country by transferring profits to London and other centres of the industrialized world" (Davidson 1973, 107). The more efficient cocoa production became, the lower the world price fell, with the result that more land ended up under cultivation (107). The upshot of this cycle was that less land was available for food production, which perpetuated reliance on imported products (107). Given the strength of the European lobbyists who fought to maintain the status quo and the reliance of Ghana's government on the availability of surplus capital held in trust by the Cocoa Marketing Board, Nkrumah had little choice but to accept the situation (107–8).

Nkrumah also had to negotiate through the maze of ethnic power structures that made up Ghana and that had justified concerns that the nationalist C.P.P. threatened their privileges and positions (Davidson 1973, 116). The scale of the problem is illustrated by the fact that "when Nkrumah took office there were no fewer than sixty-six different 'states' in the Colony alone," a problem that was exacerbated by the fact that each had its own treaty with Britain as well as its own local loyalties (117). The C.P.P., using history and religion, legitimized Nkrumah by granting him "a spiritual power as great as that of the chiefs" through the "old title of *Osagyefo*" (119). Although expedient and perhaps even necessary, given the cultural terrain within which he was functioning, the cult of personality that characterized his leadership became so influential and so widespread that Nkrumah was eventually corrupted by his own absolute power (119). For example, in an address to members of parliament at Winneba in 1964, Nkrumah reportedly remarked that

CHAPTER 5

it was natural for the people "to think of their leader as a messiah" (Omari 1970, 144). This attitude was fueled by black diasporic writers such as James, who argued that "if villagers looked upon him as a sort of Christ, they showed a far better understanding than the highly educated, not only of what should be the function of legitimate disciples today, but also of the historical Jesus" (1977b, 83). As this suggests, history is split between portraying Nkrumah as a visionary overwhelmed by absolute power or as an opportunist whose personal ambitions led him to use any ruse to achieve power.[3] Moreover, these depictions demonstrate Nkrumah's importance as a transnational black figure even as they foreshadow the emergence of the despotic tendencies that would ultimately undermine his government. Regardless of the rationale, by the time Ghana became a black African republic in 1960 and had severed all colonial ties with England, Nkrumah and the C.P.P. had given up the pretense of democratic values and were moving toward a totalitarian state (Davidson 1973, 166).

By the early 1960s, the C.P.P.'s leadership, drawn from Ghana's petty bourgeoisie, increasingly began to act in ruthless self-interest (Davidson 1973, 121, 124). Corruption became so endemic that Nkrumah gave a blistering speech in which he accused some C.P.P. members of using their power to "threaten and intimidate those whom they are trying to influence" (Nkrumah, quoted in Davidson 1973, 175). In an environment where the wages of urban and agricultural workers were diminished by a rapid rise in the cost of living, the increasing economic prosperity of the C.P.P. leaders began fracturing the very populist support that swept Nkrumah to power in the first place (175). Furthermore, Nkrumah's failure to curb these exploitive practices, which also included his own, contributed to increasing unrest and dissatisfaction (175–76).[4] This was further complicated by Nkrumah's decision in 1961 to deal with the government's growing economic crisis by deducting between 5 and 10 percent of all wages and other income as "compulsory savings" (176). Reaction against the move exploded when port and railway workers revolted illegally against the budget during the Takoradi strike, which became emblematic of Nkrumah's increasingly oppressive tactics as he ordered the arrest of the leaders and forced workers to return to their jobs or face dismissal (177).

The Problematics of Return in *Testament*

Davidson argues that the strike was foundational in Nkrumah's move from democratic politics to socialism, based on a repudiation of the poor economic advice he had received since 1951 (1973, 177–78). Although this undoubtedly played a role, it cannot be denied that the change in direction also made it much easier to suffocate rising opposition by the use of oppressive Stalinist tactics. Fueled by what Davidson has described as "an unbroken faith in his own ability," Nkrumah systematically used propaganda and oppression of the opposition to remove the old guard members of the C.P.P. who would be most likely to resist Ghana's changing direction (Davidson 1973, 184; Omari 1970, 91). This, however, did not stem the rise of political discord: in July 1962, Nkrumah was wounded in an assassination attempt at Kulungugu (Davidson 1973, 182). Because of the circumstances of the attack, the attempt was determined to be an inside job, leading to the arrest of two men, Secretary General Tawia Adamafio and Foreign Minister Ako Adjei (182). When they were later acquitted of the charges, Nkrumah refused to accept the verdict, dismissing Chief Justice Sir Arku Korsa in an act that drew broad national and international criticism (183). This proved to be a benchmark event: by 1963, now increasingly under siege by continued economic strife and assassination attempts, Nkrumah began to consolidate more and more of the government's business under his personal control, resulting in mounting isolation (189). In 1964, Nkrumah cemented his control of Ghana by rigging a referendum to overwhelmingly confirm the country's status as a single-party state, making himself president for life (191–94).

It was the complete collapse of cocoa prices between 1964 and 1965 that precipitated a serious financial crisis. Combined with the debts incurred to Western businessmen during Nkrumah's aggressive modernization of Ghana and the exorbitant repayment conditions, Nkrumah's popular support was undermined (Davidson 1973, 198). Unable to economically sustain the complex party patronage that ensured solidarity in C.P.P. ranks and the loyalty of the armed forces, Nkrumah's fall was thus inevitable: the opposition, denied lawful expression, chose to fight back with increasingly violent means of resistance and successfully planned a secret coup (Baynham 1988, 207). The end came in 1966, while Nkrumah was absent on a state visit to Hanoi (Davidson 1973, 202–3). On February 23, a small force of six hundred soldiers

CHAPTER 5

from the Third Infantry Battalion executed Operation Cold Chop by capturing key government installations in Accra, the capital city, in a virtually bloodless coup (Baynham 1988, 183–85). The fact that such a small force ended Nkrumah's regime without major opposition demonstrates both direct and indirect collusion on the part of the military and is a testimony to the widespread dissatisfaction of the civilian population as the administration and other institutions readily collapsed in the takeover's wake (182, 205). The revolution that had begun with such promise and paved the way for the independence of other African states simply seemed to disappear as if it had never existed.

Despite his contradictions, Nkrumah and his regime in Ghana remain an important aspect of African and African diasporic history. It may be observed that Nkrumah's success and his failure are linked: the drive to political independence, the struggle to escape colonial economics, and the fragmented realities of African clan divisions reinforced—or perhaps created—by colonial policy, all demonstrate the difficulty of a neocolonial legacy (Davidson 1973, 207–18). From Davidson's perspective, Nkrumah "failed in trying to reach the right goal, and not, like many of his time and later, in trying to reach the wrong one" (207). From the viewpoint of the black diaspora, Nkrumah's contribution to independence movements in Africa demonstrates the power of black diasporic thinkers and the flow of ideas between peoples of differing maps and histories to effect change in this contested space.

The problematics of return is a central contention of John Akomfrah's *Testament*. Created under the auspices of the Black Audio Film Collective, which Akomfrah helped found in 1983, *Testament* emerged from the collective's drive to reappropriate "pre-existing imagery" of black British culture after the 1981 riots that raged across Britain protesting racial oppression, most notably in Brixton (Hill 1999, 222, 219). Focusing on the development of narrative methods that challenged mainstream depictions of British blacks by "a refusal of the conventional mechanics of identification," and insisting on active spectatorship that encouraged debate, the collective has produced films that include *Territories* (Isaac Julien; United Kingdom, 1985) and *The Passion of Remembrance* (Maureen Blackwood/Isaac Julien; United Kingdom, 1986; Hill 1999, 219–22). *Testament* shares with these works an emphasis on ex-

The Problematics of Return in *Testament*

ploring the critical impact of contemporary history on black identities that exists suspended between nations and political imperatives derived from inequality and oppression.

From the beginning, Akomfrah's works have been infused with an open-ended interrogation of filmic form, identity politics, and the clash of personal and national histories. For example, his award-winning debut film, *Handsworth Songs* (United Kingdom, 1986), made under the auspices of the collective, focuses on the events of the 1985 Handsworth riots in a nontraditional documentary that emphasizes experimentation as a means of realizing a distinct black British aesthetic (Akomfrah, quoted in Petley 1989, 261). He has completed over twenty-four film and television projects since then, including the feature documentary *Urban Soul* (United Kingdom/Ghana, 2003); the much-lauded *Last Angel of History* (United Kingdom, 1995), which won the Paul Robeson Prize, awarded at the Panafrican Film and Television Festival of Ouagadougou in 1997; and the television documentary *Seven Songs for Malcolm X* (United Kingdom, 1993), awarded Best Feature-Length Non-fiction Film at the First Festival of Black Culture in Paris in 1994. Among his fictional film works is the feature film *Who Needs a Heart* (United Kingdom, 1991), which won Best New Drama at the Chicago Film Festival (1992), and the short drama *Digitopia* (United Kingdom, 2001), significant for its exploration of alienated black subjectivity in a digital universe.

Testament (1988) is Akomfrah's first feature film and, like his other works, it is a multilayered narrative that features a combination of aesthetic approaches designed to create debate and challenge established boundaries of black identity. When asked if the work is autobiographical, Akomfrah acknowledges that fragments of his family's history have been interwoven into the narrative, a process that blurs the line between fiction and documentary.[5] This approach creates a very complex and challenging structure in which personal, fictional, and national histories collide, complicating and explicating exilic identity formation in the black diaspora. The film plays on the notion that although exiles often experience rupture from origin, the fact that they negotiate new realities with the full force of the cultural histories and identities behind them makes origin an important anchor in these identity constructions. The violence within which exile is often contextualized, however, results in a discontinuity between origin, where history continues, and exilic experience, where history is arrested at the point of departure. This raises the possibility that the dissociative effects of arrested memory contribute to a problematics of return in which the disjunctures between past memories and present realities challenge the mythical concept of return to an "unadulterated" African origin.

The film delineates the experiences of Abena, a Ghanaian exile who returns to her homeland twenty years after Nkrumah's fall. An activist student in the C.P.P., Abena left Ghana in 1966 for exile in England under mysterious political circumstances. Now a television journalist, Abena's assignment in Ghana is to track down Werner Herzog for an interview during the shooting of his film *Cobra Verde* (Germany, 1987). The fruitless pursuit of Herzog becomes emblematic of the disintegration of Abena's carefully constructed facade as the time she spends in Ghana compels her to interrogate the rupture in her past. More to the point, as Abena reconnects with old friends and fellow C.P.P. party members Danso and Rashid, she is forced to confront her role in Nkrumah's corrupt regime and accept responsibility for her own acts of betrayal when it is revealed that she saved her own life by informing on Danso, Rashid, and other party members. The uneasy and even contradictory peace she strikes with her friends and the events of that time come to epitomize the profound alienation and impossibility of return created by forced exile.

Abena's experiences over the course of the film reveal that origin can be a site of rupture between journey and return, in which memory mythologizes historical and personal imperatives. As Brah observes, "'home' is a mythic place of desire in the diasporic imagination. In this sense it is a place of no return, even if it is possible to visit the geographical territory that is seen as the place of 'origin'" (1996, 192). This suggests that maps and histories are not static concepts but subject to the ebbs and flows of memory held by individuals. On a very basic level, such a view challenges the notion of history as whole cloth and linear. Furthermore, in the case of exilic experience, the trauma of dispersal creates a paradoxical relationship with origin that is always absent as home, thus implying "an involuntary or enforced rupture between the collective subject of the original culture and the individual subject" (JanMohamed 1992, 101). At the same time, there is nostalgia for

The Problematics of Return in *Testament*

Testament (Courtesy of Smoking Dogs Films)

origin that continues to pervade the identity construction of the exilic subject, causing, in turn, a disconnection from point of arrival (101). In a very real sense, exiles exist in a seemingly irreconcilable void.

These antinomies are reflected in Abena's conflicted identity early in the film as a means of capturing "the complexity of having ambivalent attitudes, both to the place you've come from and the place you've gone to" (Akomfrah, quoted in Ofori 1990, 625). Abena is first revealed in a high-angle medium close-up shot standing at the prow of a boat traveling up a river. The movement of the waves toward the boat and the hazy distant shore gives Abena a sense of being suspended above the water. A voice-over narrates: "The last midday, the last shadow of the last living fragment. Twenty years ago I started running from family and friends." This revelation of her character introduces two primary aesthetic strategies employed throughout the film as a means of exploring the psychological terrain of exile. First, the river becomes a metaphor for Abena's emotional state and for her intrinsic Ghanaian identity as she accesses past memories. An explanatory note occurring at the beginning of the film indicates that rivers are linked to the gods

Testament (Courtesy of Smoking Dogs Films)

The Problematics of Return in *Testament*

and goddesses of Ga, symbolizing memory.⁶ Thus, the introduction of Abena places her in a memoryscape that intimately connects her to African, Ghanaian, and personal history.

Second, the narration is delivered in first-person address, a mode that will come to symbolize Abena's present-day thoughts. The narration creates an interesting ambiguity since it is performed by Sally Sagoe while the character of Abena is played by Tania Rogers. As Manthia Diawara notes, the narration uses the "narrating 'I' to comment on the documentary, and yet she [Sagoe] is treated in the story/history as 'Abena'" (1999, 319). As the film's visual structure clearly sutures this narration to Abena's psychological state through the association with river images, the narration functions as a window on Abena's thoughts. As the sequence progresses and the film cuts to a medium shot of a soaring vulture, the narrative voice transits from first person to third person as the narrator observes, "One day, twenty-fourth of February 1966, twenty years ago, Abena was a student at the Nkrumah Ideological Institute." This signals a narrative movement from Abena's present-day thoughts to her personal history. Taken together, these two modes of narration make explicit the "war zone" of memory through which Abena will struggle for resolution, redemption and release from the shadows of her past.⁷ Furthermore, the two forms of address in the narration ironically play off Abena's current incarnation of self by conflating the presumably unbiased, emotionally controlled delivery of journalistic observation with the inconsistencies and unpredictability of personal recollection. Thus, the film's narrative is foregrounding the constructedness of both national and personal histories and, in doing so, questions the validity of both.

Connecting Abena to the Nkrumah Ideological Institute aligns her with the youth movement so instrumental in maintaining Nkrumah's cult of personality.⁸ The Institute was located at Winneba and opened in February 1961 (Baynham 1988, 140). Its mission was to enforce the "ideological education of all citizens, including personnel in the armed forces" by reinforcing identification with the party and producing "party stalwarts well-versed in the CPP's somewhat ill-defined brand of 'scientific socialism'—'Nkrumahism'" (140).⁹ Generously funded by government moneys and administered like a university replete with visiting lecturers from Moscow, the institute's goal was to provide a high level

CHAPTER 5

of indoctrination and took the Moscow Institute of Marxism-Leninism as its model (Omari 1970, 121). Thus, Abena, along with the characters of Danso and Rashid, are representative of the elite among Nkrumah's followers and therefore are among the most betrayed by the disintegration of the regime and the events of the coup.

The narration also implies the impossibility of discussing exile without the referent of nationalism. Exile and nationalism seem intricately interdependent as both allude to the most personal and most public of experiences, although the ambitions of nationalism often seem to drive the imperatives of exile (Said 1990, 360). The level to which exile and nationalism are entwined is demonstrated in *Testament* by the use of tinted archival footage depicting Nkrumah and the military coup that ended his government. This tack is introduced early in the film in tandem with the character of Abena and is linked to the narration. As a series of shots unfolds revealing the arrest and imprisonment of members of the C.P.P., the narration discloses that the four words "There's been a coup," uttered by Rashid, became the impetus of Abena's flight.[10] Thus, the national history of the coup is irrevocably interwoven with Abena's conflicted personal identity.

Testament is about historical events, but it is also about the intangible spaces between events, personal actions, and responsibilities. Like these unnamed, unidentified spaces, Abena's search for comprehension often derails on unseen or unspoken things in an inaccessible African landscape (Rose 1989). Hence, ambiguity plays an important role in the narrative structure of the film, engaging the spectator in both Abena's quest and confusion. For example, in a desire to reconnect with the friends of her past and ameliorate the estrangement created by her flight to England, Abena visits her childhood friend, Danso. Also a student activist and past member of the C.P.P., Danso has remained in Ghana and is now living in difficult circumstances on a ramshackle farm. When Abena arrives at the farm, Danso refuses to return her greetings and continues on with her chores as if Abena is invisible. While Danso works, Abena sits beside her, but her friend avoids making eye contact. When at last Danso acknowledges Abena's presence by sitting on the ground beside her, they are framed in a medium two-shot with Danso in the left foreground and Abena in the middle ground on frame right. Although they are physically present in the same space, the shot's com-

The Problematics of Return in *Testament*

position emphasizes Danso's refusal to make eye contact with Abena, indicating that this move is not a conciliatory act on Danso's part. The past strife that separates them is hinted at in Abena's explanation that although she received Danso's letter, she was in the same difficult position and could not help her. When Danso maintains her stony silence, Abena invites her to come and stay in her parents' house. The film cuts to a medium close-up as Abena looks at Danso for her response. The intimate scale of the shot accentuates the depth of Danso's anger as she maintains her stony silence. In the medium two-shot that follows, Danso rises and walks out of frame, abandoning Abena. Alone and isolated against the African landscape, Abena shouts Danso's name in frustration. This scene raises a narrative mystery: the exact nature of the estrangement between the two women is not explained, and the deep-rooted anger that underlies Danso's silence seems scarcely accounted for by Abena's refusal to assist her. In addition, the nature of Danso's request for help is never made clear, resulting in narrative suspense, which, in turn, invites the spectator to actively question the dynamics between the two women. More important, it is what Abena fails to verbalize that raises questions regarding her own reliability as a narrative agent. For example, she neither directly addresses in detail the events that have estranged them, nor does she ever explicitly apologize for her refusal to assist Danso. Her acknowledgement of Danso's request for help is more a defensive justification of her actions than an expression of regret. This delimits the amount of empathy the spectator feels for Abena, and the distance permits an interrogation of both the events of the past and Abena's present motives.

On one narrative level, Abena is positioned as a "specular intellectual" caught between competing cultures and seeking to subject them to "analytic scrutiny" (JanMohamed 1992, 97). Thus, from an apparently neutral vantage point she attempts to justify her activities by portraying Nkrumah and the C.P.P. as utopic social forces, a strategy not uncommon among exiles (97). On another level, however, Akomfrah effects a critique of such neutrality by generating a collision between the calm intellectual incisiveness of Abena's interior dialogue and the clear dishevelment of her psychological state. During several of the memory sequences, a group of four women dirge singers appear, indicting Abena for betraying Ghana by choosing exile. For example,

CHAPTER 5

near the beginning of the film, Abena is depicted wandering alone through the ruins of a fortress, a device that is repeated throughout the film and represents the fact that "exile is a solitude experienced outside the group" in which traumatic alienation reinforces a sense of separate existence (Said 1990, 359). As Abena moves through the ruins, she encounters the dirge singers, who chant, "Your kinfolk are dying. Or did you forsake us before you died? Had we already lost you at the time of your death? What pact did you agree to with the foreigners that they now control our lives?"[11] This encounter serves two purposes. First, the words suggest that something vital has died in Abena as a result of her decision to leave Ghana for England. Second, the dirge singers function as a means of critiquing Abena's actions, not as a personal betrayal, but as a betrayal of her essential Africanness.

Later in the film, Abena arranges to meet Danso on the "neutral ground" of their primary school, but Danso fails to appear. Over a sequence of archival images, voice-over narration reveals that after hours of silence on the farm, Danso finally agrees to share the house with Abena, but acknowledges that she may not be able to speak to her. Abena's insistence that they meet at a place of childhood memories causes Danso to look at Abena "as if something had died in her." The sequence of archival images then cuts to a medium shot of a pensive Abena seated on a bench outside the school as the voice-over admits that Abena knows why Danso looked at her in such an emotionally charged way. The image dissolves to a long shot of the dirge singers singing in a courtyard of the fortress. As the camera dollies from right to left in a long take, the dirge singers charge that a sacrilege has been committed against River Sakumo's fetish priest and that those responsible must answer to the river goddesses.[12] As they move, they pass Abena and Danso, dressed in mourning. They are seated on a bench, playing a child's game and counting in time to their chant. The singers demand a call to action, a call to Abena personally and Ghana as a nation to end their collective denial and recoup the importance of Nkrumah as history (Rose 1989). It is significant that the question of responsibility is raised directly by the dirge singers, an act that contrasts with Danso's silence. In this way, the dirge singers give voice to the unspeakable betrayal that separates Danso and Abena and, ultimately, estranges personal and national histories. This sequence underscores a

The Problematics of Return in *Testament*

schism that seems integral to exile, which is often simultaneously propelled and sustained by intransigent violent nationalist conflicts (Said 1990, 359–60). Given that exile neither heals nor resolves such ruptures, it seems that any rapprochement with origin is an illusory goal.

The severity of this irreconcilable tension is manifested in the slow dismantling of Abena's carefully crafted control. After Danso's failure to appear for their meeting, Abena withdraws to her childhood home. The depth of her depression is revealed in a later scene as she prepares to go to bed. Depicted in a medium shot, she is framed between two blue window shutters, creating a narrow claustrophobic space that reflects her psychological entrapment. Sitting on the bed in a trancelike state, she is portrayed in a medium close-up. The camera dollies slightly left to reveal a door opening on the verandah behind her, disclosing the presence of a group of young girls in white dresses playing in the background. Rashid, who has been assisting Abena with the house since her arrival in Ghana, enters her bedroom and informs her that her researcher had come by earlier in the afternoon, leaving an opening for Abena to explain why she failed to answer the door. When Abena acknowledges Rashid distractedly, he asks her if she is all right. Her distant response that she is fine prompts Rashid to suggest that she stay at a hotel where she would be more comfortable. Abena does not respond directly to his concern. Instead, she admits that she should have stayed in Ghana. As she speaks, the clapping game played by the girls in the background metaphorically connects this admission to the indictment made by the dirge singers and to the game she plays with Danso in the fortress, creating an overlapping psychological space. The significance of the girls' presence lies in its demonstration that "exilic dislocation can be experienced simultaneously both at quotidian and profound and at corporeal and spiritual levels" (Naficy 2001, 28). Hence, the girls represent a rupture between Abena's inner torment and her everyday controlled persona, signaling a breakdown in her ability to sustain the illusion that the two are separate.

The gulf between Abena and Danso ultimately remains unbridgeable, illustrating that Abena has fallen prey to what JanMohamed describes as the "desire for an 'authentic identity'" that would justify her past decisions (1992, 117). Throughout the film, Abena seeks desperately, on an intellectual level, to avoid accepting responsibility for her

CHAPTER 5

actions, despite the fact she has already recognized on a psychological level that she must. Therefore, Abena attempts to validate the actions that precipitated her exile by deflecting responsibility onto history, politics, and individual actions taken by her friends. Danso's last appearance in the film evidences this tendency. During a breakfast scene in the garden, Abena challenges the basis of Danso's silence by questioning why Danso was so affected by the events of 1966, given that she enrolled at the ideological institute with the pragmatic goal of getting a job at the end of her training. Furthermore, Abena points out that Danso laughed at the lectures on Soviet Marxism, thus impugning the intensity of Danso's political commitment. These statements critique some of the political realities of Nkrumah's overthrow, and many participated in valorizing the regime simply because the consequences of not doing so were economically and politically disastrous (Baynham 1988, 208–9). Deflecting responsibility onto Danso's materialistic tendencies, however, does not relieve Abena of her own, and for this reason the charge appears self-serving as she fails, once again, to give voice to the exact actions that lie at the heart of Danso's silence. Danso's response, therefore, is to shift impatiently and turn her back on Abena, dismissing her query as irrelevant. This exchange thus implies that Abena's attempts to deflect the seriousness of her own past actions by diminishing the validity of Danso's anger are self-serving. Danso's refusal to contest the point verbally casts doubt on the sincerity and accuracy of Abena's observations.

The power of the unspoken conflict that lies between the two women is underscored as Abena looks out into the garden, her attention suddenly distracted by the intrusion of a memory into her present space. In a series of shots tinted red, a man and a woman stagger under the weight of large rocks they carry as they struggle across the garden and drop them into a deep, dark hole. The intrusion of the past on the present suggests that, for the exile, the "expression or activity in the new environment inevitably occur against the memory of these things in another environment. Thus both the new and the old environments are vivid, actual, occurring together contrapuntally" (Said 1990, 366). The meaning of the memory is explained when Abena takes Danso out into the garden to the base of a flowering tree, revealing that a large hole once existed where they are standing. As a child, she used to ask

The Problematics of Return in *Testament*

her mother where the water from town went. Her mother's response that it went down the hole and that the hole had to be covered up quickly because the people living at the bottom of it would come up and destroy the family, caused Abena to develop a deep terror of the hole. Her final revelation that one of the only times she has thought about this memory is when her father died in 1966 suggests that the hole metaphorically represents all the guilt Abena feels over the actions that led to her departure.

If Abena's relationship with Danso functions in the narrative as a means of explicating the violence done to personal relationships in the rift between national and individual histories, then her relationship with Rashid contrasts by illustrating the clash between national history as an unbroken strand of experience and the arrested national history of the exile. As a subject of the narrative, Rashid represents a survivor who has arrived at a place of comfort with the national history of Ghana. Unlike Abena and Danso, for whom the traumatic effects of the coup are still unresolved, Rashid has emerged from the experience with a sense of the larger political picture and an acceptance of his own responsibility and place in that history. He has genuinely come to terms with Abena's actions and acknowledges the difficult context within which they were taken. This acceptance provides a safe space in which Abena can air her lingering concerns regarding their role in the political process initiated by Nkrumah's overthrow.

Although supportive, Rashid's character is the narrative agent that most directly challenges the basis of Abena's denial, ultimately providing a venue for her to come to an uneasy acceptance of her own actions. Such denial is often motivated by the exile's attempt to refuse the full extent of the rupture from origin that occurs when the past is arrested by the circumstances of departure (Naficy 2001, 77). Abena demonstrates this trait as she seeks to cling to a mythical construct of the past by nostalgically longing for a reaffirmation of the importance of Nkrumah's role in Ghanaian history. Thus, she continually searches for a definitive reason or action that explicates Nkrumah's downfall, despite the fact that the answers already lie in her own experience. An example of this denial occurs during a conversation with Rashid as they clear the garden of overgrown brush at Abena's childhood home. By clearing away the brush and restoring the garden to its previous state,

CHAPTER 5

Rashid and Abena are metaphorically opening a space to the past, which gives the activity an ironic cast. As they prepare to burn the brush, Abena expresses the opinion that as members of the C.P.P., they had their moment in history and turned and ran. When Rashid dismisses this as "exile talk," Abena stubbornly asserts that it is a fact. Rashid retorts that all the signs of a coup were present and that everyone saw them, especially after three assassination attempts on Nkrumah's life. His question, "Who were the leaders?" voices a refusal to see the C.P.P. as unwitting victims of the coup. Abena's reluctance to accept this position is evident in her response: "We've got nothing to do with leaders. I'm trying to understand what we did." The comment exposes Abena's vain strivings to find a rationale that lessens the C.P.P.'s responsibility in its own downfall by seeking to justify the coup as a failure of individuals to take action rather than accept that the source of the regime's failure lay in its corruption and unfettered exercise of absolute power. Furthermore, Abena deflects responsibility for her personal failure by using the pronoun, "we" as a means of extending that failure to include Rashid, Danso, and all the others in the party who did not resist the coup.

This scene leads to the revelation of the exact action that lies at the heart of Abena's trauma. Graphic documentary footage of conjoined twin babies being prepared for separation surgery is interspersed throughout the film. Manipulated by hands belonging to unseen forces and overseen by the masked and anonymous faces of the doctors and nurses, the separation of the conjoined twins comes to symbolize the violent forces that tear Ghana's national and Abena's personal histories apart. The footage is eerily voyeuristic as the twins struggle and cry while gas masks, connected to the anesthetic machine, are held forcibly to their faces, foregrounding their extreme vulnerability. The sequence is then intercut with a long take of Abena, dressed in mourning, wandering through the deserted fortress, virtually engulfed by the towering architecture. Finally, the sequence returns to images of the conjoined twins, now half-conscious and separated, displayed for the camera by anonymous hands to reveal their enormous scars. Taken together, these intercut sequences are emblematic of the violent exilic disjuncture Abena feels between her person and her Ghanaian origin, which has resulted in a diminishment of her sense of identity. Fur-

The Problematics of Return in *Testament*

thermore, the estrangement indicated by Abena's lonely wandering through the fortress indicates that the promise of return for an exile is illusory. Ultimately, this signals that the gap between Abena and Ghana is unbridgeable, for as Said observes, "negotiations, wars of national liberation, people bundled out of their homes and prodded, bussed or walked to enclaves in other regions: what do these experiences add up to? Are they not manifestly and almost by design irrecoverable?" (1990, 359). Thus, Abena's nostalgic desire to heal the sundered whole is not predicated on reuniting with the Ghana she has returned to but on recouping the Ghana of the past, a goal that is manifestly unachievable.

The display of the now separated twins leads to a scene in which the depths of Abena's betrayal of the cause are revealed. In a medium shot tinted blue, a group of students stand tensely in a line. As the camera dollies from right to left stopping at Abena, the tight framing of the shot creates a claustrophobic sense of entrapment, signifying the beginning of her downfall. Identified by a soldier as a potential informant, Abena is singled out from the others who are arrested and taken away to military headquarters, leaving her alone with the commanding sergeant. Abena's final capitulation is depicted in a long take that begins as a menacing low-angle medium close-up of the sergeant mocking Abena for being childish. As he turns and approaches her, the camera dollies in to Abena, first accentuating her physical vulnerability through a medium shot of her solitary figure and then emphasizing her psychological vulnerability in a tight close-up as the sergeant forces a gun beneath her jaw, causing her to recoil in fear. The implication of the threat is clear: Abena is forced to inform on her friends and the movement in order to save her own life.

Akomfrah sustains the debate by exposing Abena's paradoxical relationship to the politics she ultimately betrayed. In a scene with Rashid near the end of the film, they sit together in the garden sharing an evening drink. Abena discloses to Rashid that until her return to Ghana, all the events of the past seemed distant. Rashid asks her if she feels guilty, and at first Abena avoids the question by responding that she feels responsible and obliged to apologize to everyone she meets. Only after these defensive comments does she reluctantly admit to feeling guilty. The degree of Abena's resistance to assuming responsibility for her betrayal creates an ideological space that interrogates the question of balance between personal and national histories. In the end, Abena's categorization as victim or victimizer may be a moot point since the actions she takes are only defensible within the very specific constructs of the time in which they were taken. In effect, *Testament* challenges the spectator to answer the question of whether personal and national histories can ever be realistically viewed as separate. Rashid's response to Abena's admission of guilt illustrates this: he takes the position that blame should not be assigned to anyone, including the historical events themselves, because their group collectively failed to take action against the corruption in their midst. Hence, all the participants are guilty, either directly or indirectly of abandoning the cause, a justification that appears to abrogate Abena's responsibility.

The scene ends on a comment by Abena that her blood still boils at the sight of the American flag. Although she and Rashid share ironic laughter, the comment indicates that Abena is still indoctrinated to some degree in the cult of personality that surrounded Nkrumah. Indeed, the film seems to argue through the characters of Abena and Rashid that the failure of Nkrumah's regime lay in the people around him and not necessarily in his actions, which remain largely unexplored in the film.

The scene that best illustrates the power of Nkrumah's cult occurs near the middle of the film. In a series of full-color archival images, the celebrations of Republic Day in 1960 are depicted as a time of great promise and national hope. The narrator describes various news accounts of the time portraying Nkrumah as a man of destiny and "greater than the air we breathe." It reveals that Rashid would read the contents of the articles to Abena and Danso, who would applaud enthusiastically, an action that underscores the power of the cult to engage its members. In a very real sense, Abena fails to either resolve or put into perspective the hero worship that bound her to Nkrumah's movement in the first place. It is significant that counterarguments critiquing Nkrumah's personal leadership are not present in the film, a strategy that reflects Akomfrah's desire to recoup a leader who gave Ghana its name and identity but who has now disappeared from popular memory (Rose 1989).

Abena's final act of betrayal is ultimately revealed in a scene near the end of the film when she returns to the ruins of the institute. En-

The Problematics of Return in *Testament*

veloped in the darkness of the interior, the camera tracks with Abena as she explores what little remains of her past. She kneels, gathers torn and half-destroyed socialist literature from the floor, and then moves through the building again, barely discernable and wraithlike. This scene cuts to another from her past, which begins with a medium two-shot of the sergeant and Abena at a press conference. As the sergeant disparagingly announces that Abena is present to apologize for the inconvenience she has caused, the camera begins a slow dolly in to a high-angle close-up. The camera movement foregrounds Abena's psychological torment by visually stressing the deep shame she feels as the sergeant informs the audience that she will name names if asked while the audience responds with sarcastic laughter. The scene reflects the historical events that followed the coup in which the new leaders "engaged in a persistent campaign of propaganda against the individuals, institutions and policies of the former regime" (Baynham 1988, 219). Considered in conjunction with the scene in which the sergeant threatens her, the spectator is given the opportunity to recognize that Abena is co-operating under duress, thus mitigating her responsibility. Certainly, once the coup was a fait accompli, the populace switched sides readily, especially given the dangerously unstable aftermath (209). However, although the choice of aesthetics is clearly meant to create sympathy for Abena, the events depicted raise serious questions regarding her reliability as a narrative authority and force a reevaluation of all that Abena has revealed throughout the course of the film. For all the carefully controlled and constructed recitation of history in the narration sequences, it seems, ultimately, that Abena is not seeking to recoup Nkrumah and his historical importance. Rather, she is seeking to rationalize her own lapse of honor by creating a historical justification for her weakness. Thus, Abena seems lost in contradiction, raising the question of whether she is a victim of history or a victimizer. The dichotomy is deliberate: to resolve the contradiction that is Abena, the spectator must assume a position on her actions, thus entering the debate concerning her level of responsibility.

The ending of the film reflects Akomfrah's refusal to invoke a reductive answer to Abena's dilemma. Despite receiving absolution from Rashid, she remains lost in isolation, unable to establish any lasting peace with the circumstances of her betrayal or with herself for hav-

CHAPTER 5

ing committed it. In a scene near the end, Akomfrah uses a long take to indicate Abena's continued estrangement from the Ghana she so desperately desires to recoup. Beginning with an extreme long shot of the Ghanaian landscape from the terrace of Abena's hotel, the camera dollies right to left, ending in a high-angle medium close-up of Abena at a table, staring out at the panoramic view. The dreamlike pace of the camera movement emphasizes the grandeur and impenetrability of the landscape, serving as a metaphor for the complexities of the nation's history. In addition, the scale diminishes Abena physically and reinforces her isolation by foregrounding her disconnection from all human contact. The voice-over narration that accompanies this visual presentation is appropriately bleak as it states that the C.P.P. had become a disease in the blood of Ghana after committing many political blunders. Acknowledgment of the movement's responsibility, however, does not lead to a release or easing of the estrangement Abena feels. As the film cuts from the shot of Abena to an extreme long shot of an abandoned rail yard filled with aged, decaying rail cars, a parallel is created between Abena's dispirited state and the lost prosperity of Ghana without Nkrumah. The narration acknowledges that in the drive to create a sense of nationhood, Nkrumah's supporters were guilty of contempt for dissent, leading to more intractable factions than ever encountered in "the ancient tribalisms." Combined with the narration, the rail yard visually represents the diminishment of both Ghana and Abena.

This unresolved collision reflects Akomfrah's concern that "history is now made up of a series of log jams of events. . . . That log jam leads to an edge where, literally, things fall off and then disappear. So it becomes impossible to rescue real events with any kind of true precision" (Akomfrah, quoted in Rose 1989). The fact that Abena's return does not achieve the desired rapprochement with her past is indicative of Akomfrah's desire to leave final judgment in the hands of the spectator. This intention is clear in the final scene of the film when Abena encounters an open grave during a walk through the cemetery. As she stares down into the narrow claustrophobic opening, the weathered remains in the grave are depicted in a series of ever-tighter close-ups, revealing a human skull and tattered bones, barely discernable in the darkness. Ending the film on a close-up of Abena's intense, almost mesmerized

The Problematics of Return in *Testament*

expression, creates an open ending in which Abena remains an exile forever in transit for whom "the promise of a homecoming—completing the story, domesticating the detour—becomes an impossibility" (Chambers 1994, 5). In leaving the final disposition of Abena's return open to interpretation, Akomfrah invites the spectator to continue to debate the meaning of Abena's "war zone of memories" beyond the film's narrative space.

SIX

Slippage and Mutable Histories in *Deluge*

In chapter 5, I described exilic experience as a disjunctive state that creates a fracture between origin and exile, resulting in alienation and making the act of return problematic. Both Abdul JanMohamed and Edward Said suggest the exilic state is experienced as one of mourning, in which the exile is caught in permanent transition between a recoupment of origin that can never be achieved and arrival in a new cultural circumstance that was never desired (JanMohamed 1992, 101; Said 1990, 363). In this case, the tensions between these conflicting poles prevent the exile from becoming at ease in either nation. The destabilization of origin as a pure concept, however, is not necessarily a negative force in the development of diasporic identities. For example, James Clifford alludes to the complex interrelationship between maps and histories when he suggests that "both roots *and* routes" contribute to "forms of community consciousness and solidarity that maintain identifications outside the national time/space in order to live inside, with a difference" (1994, 308). One way of reading this position might be to suggest that Clifford is exposing a theoretical gap: if singular terms such as arrival, departure, and return marginalize by virtue of their narrowness one type or fact of diasporic experience in favor of

Slippage and Mutable Histories in *Deluge*

foregrounding another, how can one generate an adequate framework that promotes inclusiveness (303)? Instead, Clifford argues that *slippage* occurs "between invocations of diaspora theories, diasporic discourses, and distinct historical experiences of diaspora," which offers a means of transcending fixed constructions of diaspora (302). From this perspective, exilic journey and origin do not necessarily function independently of, or in conflict with, one another but create gaps that, once bridged, generate new possibilities for viewing both. Hence, the very instability of exile can prove a positive force by virtue of its hybridizing power. Moreover, since diasporas are composed of many dispersed communities that cross borders and cultures, the transnational aspects of such journeys resist inscription in discrete concepts of origin, history, and nation (304). This suggests that although historicity has a role in the discussion, it cannot entirely contain its discourses; nor can discussions of diaspora devoid of historical context adequately account for the unique range of diasporic experiences. Under this model, diasporic identities are formed in the slippage between nation, history, and individual experience. The discontinuousness of exile thus becomes a salient aspect of a complex process rather than its defining feature.

The work of Iain Chambers is complementary to that of Clifford because he views exile as a mutable state. Like Clifford, Chambers recognizes that the journey of an exile influences the construction of identity and origin. In his framework, an exile's origin and point of arrival "act as hinges that serve both to close *and* to open doors in an increasing global traffic" (italics in original; 1994, 2). From this position, it is possible to consider that both ends of the journey's axis are transformed by the individual experience of traveling across borders and cultures. Exilic experience becomes a mediated position in constant negotiation and renegotiation of the relationships between departure, journey, and arrival that are interstitially related through memory and experience. Thus, from Chambers's perspective, exilic experience "compels us to recognise the need for a mode of thinking that is neither fixed nor stable, but is one that is open to the prospect of a continual return to events, to their re-elaboration and revision" (3). In this fashion, history becomes something that is perpetually transmuted and transformed, interpreted in transit, and subject to redefinition in "new constellations" (3).

CHAPTER 6

Such an observation adds to Clifford's assertion that slippage is a salient feature of diasporic experience by offering the opportunity to map diasporic consciousness in a multivector environment that accounts for the competition, complementarity, and discontinuity of diverse transnational geographies, histories, and cultures. In considering these two concepts, one can infer that the negative experiences of discrimination and exclusion coexist with the positive skills of survival, adaptive strategies, and visions of renewal, demonstrating that "diaspora consciousness lives loss and hope as a defining tension" (Clifford 1994, 312). Thus, whether the concept is slippage or mutable history, the constant renegotiation of diasporic identities provides a creative framework in which the measurement of subjects in motion is possible.

As a documentary film, *Deluge* explores the necessity of bridging the gap between self and origin in order to reclaim the latter as one of many aspects of diasporic identity by probing the circumstances that gave rise to an African socialist regime in Ethiopia. As a specific history within the context of the African continent, Ethiopia differs from many of its neighboring nations in that it has not been subject to colonial rule with the exception of a brief occupation by Italy between 1935 and 1941 (Halliday and Molyneux 1981, 17). Thus, in contrast to the issues of neocolonialism examined in *Testament*, *Deluge* deals with violent social change that more closely resembles the French and Russian revolutions, which marked the transition from absolute monarchy to capitalist state (14). It is therefore useful to engage in a brief discussion of the Ethiopian context that existed prior to the historical events outlined in the film.

As a national history, Ethiopia's successful resistance to colonial rule resulted in the preservation of its "highly articulated pre-colonial social structures and culture," making it "a symbol of political independence and cultural continuity" in both Africa and the black diaspora (Halliday and Molyneux 1981, 51). Although Islam played a role in its development, it is Ethiopia's position as a Christian kingdom that makes it unique. Dating from the fourth century AD, Ethiopian Christianity is a fusion of monasticism, Judaic influences, and Christian mythology, which accords the nation a special place in European imaginations (52). This position was entrenched in the nineteenth and twentieth centuries with a series of Christian monarchies that culminated in the rule of Ras

Slippage and Mutable Histories in *Deluge*

Tafari Makonnen, who became regent in 1916 and was crowned Emperor Haile Selassie in 1930 (55–56). With an official title including such descriptors as "Lion of the Tribe of Judah, the Elect of God [and the] King of the Kings of Ethiopia," Selassie claimed direct descent from King Solomon and the queen of Sheba (58). As a divine emperor, Selassie assumed absolute authority over a governmental infrastructure that had more in common with medieval monarchies than contemporary states (58). This being said, Selassie undertook certain reforms intended to move Ethiopia toward a more modern era by expanding medical and educational infrastructures in the 1920s and establishing Ethiopia's first constitution in 1931 (58). Such reforms, however, did little to change a cultural structure founded on an almost feudal hierarchy of obligation based on the status of peasant, noble, and emperor (Lefort 1983, 13). Although the striated social milieu created cultural divisions that ensured the continuation of the monarchy, it also contributed to political, economic, and social gaps that resulted in a sociopolitical situation that certainly made the revolution possible, if not inevitable (Halliday and Molyneux 1981, 61).

There were three very broad elements that eventually came together to bring Selassie's reign to an end. First, Selassie's failure to implement far-reaching social and economic reforms foundered owing to the tension between his attempts to entrench power at the center and the continuation of the decentralized power wielded by local or peripheral authorities who vigorously protected traditional rights, hence frustrating real change (Lefort 1983, 14–15). Furthermore, Selassie's failure to successfully conclude the long-standing guerrilla war in Eritrea, which had become Ethiopia's fourteenth province in 1962, contributed to a sense that his hold on the throne was slipping (39). Finally, the age of the emperor and his failure to name a successor, as well as questions regarding his mental fitness for continued rule, exposed the weakness of the monarchy (Halliday and Molyneux 1981, 83; Spencer 1987, 335).

The second major element that undermined Selassie's rule was the agrarian crisis that gripped the country, culminating in a major famine that occurred in the northern provinces in the early 1970s. Land rights in Ethiopia, primarily an agricultural nation, were defined by an entrenched, complex, and almost feudal system of *rist:* land was cultivated "by communities belonging to a putative common lineage"

CHAPTER 6

that accorded access to land based on the political and social status of the families involved (Halliday and Molyneux 1981, 63). Thus, complicated systems of rent and tribute resulted in concentrated wealth at the top to the detriment of the peasants. Selassie's attempts to institute modest rural reforms were undermined by the refusal of the provincial nobility to surrender their entitlements, testifying to the power of an outmoded social structure that made Ethiopia Africa's poorest nation by 1974, despite its great potential (58, 69). The cost of this became apparent when a prolonged drought between 1970 and 1973 triggered a devastating famine. Peasants, obligated to borrow money for subsistence from landowners, merchants, and moneylenders richer than themselves by pledging part or all of their agricultural produce, were forced off the land, resulting in a migration to urban centers that left women, children, and the elderly behind without the reserves to support themselves (Lefort 1983, 44). As Lefort argues, the social disruption went well beyond the drought itself, as the food shortage would have been rectified with the return of the rains. Thus, the famine resulted when "the whole social, democratic and productive fabric was torn asunder by the break-up of families, the departure of farmers, the death of cattle and the lack of seeds" (44). Affecting over three million people, the famine became a flashpoint in establishing the ineffectiveness of Selassie's leadership (Halliday and Molyneux 1981, 67). The failure of the winter rains was known as early as March 1973, and the minister of agriculture presented a strong document outlining the crisis that had been largely ignored by an imperial government seemingly uninterested in the peasants' plight (Lefort 1983, 46). The authorities made the decision to cover up the full extent of the situation, imposing a full media blackout in Ethiopia and denying all reports of the famine's existence (46). When pressure exerted by Western nations and the presence of the dying and starving on the roadsides finally forced the state to act, it continued to minimize the situation, failing to seek a level of international assistance equal to the size of the crisis (46–47). This resulted in as many as four hundred thousand deaths, directly attributable to starvation and disease (Halliday and Molyneux 1981, 67). The emperor subsequently responded by exempting the worst areas from taxation and allowing peasants three years to buy back their lands, but this move was viewed with widespread cynicism, as the former meant nothing, given that the peasants had no means to pay taxes in the first place, and the latter was impossible, given the extent of the economic and human devastation (Lefort 1983, 47). Most important, landlords engaged in profiteering and continued to demand payment in full "despite the bad harvest of 1973," increasing the gulf between the wealthy and the peasantry (48). Ironically, Selassie's mismanagement of the crisis would ultimately lead to a rapid rise in food prices and inflation, contributing to the crisis in the military that precipitated the revolution.

The army represents the third broad factor that hastened the end of Selassie's empire. Prior to the Italian occupation that ended in 1941, mobilizing an army was the obligation of landowners who, in exchange for land grants, were required to provide soldiers when bidden to (Lefort 1983, 17–18). Hence, the state was dependent on the largesse of the provincial nobility in order to sustain its military (18). Recognizing this weakness, Selassie, upon returning from exile after his defeat at the hands of the Italians, undertook to create a modern army that was, by force of the constitution, completely under his control (18). This was not an inexpensive undertaking as Selassie ensured loyalty through compensation: for example, the salary of an army private was double that of an urban worker, and many soldiers benefited from land grants provided by Selassie from state lands as a means of retaining control (18). The army, however, was rife with internal tensions, in part spurred by imperial favoritism that allowed preferential treatment and advancement for those of Amharic lineage over other ethnic groups (18–19). Lefort suggests that the army was a microcosm of the stresses in the larger Ethiopian society, driven by "profound cleavages based on age, ethnic or social origin, rank, branches, specialization and, of course, political attitudes" (19). The divisions, especially those between senior and junior officers, began to show in late 1973–early 1974 as living conditions deteriorated in the wake of Ethiopia's worsening economic crisis. A series of rebellions began, first involving isolated units. Finally, exacerbated by the rise of inflation, widespread unrest moved through the military, initiating Ethiopia's revolution (Halliday and Molyneux 1981, 78–84).

CHAPTER 6

Deluge/Ye Wonz Maibel (United States/Ethiopia, 1997) is an hour-long documentary that offers an extraordinary account of slippage between histories, not as a site of permanent dislocation, but as a site with potential for reclamation. Salem Mekuria's film explores the impact of the ideological disconnections that occur between family members and other survivors as Ethiopia's political situation unravels during the period spanning from the final stages of Selassie's reign to the Red Terror, the name given to the tremendous social upheaval that followed the Emperor's demise. As such, the film is one of several works created in the 1990s that effect critiques of Ethiopian feudalism, the revolution, and its aftermath (Cham 2004, 54). This places *Deluge* in the company of other films such as Haile Gerima's documentary *Imperfect Journey* (1994) and Yemane Demissie's fictional film *Girgir* (*Tumult* 1996; Cham 54–55).

Salem Mekuria is an independent film producer, writer, and director based in Boston. She also teaches art history and studio courses in film history and video production at Wellesley College. Born in Ethiopia and educated in the 1970s in film and video production at San Francisco State University, Mekuria is an award-winning and leading figure in black diasporic documentary production. She has worked with *Nova*, PBS's premier science documentary series, and has numerous international film productions focusing on African and African-American women and development issues. These include *Sidet: Forced Exile* (1991), *As I Remember It: A Portrait of Dorothy West* (1991), and *Our Place in the Sun* (1988). She is acknowledged as an important voice in diaspora filmmaking as evidenced by *RUPTURES: A Many-Sided Story*, a triptych video installation depicting a century of Ethiopian history that was presented in 2003 at the Fiftieth Venice Biennale, and *IMAGinING TOBIA*, a three-channel video installation portraying Ethiopian cultural and physical landscapes.

Deluge has been viewed internationally and received many honors, including First Place in the National Black Programming Consortium's Prized Pieces award program (1997) and the Director's Citation in the Black Maria Film and Video Festival (1997). What makes *Deluge* unique is its poignant and often poetic portrayal of Mekuria's personal struggle to understand the disintegration of friends and family as Ethiopia undergoes violent change. The film interrogates the power of multiple

Slippage and Mutable Histories in *Deluge*

border crossings to shape origin and identity as Mekuria, from her perspective as an exile in America, seeks to understand how journeys outward and back to center play a vital role in creating divisions, reconciliations, and, ultimately, transnational histories and identities. In contrast to the experience of disjunctive return in *Testament*, Mekuria accepts slippage as a part of the natural articulation of time, history, and exile and takes the position that, although origin cannot be entirely divorced from identity, it is not static and acts in concert with other experiences and cultures.

Mekuria began making *Deluge* in 1991 and originally intended it to be an official history of the Ethiopian revolution and the eventual collapse of the Marxist regime that emerged from it (Ellerson 2000, 177–78). After three years of filming interviews and initial edits of the film, however, Mekuria recognized that because she was not directly involved in the events in Ethiopia, she was uncomfortable speaking directly for the participants through her film (178). As she reconsidered her approach to the film, it became obvious to her that she was not searching for the official story so much as seeking to understand what happened to her brother Selomon who died during that period (178). Thus, *Deluge* emerged as a personal documentary chronicling the collapse of Emperor Haile Selassie's reign and the rise of the socialist Derg regime. This regime, which ignited the factional disputes known as the Red Terror, fragmented Ethiopian society along political lines and pitted family members against one another in a violent struggle for power. Mekuria takes this history as a contextual frame and locates within it her own personal history as well as that of her family, friends, and other survivors of this dangerous and divisive revolutionary process.

Deluge is thus multinarrational and founded on three identifiable systems: Mekuria's own complex narration, which encompasses her personal history and Ethiopia's political one; letters from Mekuria's brother Selomon and best friend Negist; and witness testimony from survivors. These strategies allow Mekuria to avoid what she describes as "the problem of the exile telling that story" by giving her search for understanding an active role in the film's narrative structure and placing her in a mediating position between a multiplicity of colliding viewpoints (179). In addition, the multilayered approach permits Mekuria the opportunity to explore the inherent contradictions of exile, which

Deluge (Courtesy of Mekuria Productions)

Slippage and Mutable Histories in *Deluge*

Chambers describes as the "memory of primary loss," a psychological and cultural state in which "the questions met with *en route* consistently breach the boundaries" of identities buffeted by competing cultural impulses (1994, 2). Hence, her active position in the narrative gives Mekuria the ability to interrogate her status as a black diasporic subject by challenging her own illusory memories of Ethiopia in conjunction with questioning the political underpinnings and consequences of the country's social upheaval through the testimony of those who remained behind. In this way, Mekuria portrays both exile and origin as subject to ongoing processes of negotiation and hybridization.

As a subject/participant, Mekuria moves through the narrative unimpeded by classical expectations, mixing times and tenses: her narration takes place in the present, but as remembrance, is couched in the past; although Selomon and Negist's letters are used to illustrate past events, the letters are in the present tense, bringing a sense of continued immediacy to their struggle; a woman survivor, testifying to the past death of her son in the Red Terror, does so standing at a mass grave presently being excavated, and thus, simultaneously unravels both her past experience and its lingering effects in the present. The aural elements are visually illustrated by a mixture of personal photographs, newsreel footage, witness interviews, art, and images of present-day Ethiopia. These also render the divisions between past and present as imaginary lines: for example, in speaking of the past struggles of the Ethiopian people, Mekuria illustrates her point by including present-day images of Ethiopian women carrying heavy loads of wood. The overlapping nature of the above elements creates a subtly complex narrative structure that disrupts reductive linear relations of time and space. As each narrational position combines and recombines with others in the text, the spectator is empowered to question and decipher the interrelationship of the layers. For example, Mekuria intermixes different levels of time in the same sequence, as demonstrated during the narration of one of Negist's letters. The letter itself is from the past, but its language reflects the present tense, giving a sense of immediacy. The visual presentation offers a montage of photographs: those of Negist as a young woman appear to reflect a time frame contemporary with the letter, while others reflect a past childhood shared with Mekuria. A third category, those of Negist and her child, reflect a future state. This

CHAPTER 6

offers a fluid view of time that is not constrained by pure linearity but, rather, flows forward and back at will like memory.

In terms of form, *Deluge* can be described as a performative documentary. The interrelationship of historical frame and personal viewpoint in the narrative structure evidences a more open and expressive relationship in which emotion is as important as fact (Nichols 1994, 100). This suggests that while performative documentary might possess historical grounding, the aesthetic goal is not to provide a description of history but, rather, an evocation of it. Furthermore, the self-reflexive role played by Mekuria in the text reveals how her emotive connections to, and investment in, the documentary's subject matter shapes the content (96). For example, the film opens with a slow zoom through a doorway into an editing suite, revealing Mekuria in the act of assembling the very film the spectator is in the process of viewing. This motif is reprised throughout the text, functioning as a distancing device and reinforcing the perception that the text being viewed is subject to the selective process of construction. As the boundaries between objectivity and subjectivity blur, the film's structure signals a specific concern with exposing the gap between descriptive and evocative histories, generating, as Nichols has argued, "a distinct tension between performance and document, between the personal and the typical, the embodied and disembodied" (97). By openly staking out her own social subjectivity within the documentary, Mekuria transforms an act of personal remembrance into national history and provokes the spectator to actively question her very agenda: if the central narrator's "unbiased" position is potentially suspect, can any authority in the text be accepted without interrogation?

Mekuria's blend of personal and national history is instrumental in sustaining the film's unity of form: her narration provides the grammatical structure that grounds the film and creates passage between the strata of narrated letters and eyewitness accounts. Her central role as filmmaker and subject/participant places Mekuria in the metaphorical position of "griot." As she both organizes the descriptive elements of the film and adds to its overall evocation by inclusion of her own experiences, she thereby confounds any separation of art, self, and history. Furthermore, because Mekuria's exilic quest for understanding connects these disparate narrative elements, she is creating "an ongoing

Slippage and Mutable Histories in *Deluge*

transnational network that includes the homeland, not as something simply left behind, but as a place of attachment in a contrapuntal modernity" that underscores how diasporic identities are formulated (Clifford 1994, 311). Moreover, Mekuria's exilic subjectivity in combination with the multiple narrations of *Deluge* creates slippage between origin and exile, undermining the hierarchical privilege of her narration and according equal validity to all narrational points of view. It is therefore necessary for the spectator to sort through the experiences expressed before choosing a position in the debate. Thus *Deluge* accomplishes two simultaneous narrative goals: it provides insight into the machinations of Ethiopia's Red Terror while also exploring how the disjunctive state of exile can lead to rapprochement and understanding.

This intent is signaled early in the film. Over a montage of Ethiopian iconography, Mekuria relates a historical encounter between the queen of Sheba and King Solomon, which results in the conception of Menelik, the first emperor of Ethiopia. Her comment that she "grew up with this blend of legend and history," appears to suggest that myth may be inseparable from history and is equally valid in determining nation. Furthermore, when Mekuria asks, "What history is without myths and legends?" she indicates that *Deluge* is confronting the reductive strictures of authenticity by refusing to clearly delineate the boundaries between history and myth: in other words, the story of the queen of Sheba is not authenticated as either historical or mythological, but, rather, such judgment is left in the hands of the spectator. The refusal to separate myth from history also functions as a means of foregrounding Mekuria's journey as an exilic subject. Like the spectators, Mekuria is sifting through iconic memories of Ethiopia that have shifted with time and distance. Hence, her passage though the documentary mirrors what Chambers has described as the exile's "journey" toward a subjectivity that "acquires the form of a restless interrogation, undoing in its very terms of reference as the point of departure is lost along the way" (1994, 2). In response to this strategy, the film becomes a torrent of narrational levels, images, and repetitive motifs that, while directed at illuminating a grave period in Ethiopia's history, are less concerned with authenticating historical facts than with contextualizing the numinous connections between myth, history, personal identity, and nation.

CHAPTER 6

Several narrative and aesthetic elements present in *Deluge* heighten the possibility for slippage by drawing on strategies of oral tradition, including the use of repetitive images, layered points of view, shifting between past and present as a means of social critique, and use of digressions that differentiate African oral histories from Western linear history (Ukadike 1994, 203, 210). Repetition of visual elements, for example, allows Mekuria to interrogate her own vision while suturing the spectator into the ideological quest of the film. For example, images of rivers are introduced early and become symbolic on a number of levels. Early in the film, Mekuria relates how she embarks on a long-awaited journey to see Ethiopia after her graduation. Over a photograph of her youthful self standing in front of a waterfall, Mekuria narrates, "To me, Ethiopia looked eternal, like the rivers which have been flowing through it for millennia." Hence, on one level, rivers become associated with the surging of time, with journeys to and from the historical realities of an eternal Ethiopia. Such images function as transitional devices, serving to remind the spectator of an unfragmented Ethiopia of limitless possibilities.

Zooms are also employed as repetitive motifs and are used to reveal and conceal context. Mekuria uses this strategy to great effect during a scene that underscores the absolute power of Haile Selassie as a monarch. Beginning in a medium close-up of a detail from a painting of the emperor, the camera slowly zooms out from Selassie's figure, eventually revealing the painting's iconic nature. The emperor, radiating light and flanked by his ministers, is shown standing on a cloud under the protective wing of an angel while the masses are gathered below him. This camera movement is accompanied by voice-over narration explaining that an absolute monarch, who rules by right of entitlement, must never regret the use of force. As the zoom expands, and the painting's full context is unveiled, the spectator is accorded the temporal space within which to consider the implications of the narrator's remarks. The distance between the deified emperor and the people beneath him reinforces the oppression that spurs the Ethiopian revolution to life. The same shot is immediately reprised. This time, editing time code appears at frame right, and the zoom moves past the painting to unveil Mekuria at her editing suite, facing two monitors: on the right is the iconic painting and on the left is a rushing waterfall. This

Slippage and Mutable Histories in *Deluge*

represents a shift between past and present, thus laying bare the second function that the zooms perform. The camera movement, which foregrounds Mekuria's inner conflict, visually and metaphorically suspends her between competing ideological images that must be mediated in order to achieve understanding. This process is repeated in several instances throughout the film and illustrates Mekuria's use of shifting points of view to generate social critique. Later, as she contrasts her own point of view with that of Selomon, Negist, and the survivors, Mekuria suggests that the river of Ethiopia's political evolution is fed by the tributaries of multiple personal histories: it is the confluence of these histories and their points of view that inflame the revolution and raises the specter of responsibility.

Deluge returns constantly to the role of education in the revolution and its ultimate fragmentation of Ethiopian identities. Emperor Haile Selassie I undertook to modernize his feudal nation by choosing a select group of students to pursue Westernized education. This was not a purely altruistic undertaking, for, according to Lefort, the result of the educational process most benefited the state by inculcating an elite from the Amharic culture with imperial doctrine designed to serve government imperatives; it was not a democratizing effort (1983, 28). In addition, by training more students than could be integrated into the state system, Selassie created an environment of high unemployment among these individuals, spurring on further unrest (28). Finally, exposed to new ideas and methodologies in the United States and Moscow, the students who did find employment within the state were stultified by archaic systems and processes of advancement that favored those from the upper level of the social hierarchy with Amharic backgrounds (28). Forged in these contexts, the subsequent unrest of a student movement with little chance for advancement became the dangerous core element driving resistance to Selassie's rule (27).

Mekuria illustrates the paternalism inherent in Selassie's position during an interview with her father, Neburaelid Mekuria Abeyhoy, who was a member of parliament just prior to the revolution. Defending Selassie, he relates that when formal education was first introduced, the emperor enticed children to attend school by offering them cookies and sugar. When chided by one of his aides who said that the children would be his downfall, Selassie responded that it did not matter as long

CHAPTER 6

as the country grew and developed. Abeyhoy's insistence, however, that it is difficult to enumerate all the things Selassie did for Ethiopia reflects a fundamental disjunction between the ruling elite and the students' expectations and demand for real change. These students, including Selomon, Negist, and to a lesser extent, Mekuria herself, eventually precipitate the destruction of the Selassie regime through the abandonment of Ethiopian culture in favor of Western ideologies. By including herself within these elite, Mekuria is acknowledging a distant but shared responsibility not only for the overthrow of Selassie but also for the subsequent events of the Red Terror that rip apart the fabric of Ethiopian society.

Mekuria alludes directly and indirectly to the role education plays in creating distance. Negist, Selomon, and Mekuria come from a similar social background and possess similar/shared educational experiences. The journeys they take, however, both ideologically and literally, eventually rupture that similarity and result in personal strife that parallels Ethiopia's national conflict. For example, Mekuria narrates that she and her brother Selomon looked at the same things and saw them differently. While homesick in St. Paul, Minnesota, she remembers her homeland as "Addis Ababa, or New Flower, set inside a ring of wavy hills, as beautiful as its name implied. The wild daisies of September, the aroma of Eucalyptus trees permeating the air and the thick smoke of incense in the churches, were the images I carried with me." This romantic nostalgia contrasts strongly with Selomon's political activism. As the camera zooms back from the images of Addis Ababa, Mekuria's narration reveals that Selomon boycotts his high school graduation ceremony in protest against Haile Selassie's regime because he had been suspended for his participation in a demonstration. The sense of distance created by the zoom out underscores the growing separation between their viewpoints, a gulf that is accentuated by Mekuria's observation that Selomon left for college in Moscow "with different memories and visions of a future without the emperor." This is further emphasized by Selomon's letter, which is narrated over an image situating him in a group of students in front of a monument in Moscow, thus grounding Selomon visually within a socialist ideological sphere. In addition, the formal socialist language of the letter provides a strong counterpoint to Mekuria's lyrical remembrances. From these contrasting states, Mekuria and Selomon develop different expectations of what Ethiopia should be, each becoming more polarized as the film advances.

Later, Mekuria explores the circumstances of her final contact with Negist. The day before Negist leaves, they stay up all night "speculating what life would be like in a communist country." Then, narrated over a series of childhood photographs of Negist and herself, Mekuria makes the comment that she could not imagine then that they would aspire to bring the communist system to Ethiopia. This foreshadows the enormity of the fragmentation precipitated by the politicization of the students through foreign education. The diverging perceptions of Negist, Selomon, and Mekuria escalate into an ideological slippage between personal and national histories, which parallels the disjunction of political and social ideologies that tear Ethiopian society apart.

As the process of revolution accelerates and Selassie's regime buckles, a transnational vision of Ethiopia fueled in part by foreign-trained students emerges with the adoption of socialist ideology. This alone, however, is insufficient to create a single immutable view of what Ethiopia should become. The forward momentum of the revolutionary process becomes unstoppable with the mutiny of the Second Division of Ethiopia's Armed Forces in February 1974, which was soon followed by other military units (Halliday and Molyneux 1981, 84). By June, the military had assumed control and formed a governing body composed of the Armed Forces, the police, and the Territorial Army (86). Known by the Amharic word *Derg*, this committee would force Selassie's removal from the throne and take his place as the stewards of Ethiopia's future by assassinating fifty-seven individuals without trial, including members of Selassie's government and other opponents (86–88). Eventually, the Derg would select the concept of "Ethiopian socialism" as the foundation of a new society (88). Supported by student intellectuals for whom "Marxism-Leninism provided a grid for understanding Ethiopia's place in the metanarrative of modernity," the Derg gathered around leader Mengistu Haile Mariam and violently eliminated any opposition that did not support a government based on military leadership (Donham 1999, 131). In addition to the Derg, several civilian and student-based political parties arose, and chief among these were "the All Ethiopian Socialist Movement or MEISON (its Amharic acronym)

CHAPTER 6

and the Ethiopian People's Revolutionary Party or EPRP (its English acronym)" (131).[1] Both parties offered diverging views of Ethiopia's future: the MEISON pursued a tactical alliance with the Derg, founded on the belief that an immediate transition to socialism was not possible (131). Furthermore, the MEISON favored "bringing together all militants subscribing to an anti-feudal and anti-imperialist struggle" in order to pursue the priority task of "mobilizing, training, and providing cadres" (Lefort 1983, 29). In contrast, the EPRP, who regarded the Derg as fascist and argued that a military-led government was not revolutionary, argued that an unfettered democracy was the only way to ensure a revolutionary state (Donham 1999, 132). Although there were significant ethnic differences between the two groups, complicated political rivalries between student movements led to increasing conflict, and the personal feuds, group competition for leadership, and ideological differences exacerbated by education gained in different foreign systems such as France, Russia, and America contributed to the entrenchment of hostilities between the two principal players (132).

Mekuria, recognizing that distance may be measured in ideological terms, explores the slippage within ideologies as competing socialist factions vie for power. Negist, as a member of the MEISON, and Selomon, as a member of the EPRP, both journey to Moscow with the same end in sight but return to Ethiopia on opposite sides of the dispute when the EPRP condemns the ruling Derg and the MEISON elects to continue support of it. In October 1976, the EPRP "began an outright program of assassination against top MEISON leaders," resulting in retaliatory action by the MEISON and the Derg against the EPRP's party members (Donham 1999, 133). By February 1977, Mengistu initiated the Red Terror by announcing that the MEISON was at war with the EPRP, and calling for the extermination of its membership (134). The growing dislocation in Ethiopian society is illustrated in a sequence that features one of Selomon's narrated letters. As he expresses his disappointment in Negist by declaring her to be a "mere stooge of her husband," a photo of Negist appears in close-up. This pronouncement not only underscores the ideological slippage between Selomon and Negist, it also isolates Mekuria in a space between them: in the next shot Mekuria appears suspended between competing factions as she is positioned between two monitors in the editing room. On the left monitor is the close-up photo of Negist, effectively connecting the past to the present, while Mekuria comments in voice-over that the harshness of Selomon's letter caught her off guard. This image and narration place Mekuria in a position of mediation and underscore her conscious search for understanding. This is further illustrated when survivors discuss the Derg's strategy to consolidate its power by sending the troublesome intellectuals out into the countryside to "educate" the rural people in the new ways. The students, when faced with resistance from the populace became, as one survivor relates, the judges, teachers, jailers, and disciplinarians. Ironically, this resulted in the oppression of the rural populations they had intended to liberate. Consequently, the division between the regime they intended to free the populace from and their alternative political strategies became blurred. Mekuria is suggesting, in effect, that the students themselves contributed to the creation of the dynamics that resulted in the Red Terror.

Mekuria's own education in America and her decision to remain there during the Ethiopian revolution evokes distance as a means of raising the question of whether her point of view is Ethiopian or diasporic. In one sequence, Mekuria faces two monitors, one revealing a rushing waterfall and the other, columns of soldiers. Over this shot, she narrates that the "rosy foundations" of her memories of Ethiopia were eroded as she viewed graphic images of the nation's evolving crisis from her distant home in the United States. This distance sets Mekuria apart from the events in her homeland, and shifts her point of view into a space that is physically and ideologically separate from that occupied by actual participants in the revolution. She legitimately questions the historical and ideological underpinnings of the revolution in a desire to bridge the gap that yawns between her experience and theirs. The combination of Mekuria's distance—which promotes perspective—and desire to intervene—which indicates a continuing connection to origin—suggests that the concepts of *"border* and *diaspora* bleed into one another," which supports Clifford's contention that both "the historical and geographical specificity" are crucial to understanding diasporic identities (1994, 304). Thus, while it may be argued that *Deluge* shares certain diasporic concerns—and perhaps owes its genesis in part to her location on the shores of the "black Atlantic"—Mekuria possesses both

CHAPTER 6

an inscribed Ethiopian identity and an incorporated distant perception of that identity, reflecting a slippage between point of origin and diasporic recollection (Gilroy 1993a, 3).

Mekuria skillfully employs the multinarrational levels of *Deluge* to expose the inherent conflict engendered by such a paradox. As she is positioned between two monitors in the frame, a black-and-white photograph of Selomon appears on the left monitor. The camera pans left and then slowly zooms in until Selomon's image fills the frame. Selomon's letter is heard in voice-over, observing that Mekuria is losing her old buoyant and indomitable spirit, and asking why this is so. Selomon points out that Mekuria's original intention was to return to Ethiopia after completing her education, and he believes that she will do so yet. He suggests that Mekuria cannot divorce herself from the struggle of the Ethiopian people, even if she has chosen to live in America and has married into African-American culture. The segment of the letter ends with his declaration that Mekuria is an Ethiopian and should always keep that in mind. Mekuria concedes the validity of his implied criticism. Over an image of herself reflected against a monitor screen, Mekuria asks what it means to be Ethiopian at that time and acknowledges the fact that isolation in America had led to her immersion in African-American culture. In effect, she had stowed her Ethiopian self safely away, as a strategy for survival in an alien environment. Thus, *Deluge* recognizes the paradoxical necessity of occupying two points on a line at once: as a narrator, Mekuria is simultaneously Ethiopian (reclaiming African experience) and diasporic (observing from across the black Atlantic). Yet such a position, albeit understandable, does not resolve the essential dilemma: did Mekuria, as an Ethiopian, have a responsibility to return to her point of origin during its time of crisis? The interaction between Selomon's implied criticism and Mekuria's acknowledgment of its validity allows the spectator to contemplate the implications of Mekuria's delimited role in the very history she is depicting. A certain unreliability in Mekuria's position as an authority on the events is thus foregrounded by creating an ambiguity in her position. In a further demonstration of this position, Mekuria refuses to offer a defense of her actions—or Selomon's; rather, she provides only the context within which they occur. This is an important narrative hallmark, for the social critique in *Deluge* is not couched in deductive observations. The film, like many performative documentaries, relies on suggestion instead of argument in which social critique is implied or intimated rather than explained (Nichols 1994, 100).

Ultimately, the "disaporic" distance between Mekuria and Selomon contributes to estrangement between the two, a personal rupture that mirrors the political fragmentation of Ethiopia. In a narrated letter, Selomon informs Mekuria that a "campaign of elimination" has been initiated against MEISON in retaliation for the assassination of EPRP militants. Mekuria, depicted in a close-up of her reflection on a blank monitor, narrates that she is stunned that Selomon could so casually approve of the assassination of friends. Her sense of rupture from Selomon is representative of the historical reality of the Red Terror, which tore families apart. Mekuria provides context for this rupture through interviews with her sister Sehin Mekuria and Negist's sister, W. Elfenesh Adane, both of whom recall the splintering of families as members took up respective sides in the struggle. In one chilling recollection, Adane relates an incident when she and her younger brother Abraham visited Negist at her home. Abraham, a member of EPRP, took the opportunity to record Negist's license plate number, leading Adane to wonder if he was planning to murder Negist. Sehin Mekuria justifies such extremes when she explains that to be jailed or killed in pursuit of one's political ideals was an acceptable price to pay for the advancement of the struggle. This position is echoed by Adane when she concurs that Negist's life was spent for the right reason because she died for what she believed in. For Mekuria's part, her decision to question the validity of the struggle leads Selomon to refuse further discussion of the matter, which he regards as "aimless and useless." The decision emphasizes the geographical distance between them that has, in turn, created the ideological gulf that separates them. Thus, the tension between Mekuria's objections and the positions of Selomon, and others intimately involved in the struggle, remains unresolved. By refusing to privilege her own judgment, Mekuria echoes Nichols's questions, "What do we know and *how* do we know it? What counts as necessary and sufficient knowledge?" (italics in original; Nichols 1994, 97). Ultimately, such narrative tactics empower spectators to mediate between the competing positions, combining and recombining them in order to arrive at their own answers.

CHAPTER 6

Mekuria demonstrates, through a series of interviews, that the slippage between personal and national histories persists after the fall of the military dictatorship in 1991. For example, both W. Asegedeich Wossene (Mekuria's mother) and Adane express similar grief and lack of closure concerning the deaths of Selomon and Negist. The similarities of their experiences suggest the futility of violence as a means of political expression. This irony is emphasized when Mekuria later reveals that Negist was killed in the home of one of Haile Selassie's officials who was himself assassinated at the beginning of the revolution. In addition, these personal events are connected to the wider national tragedy of the disappeared through an interview of W. Negede Yeshewawork and Ato Mola Worke concerning the fate of their son. The scene begins with a long shot of what appears to be a disinterred mass grave. As Yeshewawork speaks about finding her son's body in the street on the way to church, the camera pans right and begins a slow zoom in to the couple standing on the edge of the grave. Poignantly, Yeshewawork carries a framed photograph of their son as she relates her struggle to stay by her son's body, only to be driven away by the authorities. The film cuts to a close-up of the son's photograph, visually foregrounding the son as an individual rather than a nameless victim of violence, as his mother describes his body and others being scooped up like dirt. Finally, as Yeshewawork states that she visits this location because she is certain that this is where the bodies were dumped, Mekuria zooms out quickly, finishing the scene in an extreme long shot that places the figures of the husband and wife in context with the landscape. The fact that the zooms begin and end in social space contextualizes the couple's loss within the larger scope of the Red Terror, allowing their story to stand for that of many families suffering the same loss. It is significant that Mekuria does not reveal which side of the conflict the son represents, focusing instead on the personal cost of his death to his parents outside of political considerations.

The film's epilogue frames the personal and national histories within a black diasporic context. The sequence begins with a black-and-white photo of Mekuria with her daughter Saamra as Mekuria's narration indicates that she told her daughter about Selomon when she was eleven years old. In so doing, Mekuria indicates, the survival of Selomon's history passes from her hands to her daughter's, incorporat-

Slippage and Mutable Histories in *Deluge*

ing Ethiopian identity within a diasporic construct. Subsequently, Saamra wrote a school essay about Selomon that became the inspiration for the film. As the scene progresses, Saamra is depicted sitting on the floor and selecting photographs of Selomon from a family album as she narrates the content of her essay in voice-over. Placing the photos on the closed album cover, Saamra moves them around into various arrangements, indicating her desire to understand how Selomon's history intersects with her own. The visual rearrangement of the images, which parallels Mekuria's role in collecting and assembling the histories reflected in the film, suggests that slippage remains a salient factor in integrating transnational identities. Saamra's acceptance, however, of the imperfect past with all its gaps, suggests that slippage is a natural consequence of time and distance. Thus, Saamra's desire to preserve Selomon's photographs in order to show her future children "what their family is" indicates that Mekuria is responding to certain custodial responsibilities to create a tangible link between the past, present and future. In this way, the legacy of Ethiopia's Red Terror plays a role in both Mekuria and Saamra's understanding of themselves within an evolving context of personal and national histories.

SEVEN

Transnational Gazes in *Frantz Fanon: Black Skin, White Mask*

As noted in previous chapters, definitions of the black diaspora and diasporic identities are fraught with contradictions and pitfalls that make easy generalizations difficult to establish or defend. In part, this is due to the tremendous vitality of black diasporic communities where "localizing strategies"—such as community, organic culture, region, center or periphery—are more likely to complicate rather than explicate descriptions of diasporic experience because they "obscure as much as they reveal" (Clifford 1994, 303). This chapter illustrates just how complex the interplay of intersections and difference can be through a discussion of Isaac Julien's documentary, *Frantz Fanon: Black Skin, White Mask* (1996), which interrogates the influential works of Martinican theorist Frantz Fanon. What makes this film most compelling and useful for discussion is how it examines Fanon's theories from a transnational black diasporic perspective and, by doing so, creates an interactive debate with the film's spectators over the strengths and shortcomings of Fanon's work.

From the moment of publishing his thesis in psychiatry, *Black Skin, White Masks*, in 1952, Fanon generated world-wide debate concerning the nature of the colonizer/colonized relationship, the significance of his life and works within the context of revolution, the black diaspora,

Transnational Gazes in *Frantz Fanon: Black Skin, White Mask*

Frantz Fanon: Black Skin, White Mask (Courtesy of California Newsreel)

and his own identity as a black subject. A complex and challenging individual, a major black intellectual whose thinking was instrumental to Third World independence movements, he is considered by many to be one of the most important black theorists of the twentieth century (Julien and Nash 2000, 103). According to Henry Louis Gates Jr., the rise of postcolonial theory over the past decade has once again brought Fanon's work to contemporary notice and broadened its appeal to encompass new contexts of globalization (1991, 457). Fanon's writings—particularly the books, *Black Skin, White Masks* (1952), *A Dying Colonialism* (1965), *The Wretched of the Earth* (1963), and *Toward the African Revolution* (1964)—are considered groundbreaking because they

CHAPTER 7

were among the first to successfully evoke the need for decolonization. Over time, his writings have set important benchmarks in configuring the legacies of colonization, the processes of decolonization, and how racism exists in, and is perpetuated by, both.

Fanon was born in Martinique in 1925 into a family "who belonged to the island's emerging black bourgeoisie" (Alessandrini 1999, 2). Belonging to this economic status brought with it certain expectations and standards of behavior that were modeled on the precepts of French culture. As Fanon would later write, "The middle class in the Antilles never [spoke] Creole except to their servants," a comment that dryly demonstrates the depth of his estrangement from black culture and the pressure exerted on black Martinicans to achieve an illusory whiteness by renouncing their African racial heritage (1982, 20, 18). It is therefore significant that Fanon received a privileged French-based education—one that numbered Aimé Césaire among his teachers—and thus initially developed a strong identification with France (McCulloch 1983, 2). This led to his decision to fight for the Free French forces in Europe during the Second World War, receiving "the *Croix de Guerre* for bravery" (Alessandrini 1999, 2). The racism Fanon encountered in France during this time, however, altered his sense of identity and place in the world, setting the stage for the revolutionary works that would challenge conceptions of colonialism worldwide (2).

Black Skin, White Masks was written during Fanon's training in psychiatry at the University of Lyons in France (Alessandrini 1999, 2). Upon graduating from "one of the most radical psychiatric teaching programmes then available," Fanon started his practice at a hospital in Blida-Joinville, near Algiers (McCulloch 1983, 1). At the time, Algeria was under colonial rule by France, and the struggle for Algerian independence was reaching its peak. Fanon found himself treating "both Algerians fighting for independence and French police officers, the tortured and the torturers," and the act of practicing psychiatry against such a violent political backdrop profoundly shaped Fanon's future writings (Alessandrini 1999, 3). Becoming increasingly caught up in the struggles of Algeria to violently overthrow the French colonial powers, Fanon resigned from his position at Blida-Joinville in the late 1950s and began working with the Front de Libération Nationale (FLN; Alessandrini 1999, 3). Fanon was eventually expelled from Algeria by the

Transnational Gazes in *Frantz Fanon: Black Skin, White Mask*

French and, because of his emerging power as a revolutionary theorist, became one of "the most wanted persons of the French secret police," surviving several assassination attempts (4). Taking a position in Tunis at the FLN headquarters, Fanon continued to serve the revolutionary cause by participating as ambassador to a variety of African countries as well as contributing to the movement's newspaper as editor (4). Early in 1960, he was diagnosed with terminal leukemia and produced in a period of ten weeks arguably his most famous book, *Les damnés de la terre* (*The Wretched of the Earth*) (4). Fanon died in the United States on December 6, 1961, where he was seeking treatment for his illness, and was later buried in Algeria with full military honors out of respect for his contributions to the FLN liberation struggle (4).

Given what seems to be an intimate relationship between Fanon's work and the specific historical period of African independence movements, the resurgence of interest in Fanon's work seems somewhat incongruous (Bhabha 1996, 188). The question, why Fanon? is a salient one and is perhaps best answered by Homi Bhabha when he argues that Fanon "speaks most effectively from the uncertain interstices of historical change: from the area of ambivalence between race and sexuality; out of an unresolved contradiction between culture and class; [and] from deep within the struggle of psychic representation and social reality" (1999, 181). Bhabha's litany of elements underscores Fanon's ability to expose the hidden spaces between psychologies and social movements and the presence of a style of rhetoric uniquely situated for a postmodern rereading of black identity constructs. More to the point, as globalization alters key relationships such as border and nation, these concerns have once again become of critical interest. This suggests that the issues Fanon raised as African nations pursued independence have yet to find resolution in the postcolonial era.

Throughout his life's work, Fanon was preoccupied with issues of black identity construction, consciousness, liberation, and nationalism. In addition, Fanon's work questioned how individual actions were intertwined with social power infrastructures, a frame of inquiry shared with Léopold Senghor, Césaire, and Négritude (McCulloch 1983, 36). Fanon generally concurred with Césaire that colonizers found succor in the colonial project of denigrating and destroying indigenous cultures, histories, and personalities (36). Fanon is skeptical, however, of

Négritude's fixation on a glorious past and its failure to provide for practical resolution of barriers in the present (41). He is highly critical of the quest to validate black identity by recouping past African cultures when he writes in *Black Skin, White Masks*, "I am not a prisoner of history. I should not seek there for the meaning of my destiny" (Fanon 1982, 229; see also Kruks 1996, 131). Although Fanon is wary of Négritude, he sees its potential for working through the complexities of black identity construction. Sonia Kruks argues that, for Fanon, "*negritude* is at once untenable and yet necessary" for redressing in part the negative racist stereotypes that prevail in white cultures (1996, 130). Hence, it is the contradictory state of living blackness as a white construction that leads Fanon to argue, "What is often called the black soul is a white man's artifact" (Fanon 1982, 14). Thus, despite his rejection of some of its central tenets, Fanon embraces Négritude's position that blackness is, to a degree, a white construct created for the purpose of denying black individuals equal power as subjects.

Although Fanon may share some ground with Négritude, his project in *Black Skin, White Masks* goes beyond its parameters by exploring the ethical challenges of living as a black man in a white racist context that denigrates black cultures (Kruks 1996, 128). Throughout his formative years, Fanon was exposed to white cultural values resulting in an "inauthentic identification with whiteness" (128). He was so alienated, however, by the systemic racism experienced during his studies in France that he drew on his psychoanalytic training to codify its origins and effects from the point of view of a black colonized subject/object. Fanon argues that the black subject experiences "self-objectification," whereby her or his response to acts of racial discrimination is to "internalize the white negrophobe's gaze" (129). Fanon describes his own moment of realization when he states, "On that day, completely dislocated, unable to be abroad with the other, the white man, who unmercifully imprisoned me, I took myself far off from my own presence, far indeed, and made myself an object" (Fanon 1982, 112). The fundamental problematic for Fanon then, is that a black person's existence only derives meaning through defining her or his race against the benchmark of white culture (S. Hall 1996, 18). By insisting that the black subject can only be defined against her or his white other, Fanon identifies a binary opposition that remains as relevant in a contempo-

Transnational Gazes in *Frantz Fanon: Black Skin, White Mask*

rary context as it was when he first made the observation (1982, 110).

To a degree, Fanon is attempting to describe the inexpressible and give voice to the unspoken codes of behavior that delineate power relations between the white colonizer and the black colonized subject. Central to this problematic is the mapping and dissecting of the "representational process" in which "the look" or the gaze is accorded so "central and constitutive" a position that it defines power dynamics in a way that is almost inescapable (S. Hall 1996, 19). The gaze becomes a position of power and knowing in which the colonizer, always on the defensive, reads the black subject's look as a threat to displace him (20). This perception, on the part of the colonizer, reflects the violence that has been used both to enslave the black subject and to maintain power over her or him, as violent insurrection or revolution is an inevitable response to oppression.

Fanon's work on "colonial psycho-sexuality" (Mercer 1996, 123) suggests that the colonizer's look is one of desire to possess the black subject/object and designates fear and power as binary oppositions that have inscribed black identities within a racist colonial structure (S. Hall 1996, 17–18). This position, however, mires Fanon's work in a series of immutable binarisms such as fear/desire and colonizer/colonized, creating an essentialized black subject. The inflexibility of the binarisms leaves little room for maneuvering between categories, a weakness especially evident in Fanon's absolutist stance on homosexuality and his often-contradictory position on interracial relationships.

The fixity of such binarisms has proved frustrating for gay and lesbian activists who have sought to foreground new modes of subjectivity and hybridity as a means of expanding concepts of black subjectivity in art and theory (Mercer 1996, 122). For example, Kobena Mercer argues that lesbian and gay critics, seeking to establish a link with Fanon's work, have turned his analysis of negrophobia back on itself in an attempt to expose homophobia in Fanon's work as well as account for such discourses in nationalist narratives and histories (128). Fanon's mise-en-scène of the racist colonial gaze, in which the "black man has no ontological resistance in the eyes of the white man," glosses over the potential homoeroticism of a man looking at a man, an act endemic to Fanon's concept of colonial surveillance (Fanon 1982, 110; Bhabha 1996, 202). Ironically, it is during the process of mapping out the parameters of negrophobia that Fanon's homophobia emerges when he writes, "Fault, Guilt, refusal of guilt, paranoia—one is back in homosexual territory" (Fanon 1982, 183). It is the pairing of homosexuality with such me/not-me binarisms that creates an association between homosexuality and negative colonial imperatives in which the homosexual figure comes to stand for the enemy (Mercer 1996, 125). This position has certainly created conflicted responses to Fanon's work, leading theorists such as Mercer to argue that the mapping of differences among peoples of the black diaspora cannot occur within me/not-me binary codes (122). Indeed, it is much more fruitful to consider one's self an "incomplete character . . . that can alter the story of who it was before" (122). As an example of the weaknesses in Fanon's work, the homophobia displayed in *Black Skin, White Masks* demonstrates that he is ultimately both a visionary and a subject created within a specific map and history. As Françoise Vergès observes, "The seductive dimension of Fanon's vision" is found in his dream "of a moment of pure rupture, of a revolution which would cleanse the colonial world of its corruption" (1999a, 266, 269). Although Fanon desires to escape the boundaries of history, his project, in the end, is frustrated by the inescapability of self.

Frantz Fanon: Black Skin, White Mask (United Kingdom, 1996) exposes the tensions in Fanon's work by interrogating his notion of the colonial gaze through interviews, archival footage, and experimental reenactments.[1] Most important, the film perceptively exposes the sexual taboos in Fanon's work, revealing an implicit undercurrent of homophobia that runs through his discourse. This incisive critique locates the documentary within the parameters of what Jack Ellis and Virginia Wright Wexman describe as "New Queer Cinema," a movement that first emerged in the late 1980s in Britain and later in America (2002, 463). Including such landmark films as Julien's *Looking for Langston* (1988), Marlon Riggs's *Tongues Untied* (United States, 1989), and Jennie Livingston's *Paris is Burning* (United States, 1990), documentaries in this movement foreground queer issues and theory and frequently combine elements of dramatic reenactment with lyrical documentary style. *Frantz Fanon: Black Skin, White Mask* stands out among these offerings because Julien deliberately creates a transnational space within which he critiques Fanon's biases and strengths by considering the contradictions between his words and his life events. Tracking the development of Fanon's theories from Martinique to France and on to Algeria, the documentary explores the circulation of black ideas and influence on a global scale from a uniquely black queer perspective.

Born in London in 1960, Julien studied film and painting at Central St. Martin's School of Art and Design in London. A participant in one of the most extraordinary developments of the 1980s in England, Julien became a key figure in the new wave of young black independent filmmakers associated with such London-based groups as the Black Audio Film Collective and the Sankofa Film and Video Collective, which Julien helped found in 1983. His directorial credits include *The Passion of Remembrance* (codirected with Maureen Blackwood in 1986), *This Is Not an AIDS Advertisement* (1988), and the award-winning *Looking for Langston* (1988). Julien's first feature film, *Young Soul Rebels* (1991), won the Semaine de la Critique prize for best film at the Cannes Film Festival (Cruz 2000, vi). Julien cofounded the production company Normal Films in 1992 in order further his focus on queer documentary filmmaking (vi). Julien's documentary work includes *The Attendant* (1992), *A Darker Side of Black* (1993), *Frantz Fanon: Black Skin, White Mask* (1996), and *Baadasssss Cinema* (2002). Julien is also a highly sought-after teacher, scholar, and installation artist whose multiple-screen projections such as *The Long Road to Mazatlan* (1999), *Paradise Omeros* (2002), *Baltimore* (2003), *True North* (2004), and *Fantôme Créole* (2005) have been featured in group and solo exhibitions around the globe.

Frantz Fanon: Black Skin, White Mask is intended to bear witness to the political and cultural importance of Fanon's work (Julien and Nash 2000, 104). This is not surprising because Fanon's writings were of considerable interest in the 1980s and 1990s to black diasporic artists who were looking for new ways of conceiving and exposing the legacies of slavery and colonization (Mercer 1996, 116). The attraction of Fanon's *Black Skin, White Masks* lies in what Stuart Hall has astutely described as its status as an *"open text,"* composed of "unresolved arguments" and "incomplete oscillations" that render the work as one "we are obliged to go on working *on*, working *with*" (S. Hall 1996, 34). In particular, because the work creates an association between racism and the erotic pleasure of looking, or scopic drive, it raises questions of representation

(16, 28). In effect, by politicizing the simple act of gazing and exposing it as a social construct, Fanon actively engages his readers to challenge their roles in the perpetuation of racism. Thus, the film, composed of a series of interviews with Fanon's family members and experts on his work as well as dramatic recreations, traces the development of Fanon's work as his life unfolds, covering his family dynamics and key events such as his training as a psychiatrist in France, his commitment to Algeria's revolution in the 1950s, his marriage to a white woman, and his death in 1961. Focusing on Fanon's homophobia and his pursuit of a perfect black masculinity, the film situates Fanon as a black subject constituted and shaped by the historical and cultural discourses of his time.

Devoted to working against narrow ideas of nationalism and identity, Julien founds his documentaries on his engagement with theoretical debates around culture, politics, and representation. For Julien, such transgressions are conducted on several levels—including racial, sexual, psychic, and social—in a process he describes as uncovering "ambivalent 'structures of feeling'" (Julien, quoted in hooks 1991, 171). Far from being purely reactionary or confrontational in nature, Julien's use of transgression indicates clarity of purpose that does not flinch from the political pitfalls and complexities of representation (Walcott 1997, 63). Instead, by challenging and exploding boundaries, Julien's work functions as a site of debate, exposing closed spaces as a means of initiating dialogue with spectators around significant issues of race, sexuality, and identity (63).

Given this context, Fanon's theoretical precepts offer an excellent landscape for Julien's project of "committing acts of transgression in regard to questions of race and representation" (Julien, quoted in hooks 1991, 168). The documentary, however, is not simply restricted to exploring Fanon's gaze as an immutable iconic construct. This film, like many of Julien's past works, including *Looking for Langston*, engages spectators in an open-ended exploration of sexuality as both performance and social discourse, often exposing the hidden coding of sexuality beneath the surface of cultural practices. *Frantz Fanon: Black Skin, White Mask* also seeks to uncover the notions of sexuality contained in Fanon's key works, but, most important, the film challenges Fanon's notion of the gaze by exploring the issue against a much wider canvas that

Transnational Gazes in *Frantz Fanon: Black Skin, White Mask*

invokes "the ways in which individuals, discourses, and social groupings constantly revise themselves by identifying with and also against" prevailing social attitudes (Ross 2000, 291). Hence the documentary's depiction of Fanon as a colonized subject, but also as a potential colonizer himself, renders visible fissures beneath the surface of Fanon's work formed by his own intersections with historically situated cultures (291). In particular, by drawing attention to the fact that Fanon's own view of preferred black masculinity as heterosexual is mired in the expectations and limitations of his cultural and historical specificities, the documentary demonstrates how such attitudes are affected by performance criteria as they evolve across and through distinct social spaces (291).

Frantz Fanon: Black Skin, White Mask employs several aesthetic and narrative strategies intended to probe some of the issues raised by Fanon's work and his life. First, the documentary is loosely arranged in a chronological order that follows Fanon from his early life in Martinique to his death from leukemia while undergoing treatment in the United States. The chronological order, which explores a selection of Fanon's major accomplishments over the course of his lifetime, provides a structural frame that gives the film a forward action. Several traditional documentary visual and narrational strategies are then employed to create a layered structure composed of archival footage, personal photographs, dissolves, and interviews with Fanon's family members as well as experts on Fanon's work. What sets this documentary apart, however, is the blending of fictional and factual recreations, a dramatic tactic used to great effect as a means of countering or interrogating information offered by more standard means. Thus, the staged elements, in combination with voice-over narration, flow against the interviews and archival footage, providing both a subtle and overt critique of Fanon as a means of destabilizing his work and traditional notions of its meaning.

The opening of the film immediately sets out to challenge the spectator by creating a mystery. Initially, the opening montage of shots seem disconnected from one another as they include such disparate elements as a silhouetted man circling aimlessly with his shackled arms raised above his head, a graveyard, a claustrophobic close-up of a disturbed man muttering in Arabic, and a pair of shuttered doors opening onto a courtyard. The visual presentation, however, signals to the spectator that she or he will be required to evaluate and collate information as it is presented in order to achieve understanding of the subject matter. In addition, the sequence serves as a kind of foreshadowing of narrative strands to be developed over the course of the film: each of these images will be repeated during the film, resolving their mystery and creating context for the spectator.[2] As the opening progresses, the visual presentation outlines the fictional recreation against which Fanon's historical life will unfold. Fanon, played by actor Colin Salmon, is introduced in a medium shot that places him on the right of the frame. Projected against the wall in the background of the shot is a silhouette of a man standing with his head tilted, appearing to be gazing at Fanon as he, in turn, faces forward, looking at the camera in direct address. As the camera dollies right, revealing a still image of a long corridor in the background behind Fanon, his voice-over narration states, "I do not come with timeless truths. My consciousness is not illuminated with ultimate radiances. Nevertheless, in complete composure, I think it would be good if certain things were said." The composition of the image reveals a number of preoccupations that will be developed over the course of the film. First, the visual relationship between the silhouetted man and Fanon, as well as Fanon's direct address of the spectators, indicates that looking, or the gaze, is of paramount importance. A visual device developed throughout the course of the film, the gaze links Fanon both to the past and the present, drawing the spectator's attention to how "the formal and material practices that mark sexual identity as a resource for racial identification and racial identity" function "within and across historical moments within and across cultural traditions" (Ross 2000, 291). It is therefore significant that there is a certain critical tension in this relationship: since Fanon does not return the gaze of the man looking at him, there is an absence or lack portrayed by the overall image composition. In addition, by returning Fanon's gaze, the spectator engages him as a subject but retains a voyeuristic relationship with the silhouetted man behind him. By creating what amounts to a disrupted chain of gazes, the visual aesthetics foreground the act of looking and the thin line between being a subject or object of the gaze. This introductory shot also reveals certain character traits possessed by Fanon. As he commands attention in the frame space,

Transnational Gazes in *Frantz Fanon: Black Skin, White Mask*

Fanon is in total control: dressed in a light-colored shirt and tie, he is evidently an educated man of professional standing. The precision of his appearance and the fact that he is distanced from the figure behind him suggests that, although Fanon is a keen observer of life, he is also disconnected from it. This strategy simultaneously foregrounds and interrogates the nature of Fanon's power, creating a tension that challenges the spectator to look beyond the surface of the image.

Although the decision to include recreations within the documentary was in part motivated by the lack of extant footage of Fanon, it serves a more important purpose in the work because it facilitates "a dramatic cinematic engagement with Fanon's life and ideas" (Julien and Nash 2000, 104, 106). The casting of Salmon in particular was calculated to present Fanon as an attractive black male, emphasizing his physical presence (107). Salmon does not perform the part of Fanon but rather presents him in a fashion more akin to modeling than acting (107). Thus, in this particular scene, the Fanon of the film image does not address the audience verbally: rather, Salmon's voice-over narration is layered over the image, generating a disjunction between the two that is intended to avoid the psychological suturing associated with conventional character portrayals in fictional films (107). Hence, Fanon becomes an "open sign" that invites spectators to "project their own Fanon into the film" (107). Furthermore, this device also sustains Fanon's enigmatic quality, making the film text, as well as Fanon's theory, ultimately irresolvable.

There is a strong correlation between the interrogation of theory and Julien's narrative and aesthetic approach to filmmaking. The theoretical concepts and the individuals who generate them, or are transformed by them, serve as interacting axes that connect the psychological, intellectual, and historical forces that constitute identity formation. For example, the documentary suggests that his family's conflicted relationship to their black heritage influenced Fanon's formation of the colonized subject. This is illustrated in a complex sequence beginning with a montage of newsreel footage composed of a series of shots of De Gaulle's arrival on a visit to Algeria and of the French navy firing a salute.[3] These are juxtaposed with re-created images of veiled Algerian women who raise their hands as if to ward off the sound of French artillery and a single Algerian woman, who has a photograph by French

CHAPTER 7

war photographer Marc Garanger projected on her veil (Julien and Nash 2000, 107). The interplay between the two sets of visual systems captures the binary opposition between colonizer and colonized, a conflicted state that reinforces the voice-over commentary of theorist Hall who asserts that "the struggle between the master and slave is a struggle for power." The film illustrates this point by using a long shot of black men and women carrying harvested bananas from the field to create a parallel between the French colonization of Algeria and that of Martinique. Again, Hall's voice-over strengthens the association by noting that the struggle is to determine "who possesses the products of the slave's labor," thus implying that both slavery, as represented by the banana harvesters, and colonization are underpinned by an economic imperative that privileges the rights of the slave owner/colonizer over those of the slave/colonized subject. Furthermore, the correlation between the two historical constructs foreshadows Fanon's later involvement in the Algerian revolution by suggesting that his understanding of the Algerian fight for freedom is rooted in the legacy of slavery that shaped his early life in Martinique.

As the sequence continues, Julien demonstrates how his use of reconstructions and interviews transgresses the established boundaries of his subject matter as well as documentary filmic form. Newsreel footage of French officials as they greet African dignitaries is layered with Hall's voice-over explaining how Fanon realizes that the conflict between master and slave is rooted in the slave's desire to win recognition from the master, just as the master depends on the recognition from the slave. The action of the African dignitaries exchanging greetings with the French officials suggests that colonial relations can only be supported through the complicity of colonized subjects willing to recognize the superiority of their colonizers. The film then cuts to a shot of a headless statue covered in rivulets of red paint, later revealed in the film to be a statue of Josephine Bonaparte, who played a major role in reestablishing slavery in Martinique. The contrast between the images seems to suggest that the potential for violent revolution always lurks beneath the surface of the colonized/colonizer relationship.

Hall's interview segment culminates in an assertion that Fanon is concerned with racism's depersonalization of the black subject through the master's denial of recognition. The documentary cuts from Hall to

Transnational Gazes in *Frantz Fanon: Black Skin, White Mask*

a black-and-white archival photograph of a number of black field slaves grouped in front of a thatched building. The camera dollies to the right, revealing Fanon's father, a light-skinned black man in a tropical suit. As he moves to the right, the camera dollies with him, presenting a minimalist staged space intended to suggest a large room in a Caribbean home. Most notably, there is a large open window frame on the back wall, backlit with a projection of palm trees and sky. As Fanon's father passes it, the silhouette of a woman walks left in the opposite direction, as if they are moving at cross-purposes. Fanon's father stops at a narrow table and looks down at his son seated on the opposite side, listening to a Creole song on a large cabinet radio on the table. This is followed with a close-up of the boy, emphasizing his enjoyment. The song is then linked to black culture through an archival shot of black couples dancing. Finally, a medium long shot follows that begins with Fanon's mother leaning over the table and turning off the radio and ends with a quick dolly into a medium shot of the boy, who crosses his arms and glares out at the camera in direct address in a display of annoyance. The significance of this scene is contextualized by the interview of Vergès, who relates an incident from Fanon's childhood in which his mother chastised him by saying "Don't be like a nigger" when he expressed a preference for a Creole song over a French one.

The dense layering of aesthetic elements demonstrated by the reconstruction and interviews illustrates a narrative approach that has been described "as a palimpsest of quotations written over and against each other" (Julien and Nash 2000, 106). For example, there is a cause-and-effect relationship between Hall's statement that colonization involves a refusal of recognition and the action taken by Fanon's mother as she turns off the radio, denying him access to his own culture. Vergès's comments add a further layer to this exchange as they serve to describe the process of depersonalizing black identity that begins with valorizing French culture and ends with denigrating black culture. Furthermore, the choice to portray young Fanon's resistance in a close-up signals recognition of the devaluation indicated by his mother's actions as well as the forging of what will become the revolutionary spirit that flows through his work.

The tactic has a very specific effect: given that Fanon is simultaneously posited as an originator of theory and a subject of it, it may

CHAPTER 7

be queried if Fanon, as an individual, is inherently conflicted and ultimately unconsciously heir to some of the very flaws that his theoretical writings deplore. Such a contradiction is explored during the section of the film that deals with Fanon's condemnation of Mayotte Capécia's autobiographical novel, *Je Suis Martiniquaise* (1948). The recreation illustrating this point begins with a montage of images including, among others, a close-up of Capécia, a close-up of Fanon, and a series of black-and-white archival clips showing mixed-race couples dancing. Voice-over narration is layered over the images, expressing Fanon's disgust at Capécia's love for a white man, "to whom she submits in everything. He is her Lord. She asks nothing, demands nothing, except a bit of whiteness in her life."[4] In the interview that follows, Vergès challenges Fanon's position by arguing that feminists such as Maryse Condé have cited his failure to consider the historical context reflected in Capécia's novel. Furthermore, Vergès indicates that Fanon's narrow focus on Capécia's desire for white men, without taking into consideration that she might be fleeing the brutality of the Martinican father, is also a shortcoming in his reading. She then demonstrates Fanon's double standard for male and female behavior by noting that later on in *Black Skin, White Masks*, Fanon, who has a mixed marriage, declares that it is no one's business whom he chooses as an object of desire, given that he is a free man. The juxtaposition of the narration and Vergès's interview exposes a blind spot in Fanon's work and thus assails his position of authority as a proponent of equality. The argument is furthered during an interview segment with Fanon's brother, Joby. In defending Fanon's choice to marry a white woman, Joby Fanon quotes from *Black Skin, White Masks*, indicating that Fanon does not believe that marrying a European woman results in an abandonment of his "personality," thus refusing "to consider the problem from the standpoint of either/or."[5]

Fanon's refusal to engage on this point not only indicates a patriarchal double standard with regard to interracial marriage but also indicates that he holds himself above the very influences he insists are actively oppressing others of his race. As Vergès ironically asks during the course of a later interview segment, "Why is Fanon free of choosing and not Capécia?" Following Vergès's comment, the spectator is offered an opportunity to consider the relationship of Fanon as an authority on race to Fanon as a subject of his own historical context. The documentary playfully reprises the tableau first presented as representative of Fanon's childhood. In this case, Fanon is depicted in a medium long shot, seated at the right side of a table. On the table is the cabinet radio, suggesting that the meaning of this double standard must be understood within the context of his childhood. Behind him is a large-scale projection of a photograph of Capécia, looming above him in a way that is reminiscent of his parents' framing in the first image. The effect visually suggests that despite Fanon's denials to the contrary, he remains as alienated a subject of colonialism as Capécia.

Another means of challenging the foundation of Fanon's theoretical position is found in the documentary's interrogation of the sexualized colonial gaze. As an interview segment with Hall reveals, contemporary rereadings of Fanon's work suggest that racism "partly arises when the white looker becomes aware that he, as it were, is attracted to the black subject. The act of racism is a denial of that desire which is in the gaze itself." As Vergès asserts in a later segment, however, the black male body is central to Fanon's dialectical constructs: the alienated black man, repudiated by the black woman who desires the white man, is therefore desired by those he does not want, including white women and white homosexuals. A medium close-up of Fanon walking toward an open doorway disrupts her interview. Naked and positioned with his back to the camera, the image seems to peel away Fanon's controlled persona to reveal the man underneath. In a moment of vulnerability, he half turns to the audience and covers his face with his hand as Vergès's voice-over commentary describes Fanon's longing to be free of his racialized body. Thus, the shot underscores the impossibility of achieving such a goal by providing an ironic counterpoint to the content of the narration.

The underlying values of this construct are exposed during a reconstruction that plays with the scopic power of the gaze to both recognize subjectivity and refuse its existence. The reconstruction begins with a medium long shot that portrays Fanon in the foreground on the left edge of the frame, facing the camera in direct address. On the right, in the middle ground of the image, are two black men kissing each other in a passionate embrace, silhouetted against a bright window. As Vergès argues in voice-over that Fanon, in pursuit of an idealized total freedom, discards any form of desire that threatens his sense of

CHAPTER 7

unity, Fanon turns his head and gazes at the male couple. They, in turn, break off their embrace, and look back at him. Fanon turns away, assuming his original position, an act of refusal that is coupled with his voice-over narration denying the existence of homosexuality in Martinique. The purely theatrical nature of the blocking demonstrates the use of the "tableau vivant" as an interrogative device: by looking away, Fanon not only refuses to engage the gaze of the male lovers, but also refuses them recognition, suggesting a discounting of their significance to black experience (Julien and Nash 2000, 107). In added irony, the documentary then cuts to a medium long shot of a black transvestite as Fanon's narration asserts that although men who dress in women's clothing exist, he is certain that their sex lives are normal. The combination of these images goes beyond underscoring the heteronormative masculinity underpinning Fanon's constructs by suggesting that Fanon's own "gaze" is as exclusionary as its colonial counterpart. It also raises a more serious question: is there any circumstance under which the gaze can be decolonized, given that it is driven by cultural imperatives?

In addition to the use of reconstructions, the film's aesthetic and narrative structure also offers a subtle blending of fact and fiction through referencing representations from other media. In the section of the film focusing on Fanon's life in Algeria, Julien combines selected scenes and shots from *Battle of Algiers* (La battaglia de Algeria, directed by Gillo Pontecorvo, Italy/Algeria, 1966). A seminal text of Third World cinema, *Battle of Algiers* depicts the struggle for Algerian independence from France. The film, which covers the events in Algeria from 1954 to 1957, begins with the imminent capture of Ali la Pointe, the sole remaining survivor of an FLN cell, by the ruthless French military commander, Lieutenant Colonel Mathieu. The majority of the narrative describes the spiraling effect of revolutionary violence that culminates in the general strike of July 1956 and the decision of the French command to expose and eliminate the FLN by any means necessary, including torture, retaliatory bombings, and mass arrests. The film itself has a connection to Fanon's theories of decolonization: as David Prochaska argues, Pontecorvo drew liberally on Fanon's *Wretched of the Earth*, citing Ali la Pointe's progression from street violence to revolutionary violence as evidence of the emergence of revolutionary consciousness

(2003, 135–36). In addition, the film shares a similarity to the style of narrative structure and aesthetic approach used in *Frantz Fanon: Black Skin, White Mask* as Pontecorvo augments his fictional story line with elements of documentary, such as the use of newsreel-style footage and narration to provide expositional information during the unfolding of narrative events.

Elements selected from *Battle of Algiers* are integrated into the film's text without benefit of intertitles or other devices of identification, creating a seamless merger between Pontecorvo's and Julien's texts. As Julien and producer Mark Nash explain, "*Battle* was treated like other archive material . . . there was no clear argument as to why this film in particular should be singled out [from other archival sources] for special treatment" (Julien and Nash 2000, 106). The decision allows a subtle and powerful interplay between the two texts, creating parallels that would not have been possible had the texts been separated from each other by visual titling. For example, the documentary uses a series of shots from a montage sequence in *Battle of Algiers* in which Pontecorvo illustrates the torture committed by the French against Algerian resistance fighters. The sequence ends in a striking close-up of an anonymous Algerian man silently crying as he witnesses French soldiers torturing another man. As the camera tilts up, a soldier is revealed, calmly watching the activity and smoking a cigarette. The documentary then cuts to a high-angle medium shot of Fanon and an Algerian psychiatric patient. Fanon is in the foreground, depicted in profile on the extreme left of the frame with his patient seated on the extreme right in the middle ground of the composition. The patient's physical appearance is similar to that of the crying Algerian man, thus linking Pontecorvo's reconstruction to the documentary's narrative. Furthermore, as the patient describes how his mother was killed and his sisters kidnapped by the French military forces, the obvious trauma felt by the patient connects them as victims of revolutionary violence. In a later restatement of the tableau, Fanon retains his position on the left, and a French military officer assumes the position of patient on the right. Similar in appearance to the French soldier, the military officer describes the horror of torturing prisoners. The combination of these elements advances Pontecorvo's original shot of the Algerian man and French soldier witnessing torture by suggesting, through the documentary's reconstruction, that both colonizer and colonized are psychologically traumatized by the brutality of revolution.[6] In addition, the use of the gaze in the reconstruction subtly indicates where Fanon's sympathy lies given that in the first shot, he exchanges gazes with the Algerian patient, and in the second, he looks to the left, thus refusing to engage the military officer directly.

The empathetic gaze toward the Algerian patient is emblematic of Fanon's idealization of the Algerian revolutionary as a masculine ideal. As Vergès argues in later voice-over narration that accompanies a montage of newsreel images of Algerian fighters in combat, Fanon found in these revolutionaries "an individual whose masculinity had been wounded but who had, in contrast to the black man of the Antilles, the courage to attack the castrating master." As the montage unfolds, an extreme close-up of Fanon, framed to focus on his eyes, is superimposed over the images, thus foregrounding the act of observing. Coupled with what might be regarded as scenes emphasizing the heroism of the Algerian fighters, the sequence ironically illustrates both Fanon's desire for, and distance from, the subject. The documentary develops myriad examples of Fanon's contradictory relationship with Algeria, particularly in the contestation between different interview segments. For example, Vergès notes that Fanon assumes Algerian citizenship to the extent that when he is described as a Martinican, he expresses anger. Such a repudiation of Martinique, Vergès argues, lies in Fanon's belief that "he had found the dream country, the dream people, and the men who would embody the masculinity he was dreaming of." In an interview with Mohammed Harbi, however, the image of total immersion is mitigated by the comment that Fanon was an outsider to Arab society whose identification with Algeria lay predominantly with the "intelligentsia." This observation suggests that Fanon's intense attachment was, at best, mediated through an idealized image of what he imagined Algeria should be, rather than a connection to its actual realities. This derives, as Hall argues, from a romanticized view of the new postcolonial subject arising out of the conflict "as if the revolutionary war would be a sort of blanking out of everything," including history. The interplay between these three interview segments allows the spectator to weigh the possibility that Fanon, perhaps unconsciously, is colonizing the Algerian war as a means of proving that colonialism must be eradicated by violent struggle in order to obtain a state of true freedom for the colonized subject.

The film's ending further advances this position. In the last interview segment, Fanon's son, Olivier, aligning himself with those thousands whose parents were martyrs to the Algerian Revolution, argues that present-day Algeria is in an "illogical position": brought to the edge of disaster by a two-part system made up of the army and the terrorists, neither of which is distinguishable from the other, Algeria exists in a indeterminate state that is not an insurrection, a war of independence, or a civil war. The revelation provides an ironic end to Fanon's pursuit of the ideal masculinity and perfect revolutionary act. Furthermore, it offers a powerful counterargument to Fanon's romanticized view of Algeria as the site for a new postcolonial order free of history by implying that the colonial legacy lasts well past the expiration of colonialism itself. Olivier's final comment, however, that Fanon "would never have accepted this situation," that "Fanon disturbs . . ." implies that Fanon's great strength lay in exposing and challenging the status quo.

The documentary further supports this perspective with its final image. As in earlier reconstruction shots, Fanon is depicted in a long shot seated beside a table that holds a large, old-fashioned cabinet radio. In the background, a black-and-white still photograph of a tropical courtyard is projected. As the camera dollies in to a close-up, Fanon is portrayed in profile. The image is layered with voice-over narration in which Fanon speaks the last words from *Black Skin, White Masks:* "My final prayer: O my body, make of me always a man who questions!" As the words are spoken, Fanon turns to the camera, addressing the spectators with a gaze that invites them to form their own opinions regarding the value and credibility of his work. By selecting this structure, the documentary resists narrative closure, leaving the film available for continued debate. Thus, like Fanon's work, the documentary becomes an open text, subject to multiple readings. By unseating and destabilizing conventional ways of reading film and theory, Julien is creating a new transnational gaze that places race and transgression at the center of black subjectivity and history.

EIGHT

Locality, Memory, and Zombification
in *The Man by the Shore*

As discussed in chapter 2, the unique historical and cultural processes that inform Caribbean diasporic identities have generated theory that advances a commitment to movements such as creolization, Antillanité, and *métissage*, thus creating conceptual paradigms of hybridity specific to resident needs (Edwards 1994, 29). A certain amount of care, however, must be taken in extending such terms beyond the Caribbean to the black diaspora for, as Norval Edwards argues, "hybridity often becomes the third term in a binary racial schema" determined by existing power structures that tend to reinforce them rather than go beyond their limitations (29). In other words, Edwards is suggesting current theory move beyond homogenizing strategies of hybridity to analytical frameworks recognizing differences in patterns of creolized cultures based on the specificities of racial and historical contexts (29). Thus, theorists such as Edwards argue that, unlike concepts of creolization, Antillanité, and *métissage*, which conceive of Caribbean identities based on shared experiences, the historical specificities of Caribbean cultures create distinct experiences of hybridity that must be recognized. This is certainly not an easy task, given the multiplicity of experiences and cultures in the Caribbean: if there is one element that links creolization, Antillanité, and *métissage*, it is the notion of movement,

Locality, Memory, and Zombification in *The Man by the Shore*

of variable geographies and histories that compete for voice within the auspices of Caribbean identities and realities. Shaped on a foundation of colonialism and slavery and then by subsequent migrations of different nations and cultures, the Caribbean experience remains one of shifting imperatives and influences.

This is not to imply that the maps of experience generated by the Caribbean are completely divorced from the black diaspora. Instead, Edwards argues, the "politics of location" should become a theoretical nexus in which "(dis)location, (dis)placement, travel, and diaspora" function as modal tropes to extend current conceptions of diasporic experience beyond existing boundaries (1994, 31). Similarly, the Haitian novelist and theorist René Depestre suggests that traditions and cultures of all Caribbean peoples are created in a "mixed syncretic expression, in constant change" driven by "diverse conditions of social existence" (1976, 65). For Depestre, identity in the Caribbean is multifaceted and inherently transnational in expression, combining fluid modes of European, Asian, African, and black experiences in ways that express the specifics of locale. Given this emphasis, the concepts of map and history merge to signify unique Caribbean experiences but also place those experiences within the context of global flows of thought and peoples. Ultimately, under this schema, one cannot define the first without reference to the second.

As a case in point, the Caribbean nation of Haiti illustrates the subtle interplay of map and history by its unique standing among its neighbors. It is here that the only successful slave rebellion in the Americas took place, establishing Haiti as an independent nation in 1804. In turn lionized as a symbol of freedom and decried for the violence of some of its governments, Haiti is a contested space that continues to inspire contemporary black thinking and advance notions of black experience specific to Haitian cultural realities. Because of its status as the first black independent state, however, Haiti also offers a cultural footprint that is distinct among Caribbean states: in contrast to Martinique, where white Europeans continue to contribute directly to the syncretism of the cultural *métissage*, the persistence of European colonialism has been internalized in Haiti's dominant black society and is thus encoded in subtle nuances of race. This underscores the complicated nature of slavery's legacy in Haitian national identity and fore-

CHAPTER 8

grounds difference as a factional divide between complex discourses of color.

In many ways, the historical underpinnings of Haiti's struggle for freedom offer an opportunity to explore slavery and its aftermath as a distinct product of modern industrialization in which African labor became the commodity that drove Europe's industrial revolution (Beckles 1997, 779). Hilary Beckles, for example, suggests that the constant flow of imported agricultural labor into the Caribbean during and after slavery from countries as diverse as India, China, and Lebanon created a mixing of races and cultures still affecting these nations today (786). Thus, the West Indian, as "a futuristic individual, linked to all major civilizations," is one of the first products of globalization in modern times and, as such, profoundly shaped the history of capitalist society (786, 785). As Franklin W. Knight argues, however, the highly artificial economic construct of the plantation system, managed by Europeans and depending on slavery, focused economies on the large-scale production of agricultural products and raw materials (2000, 107). Thus, founded on slave labor that ensured a flow of sugar, coffee, cotton, and tobacco, this was an industrial revolution that rested almost entirely on dehumanizing exploitation of, and cruelty toward, the slave population.

Known originally as the colony of Saint-Domingue, Haiti is considered one of the most lucrative plantation societies that France established (Mintz 1974, 262). By the end of the sixteenth century, Haiti demonstrated its dominant status as a wealth-generating center by establishing world records in sugar and coffee production (Trouillot 1990, 37). Like Martinique and other French Caribbean colonies, power was held in Haiti by a combination of white landowners and mulatto freedmen who exploited a large slave-labor force of black Africans. The role of the *gens de couleur*, or *affranchis*, a prosperous mixed-race class, however, set Haiti apart from other colonies because the *affranchis* were landowners and were thus crucial to the colony's economic and cultural life (Mintz 1974, 262; Trouillot 1990, 37). With one foot in French culture and the other in black Haitian culture, the *affranchis* would emerge as key participants in the slave revolt, eventually becoming Haiti's *mulâtre* elite, with loyalties divided between French and black Haitian cultures

Locality, Memory, and Zombification in *The Man by the Shore*

that "anticipated neocolonialism in the rest of the world by a century and a half" (Trouillot 1990, 38).

Another factor that set Haiti apart from other French colonies is the important role slave agriculture and crafts played in the colony's political and economic life. Like Martinique, slaves were permitted to work garden plots or provision grounds as a means of freeing slave owners from feeding and maintaining them (Trouillot 1990, 38). Owing to the geographical features of the colony that prevented effective large-scale production in some areas, however, more arable land was available to slave families for cultivation, resulting in surplus production and a dependence of larger segments of the population on the availability of these foodstuffs (39). Thus slave labor became "equally oriented toward subsistence and the market" within the larger plantation economy (39). As Michel-Rolph Trouillot argues, the impact of this distinction allowed slaves to maintain some measure of control because of the importance of their produce to the colony as a whole, giving them some status in a situation where they were otherwise denied rights (39). This was a critical psychological difference that distinguished the black Haitian slave population from others in the French Caribbean because it gave them a sense of economic freedom and ownership of their own goods, however slight that entitlement might be. The importance of this cannot be underestimated as this sense of entitlement led to one of the first events of the slave rebellion. By 1789, tension was rising between Haiti's white population and the *affranchis* because of growing discrimination against the mulatto population. Slaves entered into the fray by burning some of the rich plantations on the northern plains, not so much a demand for emancipation but a demand for additional days in which to cultivate their plots (39, 42). This act would eventually contribute to the creation of a revolutionary vanguard bringing together slaves and *affranchis* in order to set Haiti on the path to emancipation and independence.

It is important to consider that the Haitian Revolution was not a single event but rather the culmination of a long struggle for freedom for both the *affranchis* and the slave population. Haiti had a long history of slave insurrections beginning as early as 1522, and uprisings such as the Makandal conspiracy of the 1750s demonstrated the ability of Hai-

CHAPTER 8

tian slaves and maroons (escaped slaves) to create secret resistance organizations in defiance of white authorities and consequences.[1] These were not successful as regionalism and factionalism prevented such uprisings from gaining the momentum necessary to mount a full-blown rebellion. In the two years after the unrest that began in 1791, however, the foundation of a cohesive revolutionary movement was established, including a popular support base and a core of determined leaders aspiring to unconditional freedom (Trouillot 1990, 42–43). In 1793, under the leadership of François-Dominique Toussaint Louverture and with an organization that brought together *affranchis* and slaves, the long road to independence was undertaken. Louverture succeeded in manipulating the competing interests of Spain, England, and France, establishing himself as general-in-chief of Haiti and by 1799 successfully neutralizing the power of the *affranchis* in the west and south in order to consolidate his position (43). He was exiled to France through treachery in 1802 after Napoleon's troops landed in Haiti, providing the impetus for the final phase of the revolution (43). Replaced by Jean-Jacques Dessalines, a former slave and supporter of Louverture, a new goal was set by reorganized revolutionary forces that called for the "elimination of the white presence," which was felt to be a barrier to permanent freedom (43–44). Leading the army to victory, Dessalines proclaimed the independence of Haiti on January 1, 1804 (44).

The effects of the slave rebellion rippled out well beyond the new nation's shores. As Depestre suggests, the revolution had widespread effects, leading slaves in America to begin to challenge the racist stereotypes of Africans generated in the rationalization of slavery by white culture (1976, 64). This was recognized by colonial empires in Western Europe and by the United States, most of which imposed political and diplomatic blockades in an effort to weaken the new nation (Trouillot 1990, 50). Most important, the Haitian Revolution challenged the complacency of proslavery rhetoric by demonstrating that not only could black peoples form a state through effective resistance, they also could hold it in the face of considerable pressure to relinquish it (Knight 2000, 105). Haiti, however, remained a contested space with factionalism between competing interests. As Trouillot observes, although concepts of "state and nation were taking shape at the same time and as part of the same revolutionary process, they were launched in opposite direc-

Locality, Memory, and Zombification in *The Man by the Shore*

tions" (1990, 44). In particular, the determination of the *affranchis* and the political leaders to maintain the plantation system and the exportation of large-scale agricultural crops collided with the desire of ex-slaves and others who wanted land and the right to work for themselves (44). Furthermore, the legacy of slavery and colonialism exacerbated these divisions, creating complicated discourses of color and class that continue to be evidenced in contemporary Haiti today.

Raoul Peck's disturbing and lyrical film, *L'homme sur les quais/The Man by the Shore* (Haiti/France/Canada, 1993), offers the opportunity to explore how the historic divisions among Haiti's black population continue to shape the nation today. Along with documentarist Elsie Haas, Raoul Peck is considered to be one of "two major figures in Haitian film practice whose work has elevated Haitian cinema to new levels of excellence and maturity" (Cham 1992, 26). As a fiction film based loosely on Peck's own experiences as a child during the fall of the Duvalier regime, *The Man by the Shore* shares with later Haitian films such as Richard Sénécal's *Barikad* (2002) and Charles Najman's *Royal Bonbon* (2002) and *Haïti: La fin des chimères* (2004) a preoccupation with the complexity of Haiti's layered social structure, its tortured history and memory, and "the human costs of oppression" (Cham 1992, 27). As such, the film offers an excellent backdrop within which to explore Depestre's vision of Haitian identity as it grounds identity within the specific map of Haitian history through the desire of the main character, Sarah, to reconstruct her childhood memory of life under the Duvalier regime in the 1960s. The narrative structure of the film, which mirrors the fragmented reality of Haitian society, presents memory as a factor in bridging the dislocation created by factional violence: in order to go forward in her life, Sarah must reconstruct her memory to create perspective and initiate healing.

Born in Port-au-Prince, Haiti in 1953, Raoul Peck has had a varied career as a journalist, photographer, political activist and award-winning filmmaker. Trained at the Berlin Film and Television Academy, Peck's first fictional feature film, *Haitian Corner*, won four international awards, including the Prix Images Caraïbes du long métrage in 1988. In addition, Peck has a distinguished body of documentary work, including *Lumumba, Death of a Prophet* (1992), which was selected for official

CHAPTER 8

competition at the 1993 Cannes International Film Festival. *Lumumba* (2000), the television documentary *Profit, nothing but!* (2001), and the television film *Sometimes in April* (2005) are films that are representative of Peck's continued commitment to exploring issues of importance in the black diaspora.

As a Haitian, Peck brings to his work the sensibilities of someone who is both an insider to Haitian culture and a Haitian citizen of the larger world. Peck's formative years coincided with the rise of the François Duvalier regime, a particularly brutal dictatorship that ruled Haiti from October 1957 to April 1971. In 1961, Peck's family fled Haiti and settled in the Republic of Congo, which had recently attained independence.

Educated in the Congo, the United States, and Europe, Peck brings what might be described as an aesthetic syncretism to his film work. In this sense, Peck rejects the narrow label of Haitian filmmaker, drawing his inspiration from issues or emotions that then set him in search of an appropriate story, often framed within a Haitian sensibility (Peck and Taylor 1996, 242). In describing his approach to documentaries and fictional narratives, Peck notes that he combines the former with fiction and the latter with realism (246). From this perspective, Peck is "trying to create an active viewer that is both submerged and standing outside of [the film experience]," inflecting his work with an engaging tension between emotional identification and critique (246).

The Man by the Shore was intended by Peck to interrogate the record of the Duvalier era by producing a filmic document that would prevent Haitians from repeating the past (Peck and Taylor 1996, 246). Ironically, a violent military coup began in Haiti a few weeks prior to shooting and lasted for three deadly years until Jean Baptiste Aristide was overthrown by General Raoul Cedras (238, 246). For Peck, the real history created a tragic parallel for the fictional work as "the film was supposed to be a monument to a time *passed*" (246). This context gives a special emphasis to the issues outlined in *The Man by the Shore*.

Structured as a childhood memoir of Sarah, the film's protagonist, *The Man by the Shore* explores the desperate straits of Sarah's extended family, which has been torn apart by Duvalierism. Living with her grandmother and aunt after the flight of her parents into exile, Sarah and her sisters are terrorized by, and resist, Janvier, an enemy of their

Locality, Memory, and Zombification in *The Man by the Shore*

father and a local leader of the tonton-makout, a much-feared secret organization. The film culminates in an attempted rape of Sarah's young friend by Janvier, resulting in Sarah witnessing Janvier's murder by Gracieux, her godfather. The emotional damage and dislocation suffered by Sarah as a result of this experience becomes emblematic of the continuing struggle of Haiti to define itself as a cohesive nation in the face of competing interests (Peck and Taylor 1996, 238).

On the surface, Haiti appears to be a nation that can be easily understood in terms of such binarisms as urban versus rural populations, *mulâtre* versus black, French versus Creole, or Christianity versus Vodoun (Trouillot 1990, 81). To use such an approach, however, is to oversimplify the cultural divergences that drive the Haitian experience and runs "the risk of masking the exchanges and contacts underlying these oppositions" (81). Hence, although the existence of the social and spatial split between populations is undeniable, it is also true to say that they are connected by movement between striations, leading to a complex cultural structure that is not easily understood from an external perspective. As noted above, Depestre attributes this complexity to the syncretism of Caribbean identities in which the struggle between diverse elements underscores a nation still grappling with the effects of decolonization (1976, 65). From Depestre's point of view, Haitian identity does not involve a strict dichotomy between cultural elements but, rather, is the product of exchange, creating a historic *métissage* in which the elements of multiple cultures are synthesized (Depestre, quoted in Dayan 1993a, 144). Although exchange allows movement between levels of Haitian society, however, it does not entirely negate the divisions between different strands of Haitian experience. In particular, the historical split between urban and rural populations is a political reality that has inflected Haitian politics from its very beginning.

Although *The Man by the Shore* offers a multiplicity of readings from different viewpoints, the narrative structure does not directly explain the striations of Haitian society. Hence, a Haitian audience inculcated with the subtleties of that society will immediately identify the competing cultural forces depicted in the film that allowed Duvalier to rise and sustain his dictatorship. For a non-Haitian audience, the lack of explicit explanation creates a sense of suspense and ambiguity that intensifies the impenetrability of Haitian culture viewed from the outside and en-

CHAPTER 8

gages the viewer in an active quest to understand. The fact that the film facilitates a variety of reading positions within its narrative structure reflects Peck's own position as a filmmaker who seeks to address both local and international concerns.

Deeply affected by the violence of the regime, Sarah still lives at the epicenter of a traumatic experience that, thirty years later, continues to send shock waves through her life. Her quest to understand the shifting grounds of her childhood memories becomes the center of the narrative, and her process of reconstruction is reflected by narration that frames the fragmented action of the film. This choice gives the film's narrative several aesthetic advantages. First, as a child caught up in adult strivings beyond her comprehension, Sarah is one of the few characters in the film that does not bear some responsibility for the actions that take place. Second, the gaps in Sarah's understanding create ambiguities that must be filled in, engaging active spectator intervention in the narrative. Third, and perhaps most significantly, Sarah's fractured memories become a metaphor for the fissures in Haitian society. The film interweaves these threads right from the beginning by opening with a famous political speech by François Duvalier, presented in voice-over as the credits roll. Naming all the regions of Haiti, as well as singling out the middle class of Port-au-Prince, intellectuals, teachers, and students, Duvalier decries the fact that the traditional power groups controlling Haiti in the mid-1950s are ignoring these strands of society. The speech, delivered during a period of virtual social anarchy in the 1956–57 election campaign, marked the rise of Duvalierism (Trouillot 1990, 147). Thus, Duvalier's charge that the authorities have gone mad foreshadows the destabilized cultural and political terrain against which the film will unfold. Furthermore, it illustrates the sophistication of Duvalier's initial appeal: the speech elicits support from both the urban elite and the rural peasantry while concealing an agenda of terror that would eventually dismantle the power of the first in favor of the second. The duplicity of Duvalier's approach and the complicity of those who initially supported his rise to power before becoming victims of it would create a kind of psychological crisis in the Haitian psyche that disrupted the very fabric and limits of society.

Sarah is introduced as an unseen narrator immediately following the Duvalier speech. The sequence begins with a long shot of an idyllic

Locality, Memory, and Zombification in *The Man by the Shore*

Haitian street in the small provincial town of Port-à-Piment. Deserted except for a man pulling a cart of wares, the image of sun-washed storefronts evokes nostalgia for a simpler time. This is reinforced by Sarah's narration as she sings the melancholy words, "Three leaves, three roots. To throw away is to forget. To pick up is to remember." The song foregrounds the process of recoupment through which Sarah tries to reconstruct from disparate snatches of memory the kind of linear cause-and-effect arrangement that would give her closure from the past. Her words, "It was so long ago and yet it was yesterday," indicate how the legacy of the Duvalier era persists beyond its historical end. These images are then connected to Sarah's childhood by ending the first sequence on the closed shutter doors of an attic and beginning the next inside the attic space. The transition between the closed shutters and the dark, chaotic attic space represents the adult Sarah's disorganized psychological state as well as the literal physical locale in which her trauma began. Furthermore, the scene in the attic begins with a series of dolly shots of lengthy duration that fragment the decor as Sarah, now a child, plays in the attic space. This enhances an atmosphere of suspense and secrets as small bits of context are exposed while the camera tracks Sarah's restless movement through the space: for example, one shot lingers briefly on a photograph of a stern older woman, later revealed to be Sarah's grandmother, Camille. As Sarah picks up another framed photograph, the spectator catches a quick glimpse of two people, a well-dressed beautiful woman and an imposing man in a military uniform, later identified as Gisèle and François, Sarah's parents. By introducing them without explanation or context, the film invites spectators to enter into the narrative space by encouraging speculation on the meaning of the images. The strategy creates two interlocking quests: in the first, Sarah attempts to comprehend the events, and in the second, the spectator must put into context individuals and events in order to understand Sarah.

This is heightened by a visual strategy, which gradually reveals Sarah through a process of fragmentation that parallels the puzzle of her context. The spectator's first glimpse of Sarah focuses on a sliver of the white lacy skirt of her dress and her patent leather shoes, identifying her as a child of a privileged family. In addition, Sarah is seen once sitting in a chair, her reflection caught momentarily in a dark and dusty

CHAPTER 8

mirror as the camera tracks past. This leaves the impression of an elusive subject who is difficult to resolve in a concrete fashion, reinforcing a sense of a mystery that must be deciphered by gathering evidence of Sarah's "real" self. When the camera finally pulls back to depict Sarah as a fully realized physical subject, the camera movement is accompanied by voice-over narration in which adult Sarah's voice identifies the time period as the early 1960s. The statement, "I was eight years old and my world was already starting with a disaster," foreshadows not only the specific trauma about to unfold but also, in a more general sense, presages the larger cultural context within which these disruptions take place.

As Sarah opens the shuttered doors and steps out onto a small balcony, the framing suggests that she is physically and psychologically crossing a threshold between innocence and corruption. This passage is emphasized by cutting to a long shot of treetops and the off-screen sounds of a beating accompanied by voices of unidentified men crying, "Hit him again!" The fact that the violence itself remains unseen and must be divined from the sounds alone heightens suspense as the film cuts to a reverse-angle extreme long shot of Sarah on the balcony looking down at the action hidden from the spectator. Furthermore, the choice of shot size distances the spectator from Sarah's emotional state: when she finally screams, the spectator can only speculate as to the exact cause of her distress. Her reaction is placed in partial context by revealing a tableau of arrested action depicting a man on his knees, surrounded by his torturers. Another man in military dress tries to wave Sarah off the balcony and is beaten in turn when a scuffle breaks out between him and the leader of the torturers. Although this is not explained until much later in the narrative, three of the men in the tableau form the triangle of relationships at the heart of Sarah's trauma: the man on his knees is Gracieux,[2] her godfather; the man in the military uniform is her father, François; and the man who leads the torturers is Janvier, whose casual cruelty epitomizes rule by terror. The decision to delay identification of these men intensifies the mystery of the narrative and adds to the profound disjunction of the events.

The fact that most of the violence takes place off-screen or is otherwise masked is a deliberate strategic move to mystify its context and accentuate the terror such violence creates. The connection between

Locality, Memory, and Zombification in *The Man by the Shore*

violence and the regime was established very early in Duvalier's rise to power. For example, Duvalierists used violence as a means of assuring his election in 1957, undertaking indiscriminate bombings of residential areas (Trouillot 1990, 153). The seemingly randomness of such attacks against civilians, often occurring without obvious motivation, bred fear and paranoia on a wide scale among the populace at large. This was an intentional tactic, which destabilized the population through terror, engendered a climate of fear, and served as a means of reinforcing the helplessness of the civilians against the state and the omnipotence of Duvalier (169). Thus, the use of unseen or masked violence is a reflection of Duvalier's use of terror as a means to control the Haitian state and evokes a profound psychological disruption and societal instability.

The culture of violence was epitomized by the emergence of a "coercive force" (Trouillot 1990, 189). Arising from the loose organization of thugs that intimidated the populace during the election in 1957, these *cagoulars* were an independent coercive civil militia that operated as a semisecret police (189). As Trouillot notes, "Both the name and the methods were a direct reference to European fascist organizations of the 1930s" that assisted in the Nazi occupation of France (189–90). Notably, the upper ranks of the organization were predominantly held by middle-class officers, but operating both within and outside this organization was a second, secretive group of individuals drawn from urban lower classes and peasant ranks of the Haitian society (189–90). Ultraviolent and unpredictable, this strand of the militia came to be known as *tonton-makout* by the general populace (189). Typically clad in blue denim and wearing hats and red kerchiefs that aligned them with Zaka, the Vodoun god of agriculture, the tonton-makout often concealed their identities with masks or sunglasses and played a critical role in intimidating the bourgeoisie and middle classes (190). Furthermore, the tension between their role within the militia and their ability to function outside of it gave both legitimacy and deniability to the tonton-makout's actions, allowing the Duvalier regime to sustain a demoralizing environment of fear that paralyzed resistance to a large degree.

The Man by the Shore echoes the uncertainties and secrecy of this destabilizing terror by creating a narrative structure that frequently

CHAPTER 8

introduces a strand of development and delays the explanation of its significance until later in the course of the film. For example, in an early scene, Sarah is living in a convent with her sisters and although it is clear that her parents are not present, the reason for their absence is not explained. The dangerousness of the situation, however, becomes evident during a noonday meal in the convent's dining room. In a series of long shots and loosely framed medium shots, Sarah's sisters are shown at a table eating with the novice nuns. In a separate but connected room, Sarah is eating soup with the convent's leader, Sister Suzanne, and other members of the convent's community. The framing of this sequence creates a sense of shared social space among the convent's members, which emphasizes it as a community composed of women. In one medium shot, Sarah demonstrates her mischievous and even rebellious nature by beginning to tell a story about an old frog, Max, despite protestations from one of the nuns that her frog stories are not very appetizing. As Sarah illustrates the frog's love of singing by making guttural croaks, men appear in the doorway behind her. The camera tilts up to reveal Janvier, accompanied by several tonton-makout in street clothing. As the camera pans with him, the room falls silent, emphasizing the disruption his presence creates as he intrudes into the communal space of the women. In the other room, Sarah's sisters are able to slide under the table, their presence concealed by the long tablecloths, but Sarah is trapped where she sits. Janvier moves into close proximity to Sister Suzanne as she rises up, a move of subtle intimidation that is accentuated by the camera pan that accompanies it. The juxtaposition of these elements signals the dangerousness of Janvier's presence despite its seeming casualness as he comments to Sister Suzanne that he is just visiting. Depicted in a series of long shots and pans that preserve spatial connectedness, Janvier first briefly checks out the novices' dining room and then moves to the head of Sister Suzanne's table. The flowing camera movement gives Janvier's physical presence a predatory power as he informs the nuns that rebels have landed and some are believed to be in hiding in the area around the convent. Despite his dismissal of the rumors as just gossip and his ironic assertion that he is simply interested in their safety, it is clear that his statements are meant both as fact and as a warning. His is not an unchallenged authority, however: although the rest of the nuns lower their eyes and

Locality, Memory, and Zombification in *The Man by the Shore*

take care not to engage Janvier's scrutiny, Sister Suzanne looks at him directly and her silence could easily be read either as submission or quiet defiance.

As Janvier turns his attention to Sarah, the camera tracks toward her giving the visual feeling of Janvier stalking his prey. The high angle of the shot and the presence of the armed tonton-makout in the background behind her emphasizes her vulnerability. Like Sister Suzanne, however, Sarah's fear of Janvier is subsumed by the urge to resist his domination. When he demands her name, Sarah croaks like a frog in response, prompting a slap on the arm for her temerity. The serious risks posed by such behavior become very clear when Sister Suzanne protects Sarah and stops Janvier from entering the dining room where Sarah's sisters are concealed by asserting furiously that he has no right to do so. Janvier's response is swift: he takes out a weapon and holds it to Sister Suzanne's temple challenging her to repeat her words. A tense medium shot epitomizes Duvalierism's culture of terror as Janvier holds Sister Suzanne at gunpoint before an audience of his tonton-makout, prepared to shoot her in front of a child. The fact that his men seem completely unmoved by these events and that none of the nuns rise to Sister Suzanne's defense typifies the callousness and immobility created by such violent tactics. It is only when Sister Suzanne backs down by claiming she said nothing that Janvier releases her.

It is significant that this act takes place in a community of women. One of the hallmarks of terror in Duvalierism is the way in which it targeted individuals normally protected by social boundaries (Trouillot 1990, 167). The danger that Sarah and her sisters face from Janvier has its origins in the flight of their parents from Haiti. This places the children in jeopardy because of the regime's practice of making entire families disappear when a single family member transgressed, or allegedly transgressed, against the state (167).[3] In addition, gender did not protect potential victims as "Duvalierist violence eliminated the gender distinction that, until then, had ensured preferential treatment for women" (167). This type of tactic was also leveled against ideological institutions, especially churches or schools, transgressing another traditional barrier observed by past Haitian regimes (167). Hence, far from being extraordinary, Janvier's violent treatment of Sister Suzanne represents the kind of imminent danger faced by the most vulnerable

CHAPTER 8

of Haitians and is indicative of the degree to which Duvalierism has destroyed the social prohibitions that mark a civil society.

The film demonstrates the permeability of the lines between the tonton-makout and the militia and the endemic nature of terror in a later scene focused on street violence. The sequence begins in a low-angle medium shot of a man in a militia uniform holding a rifle. As the camera tilts down and dollies back, a truck of soldiers is revealed and, beside it, a fire truck complete with firemen who watch a burning house without intervening. Janvier is seated on the running board and as the pan continues it reveals other tonton-makout pulling a dead man from the house, abandoning him on the street. Eerily, the scene is accompanied by a soundscape of solemn music punctuated by off-screen screams of a woman who is either trapped in the fire or being tortured. Like the treatment of Sister Suzanne, the screams of the woman underscore the sheer brutality and lack of social conscience of the participants. Furthermore, the dolly serves to connect all the authorities at the scene, creating an atmosphere of complicity in the violent act whether by the direct action of the tonton-makout or the inaction of the firemen at the scene. It is ironic that the firemen are ready to intervene only if the fire spreads beyond its chosen target, suggesting a society where agencies of protection have been perverted by violence, thus transforming them into agents of destruction.

Although Haiti is the first modern independent black nation, it still suffered from the fragmentation of colonialism, which defined status by color and race, placing Eurocentric precepts at the top of the hierarchy and black culture at the bottom (Trouillot 1990, 112). Unlike Martinique, however, where pure whiteness occupies the highest rung on the social ladder, in Haiti it is not a desirable attribute. Indeed, an assumption that Haitian color politics reflect the binary oppositions of North American racism would be of little assistance in understanding the basic tenets of these cultural practices (112). Trouillot makes the important distinction that although Haitian racial discourses are Western dominated, these categories of color "refer to many more aspects of phenotype than skin color alone, even when their etymology seems to indicate an exclusively epidermic referent" (112). An example of such a set of categories are *mulâtre* and *noir*, two dominant political and sociological discourses present in Haiti since the slave revolt (112–13).

Locality, Memory, and Zombification in *The Man by the Shore*

On the surface, the distinction seems clear, as the *mulâtre* are an urban elite composed of individuals of mixed blood who speak French and practice Catholicism, while the *noir* possess a rural agricultural background, speak Creole, and practice Vodoun (Mintz 1974, 283–84). Such clear divisions, however, are purely illusory, given the influence of what Trouillot terms the *social direction* of an individual (1990, 121). He argues that Haitian society is in constant motion, and an individual's inclusion in either category may be more dependent on her or his upward or downward trajectory in social status than on color, although color remains a crucial factor as a means of securing the types of social alliances that advance an individual (121, 122). Sidney W. Mintz makes a similar observation when he asserts that, although the connection between race and color is a significant factor in determining power in Haitian society, it is based on a perception of color and race that is malleable and responsive to context and alliance (1974, 283). Nevertheless, there is a clear social hierarchy reflected in *mulâtrisme* and *noirisme* in which the former's "income, education, and social status remained inaccessible to the majority [*noirs*] and which treated that majority with arrogant indifference" (Trouillot 1990, 125). This created a wave of increasing resentment that eventually fueled the terror of Duvalierism, frequently pitting the *mulâtre* middle-class elite against the *noirisme* elements in the regime, the militia, and the tonton-makout (125).

This division is evident in the narrative structure of *The Man by the Shore*, in which the *mulâtre* are represented by Sarah's family. For example, Sarah's grandmother, Camille, is a shop owner, aligning her with the merchant class, traditionally a part of *mulâtre* society. This is also indicated by the fact that Sarah's family communicates in French and is Catholic. Furthermore, because the narrative focuses on Sarah as a locus for spectator identification, the film appears to invite empathy for the situation faced by the *mulâtre* under Duvalier oppression. This sympathy, however, is mitigated by a subtle critique, exposing *mulâtrisme*'s own role in the dynamics that brought Duvalier to power and sustained the regime. For example, following Janvier's visit to the convent, Camille is forced to hide Sarah and her sisters in the attic of her home, located above the store. Now desperate to get the children out of the country, she meets Assad, an old friend, to ask for assistance. As a Lebanese importer-exporter, Assad represents another stratum

CHAPTER 8

The Man by the Shore (Courtesy of Velvetfilm)

of power in Haitian society. Often referred to as Syrians, a term employed by Haitians to denote people of different ethnic, national, and religious groups primarily from the Middle East, these merchants have been part of Haitian society since the early 1890s (Trouillot 1990, 55). As importers and exporters, they traditionally controlled and profited from lucrative arrangements with whichever regime was in power, often providing a variety of economic services for profit (55). The evident closeness between Camille and Assad, which facilitates her willingness to approach him with such a dangerous request, demonstrates the complexities of class and the subtle connections between various strata of Haitian society that undercut the notion of absolute separation between layers.

Camille and Assad's meeting takes place in the church. Even within a space traditionally considered to be a sanctuary, they must take care to conceal their conversation from potential spies. This is indicated when Assad suggests that they sit in the pews, one behind the other. This way, if anyone appears they can disengage and pass as two strangers. Assad reveals his role as go-between when he shares with Camille

Locality, Memory, and Zombification in *The Man by the Shore*

news of her daughter and son-in-law, who are presently en route from Venezuela to Cuba. The fact that Assad has seen them and is prepared to take the risk of relating the news to Camille demonstrates a strong personal relationship that supersedes their difference in race, thus indicating the malleability of categories in Haitian culture.

A further layer of discourse is added when Madame Janvier interrupts their conversation. First introduced in a long shot, Madame Janvier has the well-dressed appearance of a middle-class woman. Her affiliation with the *noir* class, however, is evidenced by her use of Creole as she calls for her lover, creating a contrast with the French spoken by Camille and Assad. Camille's disdain for her is immediately apparent as she calls her a bitch and prays aloud for God to deliver her from evil and all the demons that profane the Church, an inference to Madame Janvier and her husband's involvement with the tonton-makout. Thus, despite her middle-class appearance and alignment with the ruling power, Madame Janvier's status is clearly that of a *noir*, and as such, she occupies a lower position on the social ladder, at least in Camille's estimation.

The position of moral superiority espoused by Camille is undercut later in the scene when she asks Assad to arrange passports for the girls. When Assad objects, wondering where he could obtain such items, Camille retorts that he is the businessman, implying that corrupt dealings are part of common practice in Haiti. Assad's cynical comment that before the current regime it was possible to get a birth certificate for a dead man further emphasizes the systemic corruption among the *mulâtre* elite. By voicing Camille's expectation and Assad's ironic nostalgia for past fraudulent practices, the film encourages the spectator to question Camille's pious condemnation of Madame Janvier's *noir* status by suggesting that corrupt power exists at every level of Haitian society.

One element that remains unexamined by the film is the history of discrimination endured by the *noiriste* strand of Haitian culture. Arguably, this is possibly influenced by the autobiographical element in *The Man by the Shore*, which reflects the terror Peck and his family experienced and hence provides the film with a position more aligned to a *mulâtre* perspective. In addition, the film is framed by Sarah's recollections as a child, and therefore it may be argued that she might not be of

CHAPTER 8

an age to comprehend the intricacies of the politics underpinning the Duvalier regime. In that sense, the depiction of Janvier as an unpredictable, violent childhood monster that remains a cipher to Sarah and the spectators seems justified. Certainly, the absence of any kind of character backstory for Janvier leaves his actions without a context, making justification difficult, if not impossible. This, however, also opens the same actions to interpretation, signaling the profound breakdown of social prohibitions.

Janvier is portrayed as a brutish peasant who appears to be nothing more than a pretender in elite society. For example, after she hires a bus driver to smuggle the girls out of the country, Camille is suddenly ordered to Janvier's office. The scene begins with a long shot of Janvier at his desk, framing him in a context of authority that is accentuated by the portrait of Duvalier occupying the wall behind him. As Camille enters, she is framed in a low-angle medium shot that emphasizes her defiance for Janvier's authority. As she stares at Janvier, the camera moves to a reverse-angle medium close-up of him glaring back at her. This exchange of silent gazes creates the sense of two oppositional forces locked in combat. As Camille approaches the desk, the camera dollies toward her underscoring the commencement of hostilities. She demands in French that he pay her for the merchandise he had previously removed from her store, adding that she does not sell on credit. Despite the polite but firm tone and the obvious danger of the action, Camille, in effect, is calling Janvier a thief. This small act of courage, however, is undercut when Janvier forces her to repeat her words in Creole. By doing so, he is subtly demeaning her and demonstrating his superior power as a tonton-makout. Janvier brushes aside Camille's demand as a joke, illustrating his contempt for her temerity and reinforcing his position as a predator that preys on weaker victims from a position of entitlement. Furthermore, the frivolousness of the items, which include handkerchiefs and fancy underwear, signal that the theft occurs more as a routine intimidation than out of need. By choosing this line of approach, the tonton-makout is portrayed as cowardly and petty, suggesting a negative moral valuation.

This is further illustrated later in the scene when Janvier's men drag the bus driver in: beaten and half-conscious, the driver's presence is meant to demoralize and force a confession of wrongdoing from Camille. When she remains calm and continues to act as if she and the bus driver simply had a business arrangement to deliver some merchandise, Janvier throws the money she paid the driver on the table and reveals that the driver has told a different story in which the money was given to him to repay a debt. In a medium long shot, Janvier takes control of the space by moving into center frame and strategically placing himself between Camille and the bus driver in order to intimidate them both. When Camille continues to lie by saying that she may have confused two different transactions, Janvier turns and strikes the driver, telling Camille, "You see what negligence can do?" When Camille attempts to intercede on the bus driver's behalf, Janvier refuses to listen, stating, "in this office I'm the one in charge." This exchange illustrates that Camille's resistance is tempered with a human compassion that urges her to ask for clemency for the driver, despite the obvious danger of further provoking Janvier. This contrasts with Janvier's cold control and seeming lack of emotion as he pits one victim against the other. On the surface, this seems to be a blanket condemnation of *noiriste* influences in Haitian culture. By refusing to humanize Janvier, however, the film forces the spectator to speculate on the motivations for such violence and to draw from her or his own experience and imagination a justification for or a condemnation of Janvier's actions. The strategy also exposes the fear and the destabilizing effect of terror as a means of controlling resistance.

As the forward action of the narrative unfolds, it is augmented by a series of flashbacks contextualizing the traumatic events of the film's opening. For example, Sarah has a flashback to a birthday party that occurred prior to the events that send her parents into exile. The scene begins with a long shot of a well-appointed dining table piled high with gifts as a group of adults and children sing "Happy Birthday" to Sarah. The gathering, which takes place in a room filled with light and full of happy adoring people, is emblematic of everything Sarah has lost in the forward action of the film. During the course of the song, Sarah's close relationship with both men is illustrated as François and Gracieux take turns singing special verses to her. It also suggests that she is a favored child and has a position of power in the family, which is subsequently obliterated when events split her family apart.

CHAPTER 8

The Man by the Shore (Courtesy of Velvetfilm)

This idealized portrait of François as an adoring father in compassionate control of his family and his profession is ultimately shattered as Sarah struggles to understand adult complexities from a child's point of view. As a military officer, François belongs to the system that brought Duvalier to power and that was, in turn, destroyed when it failed to control the regime. The support of the army was critical to Duvalier's rise, and in fact, his victory in 1957 was founded on the military's readiness to use violence to gain political power (Trouillot 1990, 152). Duvalier successfully used the *mulâtre* officers and the *noiriste* lower ranks to play one off against the other as he consolidated power by employing economic advancement to fuel the latter's hatred of the former. In particular, the elimination of uncooperative army officers "by means of imprisonment, torture, and forced (or encouraged) emigration" successfully reduced resistance to the Duvalier regime as it became increasingly violent (155). This dynamic is exemplified in *The Man by the Shore* through Janvier and François's relationship, a method used to critique *mulâtre* complicity with the excesses of the Duvalier regime.

Locality, Memory, and Zombification in *The Man by the Shore*

One example of this critique occurs in a scene set in François's office that focuses on Janvier's desire to arrest Gracieux. Shot in a long take, the scene begins with a loosely framed medium two-shot with Janvier insisting that Gracieux is a crook. When Janvier stands up and leans over François from the side of the desk intruding into his physical space, the camera dollies in quickly to a tight medium two-shot. The camera move intensifies Janvier's act of intimidation, creating empathy for François who, despite his rank and power, seems incapable of containing him. Janvier's accusation that Gracieux has covered the whole town with antigovernment slogans elicits a demand of proof from François that is dismissed by Janvier. The dismissal is symptomatic of the environment of terror in which accusation alone is sufficient proof of wrongdoing, and François responds to it by asserting that as long as he is in charge, Janvier will not be allowed to make the law. As Janvier stands up and moves behind François, the camera dollies in to a medium close-up, trapping him against the left side of the frame and creating a sense that he is Janvier's prey. Janvier leans in from behind until his head is almost touching that of François, murmuring, "You're tempting the devil, Captain." His calculated tone and menacing physical position convey his ability to reach out at any time and destroy whatever he wishes for whatever reason he chooses. Thus, François's military status and power are completely illusory and will not protect him or his family from retribution should Janvier be refused his desires.

The process of intimidation typified by Janvier's actions enabled the Duvalier regime to create paralysis among its citizens, alienating the people from the state but also isolating competing power structures in the state itself, thus undermining any resistance. Depestre refers to Haiti as "a zombified country" in which "everything has been taken, even *self-awareness*, even the awareness of your body, or the feel or value of your body" (Depestre, quoted in Dayan 1993a, 147). Linking this "mutilation of being" to slavery, Depestre argues that zombification symbolizes the treacherous reality faced by the Haitian people who are paralyzed by random violence (147). Hence, the Duvalier regime's complete abrogation of human rights reflects the legacy of commodification that continues to operate in contemporary Haitian society. As a result, the instinct for preservation of self and one's family led to a widespread culture of complicity with the most violent aspects of the regime.

CHAPTER 8

The parallel between the fragmentation of Sarah's memory and the disintegration of Haitian society is reflected in the narrative structure as a disrupted time line in which the ordering of events refuses linear presentation. For example, a scene portraying an argument between François and his wife, Gisèle, which clearly takes place after Gracieux's arrest, immediately follows the confrontation between Janvier and François. This represents a sudden leap forward in the narrative time line, as Gracieux's arrest will not unfold until later in the film. The gap between the two scenes requires the spectator to make a speculative leap in order to orient herself or himself in the story line. Consequently, the spectator must pay close attention to the details revealed implicitly in the dialogue between François and Gisèle, actively engaging him or her in the process of piecing together Sarah's memory. Furthermore, as the confrontation between the two men transitions to the argument between husband and wife, Peck uses Sarah's adult narration to foreground her struggle to resolve fact and memory. In the narration, Sarah comments, "Mother was playing the piano, I think." In the visual image, however, Gisèle is buffing her fingernails and the piano music is represented by a haunting melody on the soundtrack. In this case, the gap between Sarah's recollection and the "facts" of the scene illustrates just how subjective and imperfect memory is as a means of reconstructing history. By drawing attention to this process, the film invites the spectator to question Sarah's point of view, disrupting her position as an authority. In this way, Sarah's reconstruction of events is as open to critique as any of the competing personal or political strands of experience expressed in the narrative.

Although the two scenes present a disruption in time, the spectator's orientation is guided through the thematic link between the scenes created by a continuation of the discourse on complicity. This connection is also emphasized in the scene's visual grammar as screen space in the argument is preserved through the use of a long take, echoing the strategy chosen to depict the confrontation between François and Janvier. The camera dollies back to reveal Gisèle, clad in a dressing gown, and seated at a vanity, her face reflected in the mirror. François, half-dressed, and also reflected in the mirror, leans over the back of the chair, murmuring that he loves her. Gisèle rebuffs him by demanding that he leave her alone. Stung, he angrily defends having handed Gra-

Locality, Memory, and Zombification in *The Man by the Shore*

cieux over to Janvier, but Gisèle remains unmoved, calling his actions shameful. In this way, she critiques his complicity with the makout forces. The choice to have François's actions condemned by Gisèle signals the importance of women in the film as arbiters of resistance: like Camille and Sarah, Gisèle is uncompromising in her criticism of the tactics of terror used by the Duvalier regime, despite the obvious danger to herself and her loved ones. All three women's actions contrast with François's apparent refusal to stand up to the Duvalier regime, allowing the film to both demonstrate and interrogate the zombification of Haiti's authorities. The implication is clear: if the women can perceive the corruption engendered by terror and resist in their own ways, how can François remain blind to it or tolerate its occurrence?

As the scene develops, François's argument that Gracieux deserved arrest because of his own actions seems like an unpersuasive attempt on François's part to distance himself from his own responsibility in the situation. Near the end of the scene, François is depicted alone in a loosely framed medium shot with his back to the camera. His face is revealed only in the distant reflection of the mirror, creating an air of defeat and isolation as he admits that he really thought he could control the consequences of Gracieux's arrest. The admission has an interesting parallel for, as Mintz observes, "Duvalier appears to have become the army's choice, ostensibly because he was considered 'manageable'" and therefore François's loss of control over Janvier becomes a metaphor for the historical facts (1974, 291). There is another imperative, however, encoded within this admission, for if the army is guilty of using Duvalier as a means of achieving power, so, too, must François be guilty of the same by using Janvier. François thus becomes both victim and victimizer, suggesting that the zombification of Haiti is a historical legacy of slavery, on one hand, and, on the other, is a personal choice of individuals who perpetuate the injustices that sustain it. This is emphasized at the end of the scene when Gisèle calls François a coward for his failure to intervene on Gracieux's behalf. François immediately slaps her, an act that indicates the deep level of his shame but also links him to the makout context where violence is retaliation for speaking out or showing any form of resistance. It also underscores how the societal disintegration is mirrored in the personal lives of Haitians as Gisèle loses respect for François and he resorts to striking her in order

CHAPTER 8

to maintain control in a destabilized situation. Thus, the scene becomes an essay on how terror and violence can entrap essentially good people in an environment where fear and self-preservation undermine societal boundaries.

The conflict created by François's complicity with the Duvalier regime is integral to Sarah's emotional struggle to come to terms with her past and is played out in the realm of her subconscious mind. This is demonstrated in a dream sequence that begins with an image of Gracieux on his knees, his arms bound behind him to a length of thick tree branch. A makout straddles him from the front, controlling Gracieux's struggle by holding onto the ends of the branch, as another stands at the rear with a pole, prodding him. Gracieux's silent struggles transition to a high-angle shot of Sarah asleep in bed. As she tosses back and forth in the throes of a nightmare, the camera zooms in and slowly rocks left and right, giving a feeling of something menacing hovering over her. A disembodied voice demands to know who she is, and Sarah's reply that she is his goddaughter connects the voice to Gracieux, tying the image of torture to her dream state. As the voice asks what race she belongs to and commands her to tell him who her father is, Sarah shouts repeatedly that she does not know, indicating the psychological impossibility of reconciling the image of François as her doting father with the image of the man whose impotency results in handing Gracieux over to Janvier's makout. The reply also underscores Sarah's shame at her father's actions as the question allows her to align herself with François but her own sense of betrayal causes her to refuse such an allegiance.

The source of that betrayal becomes evident in a later scene when François, returning from an outing with Sarah, comes upon Janvier threatening Gracieux for allegedly scrawling antimakout graffiti on building walls. François intervenes by putting Gracieux into the car and driving to his home where he orders Sarah out. Gracieux, realizing that François is going to hand him over to Janvier, begs him not to. Sarah's reaction to their exchange is depicted in a high-angle close-up as she watches François explain that he has to give Gracieux up and counsels him to act like a man. As Gracieux screams that François cannot do this to him, the angle of the close-up accentuates Sarah's entrapment between two loyalties in a situation that casts both men in unfamiliar

Locality, Memory, and Zombification in *The Man by the Shore*

light. Finally commanded to leave the car by a furious François, Sarah is portrayed in a long shot standing with her mother on the sidewalk. The shot scale diminishes her physically, emphasizing her confusion and helplessness as well as the scale of François's betrayal of her heroic image of him. This act raises a question of responsibility that is repeated later in the film when Gracieux, openly drunk and careening down the street, asks an imaginary audience who invented the makout. His response that God and Satan deny it and that Duvalier's reply is, "Haiti . . . fuck you," suggests that no one in Haitian society seems willing to take responsibility for the continuation and cruelty of the Duvalier regime. In addition, Gracieux's riddle allows the spectator to actively question whether the regime could have survived at all without complicity through fear or ambition. Such a position challenges François's status as a victim, and although there is empathy for his family's situation, there is also space for consideration of his failure to do the right thing.

One of the most important metaphors in the film is that of rape, which functions as a symbol of the destruction of Haiti's social fabric, expressed as sexual cruelty in the lives of the characters. For example, after Camille is arrested for a confrontation with Madame Janvier, her daughter Elide takes Sarah with her to the militia headquarters to confront Janvier about Camille's whereabouts. Elide recognizes the full danger of the situation when she defiantly declares that Camille is innocent of the charges and Janvier responds dismissively, "Who cares?" Framed in a medium two-shot facing off against Janvier, Elide offers him a bribe to secure Camille's safety. Janvier informs her that he will need double the offered amount for the men who are interrogating Camille, but he himself is the romantic type and can live with very little. As he touches her face despite her evident disgust, it becomes clear that Elide will be forced to sleep with him in order to free Camille. By placing Elide in this position, the film alludes to the fact that it was common for members of the Duvalierist regime to engage in the "sexual 'conquest' of females associated with the political opposition," resulting in torture and acquaintance rape that "infused the politicization of gender with violence" (Trouillot 1990, 167). This treatment, however, is not restricted to women. In the scene that follows Janvier's sexual victimization of Elide, the mystery of what traumatizes Sarah during

CHAPTER 8

Gracieux's torture is fully realized, thus linking the two events. Gracieux, surrounded by Janvier's tonton-makout, is beaten with a stick. When François tries to intervene, Janvier retorts that Gracieux is simply a heap of meat that he can make disappear at will, like any subversive he chooses to destroy. The threat is quite clear: if François persists, he will share Gracieux's fate, forcing François to back down. Janvier then pulls down Gracieux's jeans and brutally sodomizes him with a pole while François looks on. Taken together, the rape of Gracieux and the sexual exploitation of Elide symbolize the level of destabilization in Haitian society where social prohibitions have ceased to have any real meaning.

On the surface, it may appear *The Man by the Shore* is arguing that in a society without rule of law or limits, predation becomes an automatic right of the strong. This position, however, is tempered by offering the possibility that even the weakest can mount a successful resistance. After Camille's arrest, Sarah begins to carry her father's revolver concealed under her dress as a means of bolstering her sense of security. When she and a young friend cycle to the beach to play, Gracieux, who is aware that the tonton-makout use the area for killings and torture, trails them. Janvier, seeing the girls pass, follows them to the beach and surprises them, grabbing Sarah's friend as Sarah escapes into the trees. Beating the child, he throws her down and prepares to rape her. Sarah, drawn back by her friend's screams, pulls the gun on Janvier. As he advances, holding his hand out for the weapon, Sarah pulls the trigger and it clicks on an empty chamber. Janvier realizes the weapon is not loaded and rushes her. Suddenly there is a gunshot offscreen and Janvier falls dead at Sarah's feet. Depicted in a medium shot, she helps her friend up and they disappear in the trees. The camera slowly pans left, passing Janvier's inert body and revealing Gracieux on his knees sobbing, with a gun in his extended hand. The camera moves past him and the film ends on a long shot of the ocean and distant blue sky. Although Gracieux is able to extract a measure of revenge for his rape at the hands of Janvier, his breakdown raises the question of the psychological costs of both his trauma and his actions: Janvier may be dead, but Gracieux's memories of the events will continue to haunt him, just as Sarah's own will continue to haunt her.

This is emphasized by Sarah's narration at the end of the film. She likens her story to that of all who have suffered under similar political conditions, suggesting that it can be viewed in a context beyond Haitian boundaries. In addition, her admission that she still awakes in a sweat after many years, hearing Camille's voice telling her that it is only a bad dream, indicates that the legacy of such oppression exists long after the historical events that spawn them. Ultimately, the persistence of Sarah's trauma creates an open ending that allows for a variety of readings, encouraging the spectator to continue the debate beyond the frame.

NINE

Mapping New Boundaries
Discourses of Blackness in *Rude*

      Black Canadians have a long and varied history in Canada that is almost as lengthy as that of African Americans (Winks 1997, ix). The cultural differences between the United States and Canada, however, have led to very different experiences of blackness in Canada, where "spaces and places speak to each other in ways that gesture to various historical, political, and social geographies inside and outside the Canadian nation-state, and inside and outside multiple black Canadian geographical locales" (McKittrick 2002, 31; also see Mensah 2002, 38). What is truly astounding about these black communities and histories is that "Canadian historians have generally attempted to black out the Black experience in Canada" by frequently glossing over, or simply ignoring, them in official or conventional histories of Canada (Mensah 2002, 43). Joseph Mensah argues, for example, that many Canadians do not believe that slavery existed in their country, considering it to be an American phenomenon (43). This is a troubling position because it seems to suggest that mainstream Canadian histories are deliberately refusing to acknowledge Canadian responsibility for participation in the global slave trade.

      Previous chapters have dealt with slavery as a black diasporic phenomenon, and chapter 1, in particular, focused on the role of the Middle Passage in establishing New World economies, specifically in the United States. Canada is no different: the nation's backbone, in part, was established through the exploitation of black slave labor (Mensah 2002, 44). The first black slave arrived in 1628 as "property of David Kirke, an English privateer conducting raids on the French colony of the St. Lawrence River" (Alexander and Glaze 1996, 37).[1] Slavery expanded slowly until labor shortages resulted in the importation of a considerable number of slaves by the end of the seventeenth century (Mensah 2002, 44). Had plantation-style agriculture developed in Canada to the extent that it did in the southern United States and Caribbean, it is speculated that "thousands more slaves would have been imported" to Canada (Alexander and Glaze 1996, 37). Although some slaves were forced into agricultural labor, shipbuilding, or mining, most were relegated to the domestic realm of upper- and middle-class homes (Mensah 2002, 45). The result was that many African slaves found themselves in cultural and geographic isolation without ready access to community (Alexander and Glaze 1996, 38). Hence, the absence of plantation culture and the isolated pattern of settlement meant that a community-based concept of black identity did not develop, a difference that distinguishes black Canadian experiences from those in the American or Caribbean context.

As slavery became more firmly established as a practice, the Code Noir, established in 1685 in the West Indies to protect the rights of slave owners, was adopted in New France to regulate the status of slaves (Mensah 2002, 45). Although some protection and privileges were afforded to slaves under the code, these virtually disappeared by the time slavery was legalized in New France in 1709 (Winks 1997, 23). When New France was ceded to the British in 1763, the status of black slaves was not transformed, as they continued to be "non-persons under the law" (Alexander and Glaze 1996, 40). Slaves were sold and traded at will, especially in the Maritimes, where black slaves contributed to the building of Halifax. At the close of the American War of Independence in 1783, Canada developed a reputation as a refuge for blacks, and some three thousand, who earned their emancipation by supporting the British cause, relocated to Nova Scotia, where they were known as Black Loyalists (Mensah 2002, 46). Although the Black Loyalists were important to the British war effort and joined it on the basis of receiving land

CHAPTER 9

and full and equal status as citizens, these promises were never fulfilled (Alexander and Glaze 1996, 41; Mensah 2002, 46). As a result, most Black Loyalists were forced into sharecropping, casual labor, or domestic service (46). Completely disillusioned with perpetual servitude and racism, some twelve hundred Nova Scotian blacks set sail for Sierra Leone in 1792 under the sponsorship of the Sierra Leone Company who needed black settlers to assist in the founding of Freetown, the capital of Sierra Leone (Mensah 2002, 47; Alexander and Glaze 1996, 49).

Four years following this exodus, the British government decided to transport approximately six hundred Jamaican Maroons to Nova Scotia (Alexander and Glaze 1996, 50). These Maroons (runaways) were the descendents of escaped slaves who rebelled against the British in order to gain their freedom. Fearing the Maroons might join the French in battle against the British and cause uprisings throughout the Caribbean, the British arranged for their deportation to Nova Scotia on the grounds that such an isolated locale would nullify their threat (Alexander and Glaze 1996, 50–51; Mensah 2002, 48). The Maroons failed to integrate with the existing black community and, in an ironic twist of history, were eventually deported by the British to Sierra Leone where they were expected to offset the original blacks who had migrated there from Nova Scotia (Alexander and Glaze 1996, 50; Mensah 2002, 48). The next major influx of blacks to arrive in Nova Scotia occurred around 1815 after black slaves were encouraged, during the War of 1812, to desert their American masters and move north to promised plots of land. This, too, proved to be an empty promise since they were not awarded title to the land they were allocated. Furthermore, the size and quality of the land barely allowed for subsistence, and many were forced to live off charity or public assistance (Mensah 2002, 48).

The early 1800s saw another significant incursion of blacks into Canada who were fugitives and who arrived through the Underground Railroad (Mensah 2002, 49). Harriet Tubman, a seminal figure in the success of the railroad, acted as a "'conductor,' assisting and escorting more than three hundred Blacks to relative freedom in Canada" (49). It should be noted that the passing of the Emancipation Act by British Parliament in 1833 outlawed slavery in Canada, a factor that added to Canada's desirability as a safe haven (Alexander and Glaze 1996, 275). As the United States became increasingly dangerous for fugitive slaves following the declaration of the Fugitive Slave Act of 1850, some twenty thousand blacks entered Canada between 1850 and 1860 and settled in Ontario near the American border (Mensah 2002, 49–50). This considerable immigration caused significant stress on the Ontario economy, resulting in increased levels of discrimination against blacks. (50).

During the early twentieth century, the Canadian economy began to prosper, and white people from the United States and Europe, responding to the 1896 open-door immigration policy, poured into the nation in search of a better life (Alexander and Glaze 1996, 26). Ironically, blacks from the United States and the Caribbean were discouraged from immigrating: a serious campaign, launched on a number of fronts, was successful in minimizing the influx of black immigrants by allowing entry only to fill specific labor market shortages (26). For example, in 1955 the domestic-worker crisis forced Canada to establish the West Indian Domestic Scheme, which, until the 1960s, provided one of the few opportunities for Jamaicans to legally immigrate to the nation (Mensah 2002, 98–99). Jamaican immigration peaked in 1974 with upward of 11,286 immigrants, and by the late 1970s, when renewed restrictions on immigration were imposed, Jamaicans had a widespread presence in Canada, with heavier concentrations in the area of southern Ontario, including such cities as Toronto, Mississauga, and Scarborough (99–101).

Just as the history of black Canadian settlement in Canada is complex and varied, so, too, are the ways of "understanding community" when that community is composed of many black cultures (Sooknanan 2000, 140). In fact, the notion of black community in Canada is a highly contested one and, some contend, an impossibility. Given the diversity of cultures and the varied and complex histories of arrival, to state that there is a monolithic black community is extremely misleading (140, 141). How then, can notions of black community, blackness, or black be framed within the Canadian context? (141). Given that black histories are largely absent from mainstream historical narratives, there is "little, if any room for imagining Blackness as constitutive of Canadianness" (Walcott 2000, 7). Moreover, the presence of black communities from the early 1600s makes it difficult to imagine blackness as a "recent phenomenon within the nation" (7). At the same time, there are black communities with more recent roots in Canada whose contributions are negated if the definition of community is determined solely by duration of history. Regardless of length of presence, all these communities share the need to resort to methods that "resist this erasure in their personal, collective and everyday histories" (7). This is not to say that the quest for an unadulterated origin or "African authenticity" is the antidote to histories of erasure (Sealy 2000, 91). Addressing issues of blackness in Canada is a risky but necessary business, and resisting attempts to authenticate black community by harking back to a glorious African origin seems problematic (Sooknanan 2000, 143).

If origin is not the solution, then where else can succor be found? George Elliott Clarke suggests that this quandary has led African Canadians to seek answers south of the border by looking to African America for a system of blackness to shape their own identities (1998, 2). Clarke contends that DuBois's concept of *double-consciousness*, in which one must constantly negotiate two states of being, has profound ramifications for African Canadians. He argues, however, that the African Canadian experience is subject to more than the duality between black and white. Instead, African Canadians possess *poly consciousness* because of the complicated cultural milieus that must be negotiated in Canadian society (17). Cecil Foster supports this contention by acknowledging that the small pockets of black culture in Canada have resulted in a tendency to look to models of affirmation in black cultures located south of Canadian borders (1996, 18). Despite sharing Africa as a common origin, however, the divergent histories and specificities of Canada as a nation make adopting African American solutions unworkable (25). From Foster's perspective, the Caribbean, with its focus on hybridization, might provide a better model (25).

Clarke shares with Foster this yearning to look to the Caribbean for the means to frame African Canadian identities (1998, 25). He suggests that Edouard Glissant's concept of Antillanité[2] is useful in the African Canadian context, given that it shuns the primacy of a universal black consciousness in favor of identities located in specific geopolitical maps and histories that are in constant processes of transformation (1998, 25–26). Inspired by Glissant's approach, Clarke proposes that the experiences of African Canadians reflect what might be described as *"African Canadianité*, a condition that involves a constant self-questioning

Discourses of Blackness in *Rude*

of the grounds of identity" and that foregrounds heterogeneity as a defining element (26–27).

Clarke is not alone in recognizing that transnationality plays a pivotal role in African Canadian identities. For example, David Sealy contributes to the debate by sketching out a "provisional 'reading' of Black Canadian identity" that is based on acknowledging the varied histories of black cultures in Canada and suggests that "an understanding of 'border-crossing'" is crucial to understanding those cultures (2000, 91). Rinaldo Walcott offers a different perspective when he advocates resistance to all forms of domination and theorizes black Canadian as a counternarrative, "as wholly outside the biological and the national" (1997, 120). The polyphony of voices expressed in this theoretical debate indicates the impossibility of locating black Canadian identity within monolithic or static constructs: in a very real way, black Canadian identities forge themselves in a space that is paradoxically monolithic and white, on the one hand, and inherently transcultural, on the other. Given this context, it is not surprising that black Canadian identities are constantly in flux, both in terms of theoretical positioning and in terms of the multiplicity of realities they must address.

Within this context, Clement Virgo's film *Rude* (Canada, 1995) offers the opportunity to investigate how multiple black Canadian identities are forged in response to overcoming barriers presented by lives lived in a shifting diasporic context. As one of the first full-length fictional features directed by a black Canadian, *Rude* could be considered the beginning of black Canadian cinema. Black Canadians, however, have contributed significant documentary and short fictional works to the landscape of Canadian cinema in the period prior to *Rude*'s release. For example, documentaries such as *Home Feeling: Struggle for a Community* (Jennifer Hodge da Silva; Canada, 1983), *Speak It from the Heart of Black Nova Scotia* (Sylvia Hamilton; Canada, 1992), and *The Road Taken* (Selwyn Jacobs; Canada, 1996) present the struggle of black Canadian communities to define themselves in the face of adversity and racism (Gittings 2002, 255). Similarly, Colina Phillips's film *Making Change* (Canada, 1994) and Dana Inkster's *Welcome to Africville* (Canada, 1999) demonstrate the power of experimental short film to raise historical

CHAPTER 9

and personal issues affecting black Canadian experience. Furthermore, when viewed in context with feature fiction films arising in the same period, such as Stephen Williams's *Soul Survivor* (Canada, 1995) and Christene Browne's *Another Planet* (Canada, 1999), it may be argued that *Rude* arises from an ongoing tradition of black Canadian filmmaking that has always sought to give voice to cultural and historical concerns often marginalized or dismissed by white Canadian society.

Clement Virgo was born in Jamaica and immigrated to Toronto when he was eleven years old (Glassman 1995, 20). After high school, Virgo initially worked in the fashion industry as a window dresser because he felt that filmmaking was not within his reach (20). While attending a night course in film at Ryerson University, however, he met Virginia Rankin, a filmmaker known for her unique documentary and short-film work (20). Rankin's acceptance into the Canadian Film Centre created an opportunity for collaboration with Virgo on the short film *A Small Dick Fleshy Ass Thang* (1991), which achieved success on the film festival circuit (20). In 1992, Virgo was accepted into the program himself and created the critically acclaimed short film *Save My Lost Nigga' Soul* (1993), which was subsequently named best Canadian Short Film at the Toronto International Film Festival, garnered a Gold Plaque Award at the Chicago International Film Festival, and won the Paul Robeson Award for Best Short Film of the Diaspora at the 1995 Festival Panafricain du Cinéma et de la Télévision (Fespaco). Beginning with *Rude* (1995), Virgo has gone on to a successful feature filmmaking career, and his works include *The Planet of Junior Brown* (1999) and *Love Come Down* (2000), which won three Genie Awards from the Academy of Canadian Cinema and Television, *Lie With Me* (2005) and *Poor Boy's Game* (2006).

Premiering at the Cannes Film Festival in 1995, Virgo's first feature film, *Rude*, was made under the auspices of the Canadian Film Centre. Awarded a jury citation for best feature at the Toronto International Film Festival, selected for the Sundance Film Festival and nominated for eight Genie Awards from the Academy of Canadian Cinema and Television, *Rude* broke new ground in Canadian filmmaking. In addition to being the first feature film directed by a black Canadian filmmaker, *Rude* also sparked a vigorous debate among film theorists interrogating the nature of black identity in Canada. As Walcott notes, the

Discourses of Blackness in *Rude*

film "opened up the space for thinking differently about Canada as a racialized space, and more specifically, a Black space" (2000, 7). Seen alternately as brilliant and flawed, groundbreaking and belonging to the canon of Canadian art film, *Rude*'s imaginative and challenging use of space and ambiguity demonstrates the tensions inherent in African Canadian identities forged in a poly-conscious framework.

Rude follows the events that take place over an Easter weekend in the lives of three black Canadian characters living in Toronto's Regent Park projects: Luke, an ex-convict just released from prison, seeks reconciliation with his family; Maxine, employed as a window dresser, struggles with the breakup of a relationship and the deeply personal decision she must make regarding an unplanned pregnancy; and Jordan, a young boxer, is forced to confront his own homosexuality in a hostile environment. The struggles faced by each of these characters, whose lives unfurl in parallel with each other, become emblematic of the barriers facing black Canadians within the often racist context of Canadian society.

This is reflected in the way the film simultaneously constructs and deconstructs the city of Toronto as the geographical setting of the film. The film brings together three independent motifs that provide the narrative's external frame. The film opens with a long, slow-motion medium shot of a male lion walking toward the camera. The lion, depicted against a black background, strides into a pool of light, looking into the camera in direct address. This action, along with the use of a low angle, emphasizes the lion's powerful nature. Referred to later in the film as the Lion of Judah, he is connected to Rastafarianism, "a movement that is concerned above all else with black consciousness, with rediscovering the identity, personal and racial, of black people" (Clarke 1988, 17). This movement, with its belief that all black people are connected to the ancient Israelites and that contemporary black populations are direct descendents of God's chosen people, arose in Jamaica and was heavily influenced by the teachings of Marcus Garvey who believed that the only solution to the oppression of black diasporic populations was to return to Africa (17, 36).[3] Within this context, the lion's movement into the light, highlighting its magnificent mane, reflects the Rastafarian belief that the lion, as the "Lion of the Tribe of Judah," is an important nature symbol evoking Africa and a locus of

CHAPTER 9

transcendental authority (Johnson-Hill 1995, 153). The lion thus evokes several meanings at once: it is a source of power and pride as well as a symbol of community based on a shared African heritage.

The second narrative motif introduced in the film is the character of DJ Rude, a young female radio pirate who takes over the radio waves of the community every Easter weekend. Described by Virgo as the collective consciousness of the community, Rude becomes the epicenter of debate connecting the multiple black discourses present in the film's urban environment as she interacts with various callers and expressively comments on the state of contemporary black identities (Gittings 2002, 257). Furthermore, Rude's commentary, often apropos the issues Maxine, Luke, and Jordan are confronting in their personal lives, serves to function as a connector between their stories. When initially introduced, Rude is sitting at a large mixing board in what appears to be a studio setting.

Depicted in a circular dolly shot, Rude remains a mysterious entity as her features are all but obscured by shadow. Fitful backlighting teases the spectator with details as the camera circles, allowing identification of Rude as a young black woman but otherwise refusing a clear resolution of her image. The circular movement also reinforces her position as a contemporary griot who organizes the screen space and provides context for the film's disparate story lines by virtue of her running commentary.

Like the lion, Rude is also connected to the Caribbean, both by her accent and by the Rastafarian references she makes throughout the film. Yet she also signifies a diasporic space that extends beyond the confines of a specifically Jamaican community. During the long take that introduces her, Rude's dialogue sets out the parameters of the film's conceptual landscape: her words describe her as speaking from "the last neighborhood in the world," which stretches from "the land of the Zulu nation to the Mohawk nation," a reference that locates the context of her black community within previously colonized lands of Canada's First Nations peoples. This is further emphasized by Rude's comment that "for the next two nights we steal Babylon's airwaves and let them reevaluate their immigration policy." The reference to Babylon, used here in its Rastafarian sense, evokes the corrupt social and governmental institutions forced on black peoples by the West as

Discourses of Blackness in *Rude*

Rude (Courtesy of The Feature Film Project;
photography by Michael Gibson)

a means of ensuring continuing oppression (Gittings 2002, 259).⁴ This reference suggests that the space in which Rude addresses her listeners simultaneously delineates an African Canadian specificity and the larger diasporic context within which it resides, making Rude's "community" both local and worldwide in scope. Furthermore, because the act of speaking is described as stealing and inscribed within a "pirate" radio broadcast, Rude's commentary indicates a direct challenge to a society that would otherwise censor black voices. Thus, Rude's exhortation to her listeners to "cock the hammer, sharpen your spears, throw stones" is a call for a coup d'état aimed at dismantling an oppressive dominant society.

The third visual construct supports the tension between specific locale and broader diasporic perspective through a montage of long shots of the Toronto skyline and neighborhoods. Although these brief images include recognizable landmarks such as the CN Tower, in general, these are accessible only to spectators familiar with the city. Outside of this narrow scope, the series of images evokes a generic urban setting promoting the notion that Toronto is a particular place but also an extension of Babylon as a worldwide oppressive phenomenon. Although some critics take issue with the universalization of Toronto's specificity as a locale as shortchanging the depiction of local realities, this may be quite beside the point (McCullough 1999, 21). Rather, the tension between local specificity and diasporic context exposes the paradoxical state inherent in being from "elsewhere (remembering, imagining, travelling) and here at the same time" (McKittrick 2002, 31). Thus, the visual presentation underscores the way geography reflects cultural separation between races and foregrounds the difficulty of negotiating a space dominated by agendas set by white European imperatives (28). In doing so, the urban spaces of *Rude* connect African Canadian consciousness to other black diasporas (28). Thus, if DJ Rude and the lion represent the powers of black identity, the cityscapes represent the collective powers of white Eurocentric oppression they defy, positing black Canadian reality as "a counter-narrative or utterance" that challenges the concept of Canada as an inclusive nation by rendering visible the very blackness history has sought to make invisible (Walcott 1997, 120). In a very powerful way, black Canadian identity can never be fully inscribed in "real" Canadian neighborhoods or geographies precisely because they are participants in the global flows of the black diaspora: hence self is both local and distant. Within these constraints, DJ Rude's actions are necessarily clandestine and disruptive, metaphorically taking Babylon hostage for purely black purposes and staking a claim on the shifting sands of colliding nations.

Given the prominence of Christian religious symbolism in the many murals that are featured on walls throughout the film and the fact that the action of the film takes place over the Easter weekend, it seems reasonable to read *Rude* as a parable of redemption. The full scope of the film, however, is not so easily encompassed by this singular description. Instead, *Rude* presents a complex structure that more closely resembles redemption from a Rastafarian perspective, in which "exile in Babylon is the worst form of evil imaginable, the one which gives rise to the most intense suffering" (Clarke 1988, 69). Salvation from this suffering can only be achieved by turning to Africa, thus emphasizing a return to, or embracing of, African values (69).

As a triptych of characters, Maxine, Luke, and Jordan must each face personal trials that test and fundamentally alter their sense of identity. The plot structure, however, departs from mainstream cinematic norms as the characters never meet during the course of the film; nor do their story lines directly affect one another. Instead, a sense of narrative unity is created by sequencing each plotline with care, matching key crisis points in terms of screen time and bringing them to climax within close proximity of one another. This creates a defamiliarized classical narrative construct that is simultaneously linear, because of event sequencing, and non-linear, because the narrative possesses three separate plot actions that do not fold into one another in a conventional plot and subplot relationship. Instead, the three plotlines are linked thematically through Rude's dialogue and interaction with callers from the community, and her comments often raise debate around the larger social issues that are personalized through the trials of Maxine, Luke, and Jordan. More significant, this arrangement creates polyvalent black Canadian identities by exploring the different ways in which each character positions herself or himself in regard to Canadian society and the black communities in which they abide. As Walcott notes, being black Canadian means dealing with the persistence of an "ideology that suggests that black bodies can and must be abused, misused, regulated, disciplined and over-policed" (1997, 37). *Rude*, however, goes beyond a mere indictment of that ideology by examining how it relates to the relationship between self-destructive behaviors and the notion of individual responsibility within the black community itself. Thus, although systemic racism plays a major role in the film's unfolding, so do issues of gender, sexuality, culture, and the nature of community.

The film's plotlines are initiated in short scenes commingled throughout a long monologue by Rude as she explicitly describes an act of sexual intercourse between a man and a woman, referred to in slang as a "dog" and a "bitch." The masculine explicitness of the language in this, and other sections, leads Marc Glassman to question Rude's authenticity as a character because her "speeches are too macho, too male," to possess "psychological verisimilitude," indicating that "Virgo is still too much of a 'guy's guy' to get Rude's rap right" (1995, 21). Although this is certainly a valid perspective, it also overlooks the equally valid fact that the content of these same raps often challenges masculine stereotypes through the use of irony and appropriation. For example, Rude's usurping of a masculine point of view as she describes the

CHAPTER 9

sexual encounter from the man's perspective shifts the responsibility for contraception from the woman to the man. Specifically addressing her comments to the men in her audience, Rude asks them to consider the fact that ten thousand single women will be raising children from among the fifty thousand conceived on this night. She sardonically suggests that if they are "tired of rolling a sock on to your pickle," then uncertainties of using withdrawal might form an alternative, albeit dangerous, mode of contraception. Furthermore, Rude's description of the incident as a single-minded pursuit of release on the part of the male partner implies that sexual pleasure should have a societal price for men as well as women.

By focusing on the description of a sexual act, Rude's comments implicitly incorporate each of the three story lines, the introductions of which are framed within a relationship discourse. A talented artist, Luke is first portrayed in a tight close-up lighting a match and then in an extreme high angle as he stares down at his self-portrait burning on the sidewalk.[5] This act underscores Luke's ambivalence as he is accosted on the corner by a young black man who pesters him for drugs, having recognized him from his past life as a drug dealer. Finally, the image of the burning painting dissolves into a close-up of an intact portrait, located in the bedroom of a young black woman dressing in a police uniform. The act of burning the painting therefore raises a narrative question: which part of Luke's life is he trying to shrive himself of, and how does the woman from his past fit into that act?

In Maxine's introduction, she is portrayed in a long shot walking past a mural featuring a Christ-like figure surrounded by disciples. She strides purposefully, carrying the arms and legs of a mannequin. The image, which is repeated through a jump cut and shot in slow motion, has a haunted, floating quality that reflects Maxine's state of mind. This is reinforced through the jerky, handheld shot that follows, portraying Maxine sitting in the middle of a rumpled bed. A masculine voice is heard off-screen, and the set-up implies that she is being filmed by a video camera held by an unseen man, later revealed to be Andre, her lover. The high-angle shot has a voyeuristic quality as Maxine looks into the camera in direct address, an effect heightened by the fact that he asks her to take off her clothes. She responds to the command with discomfort by saying no and covering herself with the blankets. The shot raises questions concerning the context of the videotaping, the identity of the unseen man, and the nature of Maxine's relationship to him.

The third character introduction involves Jordan, who is wearing boxing gear and shot from an angle that would approximate an opponent's gaze. The film then cuts to a low-angle long shot of Jordan's practice session in the ring as he boxes with a partner. As the camera dollies past in slow motion from left to right, the camera movement foregrounds Jordan's physical prowess. In contrast to the voyeurism in Maxine's sequence, in which her spectator is an active participant in the process, the long shot of Jordan places him within the context of impersonal surveillance, as if capturing a public performance. Later in the opening, he is depicted in a medium two-shot, sitting on the edge of the ring with his fellow boxer and friend, Curtis. It appears, on the surface, that this is a moment between friends, but there is an easy intimacy between them, especially evident in the lingering look that Curtis gives Jordan as he leaves, suggesting there is more at play than simple male bonding.

By using crosscutting as a major organizing principle to intertwine the plotlines throughout Rude's rap, the visual presentation maintains the independence of the story strands while at the same time creating thematic associations between the stories through screen proximity. Rude comments, "There are ten million Nubian tales in the projects on this Ojibway sacred ground," a statement that signals the film's goal of personalizing specific issues that are of importance to black communities through the characters of Maxine, Luke, and Jordan. The pull generated between concepts of specific locale and everywhere is echoed in the narrative construction by the creation of a similar tension between the characters and the issue each represents. Furthermore, this strategy enables the film to explore the competing impulses in the black community by grounding the struggle in a certain level of ambiguity that leaves room for the spectator to question the choices and motivations of character actions. For example, very little information is revealed concerning character backstory: we are never told how long Maxine has been with her lover or how serious their relationship was; Jordan never directly gives voice to his own attitudes regarding his homosexuality; and Luke's motivation for drug dealing in the first place is

CHAPTER 9

never directly addressed. The lives of the characters are simply picked up as they are unfolding on that Friday night without explanation. Instead, the narrative seeds subtle clues to these questions that can only be discovered by the spectator's close attention to the narrative, thus engaging the spectator as an active participant in making sense of their choices.[6]

The emphasis on personal choice and suffering as a necessary process for self-understanding places *Rude* on a different footing from other films discussed in this volume. One of the criticisms leveled against the film is that its politics are implicit rather than explicit in nature. For example, Walcott has questioned the specifics of what makes *Rude* a black Canadian film, given the de-emphasis on larger political issues (1997, 56). *Rude*'s political discourse, however, does question how different strands of black experience interact and affect the development of African Canadian identities. Hence, although race relations and the challenging of systemic white racism play a role in *Rude*'s ideological construct, the film is far more focused on interrogating the responsibility of black Canadian individuals for choices that affect their families and their communities. For example, Gittings argues that Virgo is concerned with the "psychic deconstruction of the internalized white stereotype of 'nigger'," and this is certainly true in the case of Luke, who must resist being pulled back into the realm of dealing by Yankee, a white drug lord and Luke's ex-boss (2002, 260). This analysis, however, does not account for Maxine and Jordan, both of whom are struggling with expectations more closely allied with the black community than with white society. Here, racism is de-emphasized (although always present) in favor of a critique that delimits the parameters of acceptable black identities.

The film lays out Maxine's struggle like a puzzle, providing bits of information and delaying contextualization of her actions until late in the film. In this case, the story strand is composed of layers that combine past backstory, as represented by the video clips, with a forward action of a weekend spent by Maxine alone in her loft. In the forward action, Maxine is coping with a nasty split from her lover, Andre. This is illustrated by a scene early in the film where Maxine is in her bathroom changing her clothes. Depicted in a long dolly shot, Maxine walks from the darkened foreground of the loft's kitchen into the bright rectangle

Discourses of Blackness in *Rude*

of light coming through the open bathroom door. As her answering machine plays messages, Maxine sits on the toilet, and her body all but disappears, masked by the bathroom doorframe. She is in this position when she hears an angry message from Andre, informing her that he came over in her absence to pick up his belongings only to find that she had taped over some of his videotapes. Maxine's masked physical position within the rectangle of light provides a marked sense of entrapment as she angrily yells to the message that the video camera was hers to do with as she pleases. This scene serves several functions. First, it demonstrates that Andre and Maxine had a long-standing relationship. Second, and most important, it raises the question of who controls the video images. This is particularly significant when considered in conjunction with earlier scenes in the introduction that place Andre in control of "constructing" Maxine by "capturing" her image on tape. The fact that this struggle is played out on the canvas of Maxine's body is significant: as Walcott suggests, "The discourse(s) and realities of slavery have come to mark how we see and think about bodies, especially black bodies, and blackness" (1997, 54). By treating Maxine as an object to be fashioned after his own desire, Andre's capturing of Maxine's image against her will can be read as an expression of ownership and a denial of her right to personhood. Thus, control of Maxine's image and, by extension, recoupment of her real-life body are central to Maxine's struggle.

The notion that Andre views Maxine in a proprietary fashion without general concern for her needs as a person is evident in several scenes from the videotapes that are scattered and repeated throughout the progression of the narrative. For example, during a phone call from her sister, Maxine tells her that Andre is moving out and expresses anger at his insistence on removing the fish tank. As she does so, one of his videos plays on the television. Andre is filming Maxine's backside in long shot, lingering on her physical beauty and making suggestive remarks as she bends over to adjust a mannequin. When she realizes what is going on, she stands up in the frame, holding her hands out to block Andre's view, and tells him not to film her in this manner. The fact that she is framed in direct address accentuates her discomfort and annoyance at such a voyeuristic action, but Andre is not deterred as he continues to follow her through the loft. Taken together, Maxine's

CHAPTER 9

description of Andre in her phone conversation as a selfish man and "an asshole" appears to be confirmed by his continued insistence on filming her.

Another sequence from the videotapes plays a significant role in the final scene revealing Andre and Maxine's breakup. This is first introduced as a transition sequence following the scene in which Maxine listens to Andre's angry message. It begins as a brief video close-up shot of Maxine sitting in bed with her hand covering her face and then dissolves into a low-angle medium shot of her sitting on the bed, naked under the blankets. Looking up at Andre, who is off-screen controlling the camera, Maxine holds up her hands protectively in front of her as if warding him off. This sequence is then connected to the following scene in which Maxine, still in the bathroom, listens to a message from her sister, who inquires after her weekend plans. This time, Maxine is on the far right of the bathroom door, and as she strips off her clothes revealing her nakedness, her sister's message invites her to go to church with her on Easter Sunday. Maxine steps to the left, disappearing from sight just as her sister adds jokingly that she has a lot of sins to repent. Simultaneously, a young girl in a blue dress and braids steps into frame right, and, as she does so, the bathroom light fades to black, leaving her figure prominent in the dark frame. The presence of the girl, who continues to appear at moments of crisis or contemplation in Maxine's story strand, initiates a narrative mystery: how is she related to Maxine and why is her appearance often associated with the video clip of Maxine raising her hands to ward off Andre?

By refusing to immediately resolve this question, the film opens the narrative to speculation. Certainly, Andre seems to bear primary responsibility for the breakup: his anger and his decision to clean out the loft completely while Maxine is passed out on the bed from a night of drinking and despair definitely appears to cast her as a woman who has been sexually exploited and then abandoned. A very different picture, however, emerges when the full context of the scene from the videotape is disclosed. The sequence begins with a medium close-up of Maxine pensively sitting in the darkened loft smoking and drinking beer. Her framing, in the right corner, suggests a sense of entrapment as she is heard murmuring in voice-over that neither she nor Andre is ready to have a child. The shot fades out and a long shot of Maxine

Discourses of Blackness in *Rude*

sitting naked under the covers of the bed fades up. Andre is positioned on the far right of the frame with his back to the camera, masking his face. The sequence continues to cut back and forth between these two scenes as Andre's anger grows until he demands to know if she intends to have an abortion. The sequence climaxes as Maxine holds her hands in front of her face as if to ward off his furious barrage. The final fade leads to a long take of the young girl as she dances across the loft toward the chair in which Maxine is sitting. The long take is composed of a dolly shot that moves from the child to focus on Maxine, connecting their space. This reveals the child as Maxine's unborn daughter and the source of the breakup. Although Walcott comments that the girl is an intentional reference to the unborn child in *Daughters of the Dust* (see chap. 3), there are significant differences: unlike Dash's creation, who is an active structuring force in the film, Maxine's unborn child is more directly, and passively, symbolic of her repentance (1997, 61). Although the child is present in many of the scenes, she does not speak, nor does she directly influence the narrative flow until her final contact with Maxine in the film's resolution.

The fact that Andre's face is either masked or his presence kept offscreen prevents the spectator from identifying with his character, except as a negative force in Maxine's life. Although this renders Andre a cipher, it has the narrative benefit of clearly focusing on the issue of Maxine's control of her own body. Furthermore, the strategy offers a site for debate surrounding the appropriate rights of men and women in such a decision: although it is clear that Andre feels strongly that Maxine should have the child, his powerlessness to alter the decision by anything but his choice to leave expresses the inherent difficulty in balancing such competing interests. The film, however, clearly demonstrates that the final decision should be Maxine's alone. Clues to this are scattered throughout the text and often encoded in Rude's raps, which mark transitions to key scenes. For example, in the second scene involving an appearance by Maxine's child, the child materializes on the bed as Maxine enters from the right, in a housecoat. Rude's broadcast is heard as diegetic sound, coming from an unseen radio, as she says, "This one goes out to the bitches. If you've lost the sound of your disenfranchised diasporic voice, maybe I have it." Her words wrap onto a tight two-shot close-up of Maxine and the child. In this case, Maxine

CHAPTER 9

is out of focus in the background on the right, with her naked back to the camera while the child is in focus in the foreground and positioned tight against the left frame, looking back at Maxine. The sequence ends with Andre, off-screen, filming Maxine and asking her to make love to the camera. Portrayed in a medium shot, Maxine laughs and, in direct address, tells Andre that she is not going to comply. Thus, the visual structure links Andre and the child to the loss of Maxine's "diasporic" voice, which, arguably, must be rediscovered before she can move on with her life.

The film further advances the position that the choice must be Maxine's alone in a later scene when Maxine informs Andre that she has had the abortion. Portrayed in a high-angle long shot, sitting on the floor with her back to the wall for support, she speaks to Andre on the phone in an exhausted voice saying, "I didn't ruin it." She listens for a long beat of screen time as the camera slowly tracks from right to left and finally struggles out the words, "I couldn't have it. I wasn't . . . ready. . . . I didn't ruin it." Propped against the wall next to Maxine is a female mannequin, whose physical position mirrors her own. Dominant in a shaft of light, the mannequin seems to offer a contrast between a stereotypical and unachievable ideal of female perfection and the complicated reality faced by Maxine as she confesses to an action she knows will end her relationship permanently. Maxine's repetition of the phrase "I didn't ruin it" indicts Andre for leaving her because of her decision, a meaning foregrounded by the filmmaker's decision not to allow the spectator to hear Andre's side of the conversation: in the absence of his responses, the spectator must speculate on his motivations. Finally, the shot scale distances the spectator from Maxine's emotional state, inviting her or him to consider the correctness of her decision.

As a young boxer, Jordan shares with Maxine in his story strand the notion that "what is at stake in *Rude* are bodies and their histories or bodies in history" (Walcott 1997, 66). In this particular case, Jordan's homosexuality and his position as a promising athlete serve to expose the hypocritical stereotype that demands a specific, exaggerated type of heteromasculinity in black men. Virgo alludes to this intention when he states that, "when we think of young black men, we think that they are the ultimate symbols of machismo, of masculinity" (Virgo, quoted in

Glassman 1995, 20). Thus, from Virgo's perspective, Jordan's character critiques the homophobia present in black communities by challenging the perception that one cannot simultaneously be a strong black man and be gay (1995, 20). This stated goal, however, has proven to be controversial in and of itself: although critics such as Glassman have considered *Rude*'s treatment of Jordan as "rendered in an interesting and impressive manner" (Glassman 1995, 20), others, such as Walcott, have taken exception to the "black/queer body [being] asked to stand in as the site upon which the inscription of violent heteronormative desires are lived out" (Walcott 1997, 63).[7] There is merit in both sides of the debate, a fact that attests to a certain level of underdevelopment both in Jordan's character and in the context of the story strand itself.

Unlike Maxine and Luke who are accorded a certain amount of personal background, Jordan remains a total cipher: it is unclear whether or not he has family, what his relationship is to them, or even how he supports himself outside of boxing. Furthermore, Jordan is not given a personal living space and is portrayed only within the confines of the boxing club or Riverdale Park, where he joins in the gay bashing of a black man. Hence, the character's screen identity is narrowly tied to his pursuit of boxing, a decision that makes his physicality the main determinant of his identity. In addition, Jordan is not provided with an opportunity to openly discuss his own attitudes toward his homosexuality, rendering him mute on the very issue that shapes the story strand. Although this is a legitimate strategy intended to raise debate surrounding the issues, the effect of Jordan's failure to speak even briefly on his own behalf is to normalize the very prejudice Virgo seeks to mitigate, as the "diasporic voice" of homosexuality is not openly expressed or recouped.

This shortcoming is further highlighted by the decision not to contextualize the evident homophobia of the black community depicted by the film. As Walcott argues, the centrality of the body and performance in black youth culture "echoes the various ways in which black cultural practices have always treated bodies as a canvas upon which historical and contemporary social relations may be signified, inscribed and rewritten" (1997, 64). Walcott's contention that the black body can also serve as a symbol of resistance to those same social relations is useful in codifying Virgo's depiction of black homosexuality and its rela-

CHAPTER 9

tionship to the community (64). For example, in a scene near the beginning of the film where Jordan and three fellow boxers are showering, Virgo uses a loosely framed medium shot of the four men as one of the boxers recounts how he was approached by a gay man in the park. Jordan is positioned on the midleft of the frame, and the other boxers are blocked in such a way that he is the focus of the shot. On the surface, this could be considered a means of demonstrating that Jordan's masculinity is indistinguishable from the heteronormative male bodies that surround him. Furthermore, when the boxer telling the story refers to women as "bitches," Jordan challenges him by asking why he feels it is necessary to refer to women in this manner. Although his companions tell him to shut up and continue with their behavior, the exchange suggests that Jordan is capable of actively expressing opinions that are contrary to those held by his peers.

Jordan, however, remains silent on the subject of homosexuality: as the scene progresses, he is depicted in medium close-ups, turned away from the others, visualizing his discomfort at the way in which his companions characterize the gay man in the park. This composition emphasizes Jordan's estrangement from his peers but also serves to underscore his isolation and the fact that his heteronormative behavior is a mask for a "shameful" secret. Hence, both his sensitivity and his concealed reactions challenge the presumption of hypermasculinity associated with elite sports. The actual difficulty arises in accessing Jordan's role within the black community from which he is concealing his homosexuality. The cultural genesis of the extreme masculine social construct reflected in the shower scene is not explored, nor does the film provide any motivation or deeper understanding of the violent reaction of the others when the storyteller reveals that his genitals were fondled by the man during the encounter in the park. Although it might be argued that the intent is to create discussion by allowing the spectator to draw her or his own conclusions on the subject, the film also fails to acknowledge the cultural or historical roots of this extreme homophobia (Walcott 1997, 64). Thus, the film makes it difficult to see Jordan as anything other than passively complicit in his own victimization.

A similar dynamic is expressed in the scene where Jordan and his fellow boxers accost the gay man in Riverdale Park. The latter is first

Discourses of Blackness in *Rude*

introduced in a long shot that dollies in as the gay man sits at a picnic table, exchanging a kiss with a young man. This is crosscut with a scene of Rude, as she confronts an angry male caller's characterization of her as a "pussy sucking whore" by explicitly describing a sexual encounter she had during a lesbian affair. Her closing comment, heard as voice-over, ironically asks the caller, "Haven't you heard, nigger? We got no fags, lesbian, dykes, queers, homosexuals in the black community." The pairing of Rude's words with the visual image of the men kissing seems intended to underscore the impossibility of denying the existence of a black gay community. Furthermore, the blatant homophobia of Rude's caller, associated visually with an image of the young boxers arriving in the park, suggests that the prejudice expressed by both is an inherent aspect of the black community in general. Neither connection, however, serves to add substantively to the debate the film appears to want to generate: the fury of Rude's caller reflects an absence of social context similar to that of the young boxers, and Rude's graphic description of her domination of her partner is presented only within a sexual frame, which serves more to objectify the gay encounter than humanize it. If Rude's openness concerning her encounter is meant to demonstrate that the black community is not monolithically homophobic, it fails because she speaks as a subversive adventurer and not as a member of the gay community.

Jordan's estrangement from his peers is further illustrated through the creation of divided space during the mugging. As they approach the gay man, Jordan lags behind the others. The confrontation begins in a medium long shot as two of the boxers take up positions on the picnic table to the right and left of their victim while a third stands behind, effectively cutting off all escape. Jordan is depicted in a medium shot, standing a short distance away from the struggle which takes place like a tableau in front of him. The visual presentation accentuates Jordan's passivity: although he urges the others to stop the attack, he fails to step into the space of confrontation or take any direct action that would require him abandoning his position as observer. This contrasts sharply with the defiance of the gay man who, despite the obvious danger, stands up verbally to his assaulters by openly admitting his homosexuality. When Mike, one of the boxers, demands the gay man's chain and ring, the latter rises, defiantly refusing to hand it

CHAPTER 9

over in a face-to-face confrontation, declaring, "You know what you niggers' problem is, no one's ever come in your mouth. You should try it some time. It's liberating." The words, wrapped over a close-up of an obviously frightened Jordan, indicate a kind of courage and pride in self that serve as a counterpoint to Jordan's passivity.

As the gay man challenges Mike by declaring, "You're going to have to either kiss my black ass or lynch it," Jordan attempts once again to urge the others to stop and begins to walk away himself. The use of the word "lynch" appears to link the violence in the park to past unjustified violence against blacks, most notably in the American South. Furthermore, the film's violence is connected to the power of peer pressure as Jordan is drawn into the fray in a desperate act of fitting in. As Mike rips the chain from the gay man's neck, one of his companions grabs the gay man's arms, holding him forcibly in place. As they begin to beat him, Jordan's reaction is depicted in a medium shot. As the camera dollies swiftly into a close-up of Jordan, emphasizing his horror, the screen fades to black. This initiates a series of short images connected by fades in a visual presentation that is reminiscent of the revelation scene in Maxine's story strand. A long shot of the beating filmed in slow motion fades in as the camera slowly dollies toward the action, lingering on the violence of the beating. At the end of the shot, the gay man is held down on top of the picnic table and presented to Jordan as if he were an offering. Jordan looks swiftly from side to side, indicating a vacillation between the desire to flee and a paralyzing fear holding him in place as the off-screen voices of his companions urge him to participate. Depicted in an extreme low-angle close-up, and raising his fist, Jordan is forced to face his victim directly. This suggests that Jordan is confronting the part of himself he fears most, a psychological conflict underscored by the reverse high-angle close-up of the gay man as he defiantly shouts, "Fuck you" at him. Unlike depictions of the other characters, Jordan's beating of the gay man is not directly presented onscreen: it is implied by having Jordan's fist come down toward the camera as if he were landing a blow. Instead, the film focuses on the effect of that violence on Jordan by a series of jump cuts of him running through a field, away from the scene of the beating. The sequence of shots, which take Jordan from the midground of his run and progressively backward as if traveling in reverse, allows the spectator time to contemplate the depth of Jordan's confusion and shame at his participation in the beating. Furthermore, as Jordan's motivation for participating is somewhat ambiguous, given that he was free to leave, it also allows the spectator to question his motives and the correctness of his actions. Hence, the violence becomes a means of not only critiquing the homophobia in the black community but it also challenges the passivity of those who allow such violence to unfold without intervening.

The correlation, however, between homosexuality, self-loathing, and violence present a less than satisfactory reading when considered in tandem. By creating a relationship between Jordan's participation in the gay bashing and the deep shame he feels at being outside heteronormative masculinity, the film appears "to inscribe upon the queer body the very hatred that the writer/director hopes to dismantle" (Walcott 1997, 65). For example, after the beating, Jordan is presented in a number of long and medium shots as he takes out his anger on a punching bag. Later, he viciously spars with his close friend, Curtis. The sequence, visually reminiscent of the gay man's beating in the park, is composed of a series of short images filmed in slow motion and connected by the use of fades. In particular, the medium shots of Curtis reeling from furious head and body blows link his beating to that of the gay man's and are indicative of Jordan's self-hatred. In addition, a long shot taken from ringside shows Jordan taunting a woozy Curtis to continue, echoing the taunts hurled at the gay man prior to the commencement of the beating. The significance of the sparring session is revealed in a later scene set in the locker room when Jordan apologizes to Curtis for letting things get out of hand. Portrayed in a medium two shot, they sit on benches facing each other as Curtis removes Jordan's gloves. The camera slowly dollies in as Curtis removes the wrapping from Jordan's left hand, which was injured during the beating of the gay man. The camera movement intensifies the feeling of intimacy created by Curtis's tender handling of Jordan's injury, a closeness that prompts Jordan to first touch Curtis's face and then exchange a brief kiss and embrace. The exact meaning of the gesture is left somewhat ambiguous: although Curtis does not pull away and returns the kiss, he quickly goes back to the business of treating Jordan's injury without

CHAPTER 9

either of them commenting on what has just happened between them. Thus, although both feel an attraction to one another, it is still undeclared and, ultimately, remains a closeted act.

At this point in the discussion, it is worthwhile considering how these three story strands contribute to notions of black Canadian identities. One of the unusual aspects of the film is that ethnicity is only openly coupled with blackness in Rude's raps, where a diversity of cultural backgrounds are evident in the accents of the callers into the program. The ethnicities of Maxine, Jordan, and Luke, however, are never explicitly broached by the film, resulting in a homogeneity among the characters that refuses reading within a narrow construct. Walcott argues that the film's obsession "with the properties of producing and explicating a 'correct' black masculinity" results in a failure to advance beyond "a moralizing conservative politic" (1997, 60, 66). Although Walcott's comments are certainly salient, the extent of Virgo's "failure" is actually dependent on the degree to which one believes that he should be held to a specific type of political expression. Ultimately, however, *Rude* does stake out a central, normative position of black experience through the character of Luke that, in effect, relegates the depictions of both Maxine and Jordan to the margins of the narrative structure.

Luke's story strand is the most developed of the three, occupying more screen time than those of Maxine and Jordan. It is also the most complex: the central action involves Luke's attempts to reconnect with Jessica and his son, Johnny, as well as subplots encompassing his brother, Reese, a wannabe drug dealer, and Luke's old employer, Yankee, a white drug supplier. Having just been released from prison, Luke faces the economic difficulties of reestablishing his life and must ultimately make what is essentially a "moral" decision concerning the tempting possibility of resolving these problems by resuming his occupation as a drug dealer (Walcott 1997, 60). Cast within the conventions of the so-called hood film genre, Luke's struggle links questions of black masculinity to issues of economic deprivation and its impact on the cohesiveness of the black family unit. As Walcott argues, this has become a stereotypical construct within the genre, based on the contention that the social disintegration of black communities is linked to racism and the resulting impoverishment that prevents black males from adequately supporting their families without resorting to crime (60). Luke's character, articulated within the framework of fatherhood, initially seems to reflect this stereotype. In this circumstance, however, Luke's criminal behavior is not cast as an act of defiance against an oppressive society as is the case with many hood genre films. Instead, Virgo goes beyond simply reiterating "the virulent strain of anti-Black racism in Canada" and seeks instead to ask the complex question of whether resorting to such violent lifestyles actually implies collusion with, versus a defiance of, the systemic devaluation of black Canadians (Foster 1996, 7). Hence, as imperfect as Virgo's strategy may be, it is precisely because this is a moral choice that Luke's character deconstructs the stereotypical depiction of black masculinity.

Luke's story strand possesses, to a degree, a thesis/antithesis structure where other characters represent the extremes of the moral continuum in which Luke's choice must be made. For example, Jessica, the mother of Luke's child, is a policewoman and hence representative of the very societal authority that imprisoned Luke in the first place. Jessica signifies the values of a silent majority for, as Foster argues, "despite the very obvious macho attempts by some members of the black community to appear to be *different*, nobody can deny that most of us in the black community are law abiding and want the same successes as the wider community" (1996, 68). Jessica is portrayed as a positive force through her belief in law and order and her commitment to providing a stable home environment for her son, based on mainstream mores such as a strong work ethic and respect for social institutions. This places her character in moral opposition to the values underpinning the drug world. Her position as a good black woman is further advanced by the fact that her visual presentation does not generally possess the type of sexualized fragmentation used to portray Maxine and Rude, who are both objects of desire framed predominantly for a male gaze. For example, the visual depictions of Rude delivering her often sexually charged raps take place alone in the limbo space of a room, an apartment, or a studio and frequently contain extreme close-ups sexualizing such physical attributes as her mouth. Similarly, the video clips of Maxine objectify her physical beauty from Andre's perspective. In contrast, Jessica and Luke are often portrayed in medium two-shots, physically positioned with similar screen space and character blocking,

CHAPTER 9

suggesting they are equals in the relationship. Medium two-shots also predominate in the scene where Jessica and Luke make love, emphasizing both male and female pleasure. Such a departure places Jessica in a very different category of female experience and valorizes the heteronormative values presented by her relationship with Luke.

Although Jessica is generally associated with what might be termed as positive mainstream norms, hers is not a totally stable position. At issue here is her relationship with Luke's brother Reese and the role he has played in Luke's absence. It is clear from evidence provided by the narrative that Jessica is both well aware of Reese's drug dealing and yet has continued to encourage a relationship between him and her son. This intimacy is clearly indicated during a scene at night when Reese arrives looking for Luke and appears in the doorway of the bedroom, disturbing Jessica's sleep. She invites him in and he sits on the edge of the bed as they converse. During the conversation, Reese hands her some money to give to Luke, which Jessica does not refuse outright, stating only that she will not ask where it came from. Her warning that she will arrest him if she catches him, however, indicates that she is very aware of his criminal activities. She adds that she will not tolerate Luke becoming involved in drug dealing again, implying that Reese is not to entice him back in. What is striking, however, is her failure to ban him from the premises unless he cleans up his own life or issue a directive telling him to stay away from her family. Instead, the scene ends with the two of them embracing, indicating affection for one another. Jessica's continued acceptance of Reese's presence in her family's life decenters her as an arbiter of positive social values by demonstrating the inherent contradictions faced when balancing competing imperatives within the black community.

Luke's white ex-boss, Yankee, represents the opposite side of the moral spectrum. A cruel and predatory man, Yankee is first introduced in a scene that begins with two medium shots of the anthropological drawings of Africans adorning the wall of his space. In addition, in the foreground of one of these shots are objects of African art that, taken in conjunction with the loosely framed medium close-up of Yankee that follows where spotlighting on the wall behind him illuminates a collection of African masks, clearly connect Yankee to slavery and colonialism. Yankee's collection of African art therefore signifies how "the

Discourses of Blackness in *Rude*

operationalization of power on bodies to mark, discipline, and control can be understood as enacted through the very enslavement of [black] bodies" (Walcott 1997, 54). This connection is strengthened in a later scene when Junior, a young black man who owes Yankee money, asks for a drug fix on credit. Yankee's response is to stick the syringe into another of his employees who is potentially infected with HIV and mix his blood with the drugs. Depicted in a series of canted two-shots that emphasize his physical control of Junior, Yankee draws Junior in close and puts the needle to the side of his neck, asking him if he is sure that he wants it. When, in desperation, Junior says yes repeatedly, Yankee empties the contaminated syringe into him and shoves him aside contemptuously. Yankee's casual debasement of Junior demonstrates that he regards the black men in his employ as less than human, using their "bodies as machines" or "as a blank canvas to be written on and inscribed with the desires of the master" (Walcott 1997, 54). In addition, the portrayal of Yankee as a predatory enslaver of black men attempts to demystify some of the glamour attached to the drug business by popular music and media: trapped by his addiction and exploited for profit by Yankee, Junior presents a strong counterargument to the notion that dealing drugs leads to power and economic freedom.[8]

However broadly drawn Yankee's villainy is, Virgo does not overlook questions of individual responsibility for, or complicity with, this new form of slavery. These questions are played out against the backdrop of Luke's relationship with his son, John. For example, in a scene that takes place after Jessica leaves for work, Luke attempts to bond with John. Character blocking places them on either side of a kitchen table that visually accentuates the awkward emotional gulf between them as John asks, matter-of-factly, where Luke has been. Luke's uncomfortable reply that he was in jail is countered by John's acknowledgement that he has known all along, having been told by Reese. In addition, John's statement that he was only pretending not to know indicates that he has been well aware of the attempts to shield him from the consequence of Luke's drug dealing. This suggests that despite the best efforts of the adults involved to protect him, John understands what is going on in the household and is affected by it. Virgo expands on this theme in a later scene, when Reese and Yankee arrive to talk about Luke returning to his old habits. After a failed attempt to make

CHAPTER 9

dinner, Luke makes John a peanut butter sandwich at the kitchen table. Virgo initially uses a long shot to depict the activity as John complains that Luke is putting on too much peanut butter, forcing Luke to scrape some off. This small action further reinforces the effects of Luke's absence as it indicates his unfamiliarity with John's likes and dislikes. As John eats and Luke watches in silence, the camera slowly dollies into a tight medium two-shot that creates a sense of shared space between the two and focuses on the emotion Luke feels in sharing this simple, commonplace moment with his child. The moment is disrupted by the arrival of Reese and Yankee, and the easy rapport that exists between John and Reese as they joke together provides a poignant counterpoint to the awkwardness between father and son. Furthermore, the relish with which John accepts the fast food Reese had brought him suggests Reese's intimate knowledge of John's tastes.

Luke's disconnection from his son is illustrated through a long shot that places Yankee, Reese, and John on one side of the room and Luke, separated by the table, on the other. John's alignment with Reese indicates the boy's admiration for an uncle with the economic wherewithal to indulge him, regardless of the source. Luke's discomfort with the situation is underscored by his terse comment to Reese, asking if he always just walked into the apartment without notice. Reese's reply that Jessica gave him a key because he looked after the boy in her absence provides further indication of his intimate role in John's life. Furthermore, when Yankee reaches over, rubs John's head and calls him, "little man," Luke responds by calling the boy over and telling him not to eat the food because it is bad for him. By drawing John away from Yankee and separating him from Reese, Luke is indicating that he wishes to keep John separated from the seductive aspects of drug culture and its predators.

Virgo restates the economic aspects of drug culture several times during the course of the film. Later in the scene described above, Yankee and Luke, now alone, discuss the possibility of Luke returning to work for him. When Luke indicates that he does not want to talk about the issue with John present in the apartment, Yankee argues that the discussion concerns John's future as well as Luke's. His comments, "I mean, you gotta make money to take care of the kid. You gonna make Reese keep doing that?" are intercut with a high-angle close-up of Luke, who is positioned on the far right of the frame, indicating a sense of entrapment. Connecting the issue to John's welfare suggests that the economic imperative of looking after his family is a very real concern for Luke. The pressure to provide materially for John is further developed in a scene that takes place as Luke, with John looking on, continues to add to the street mural he had started painting prior to going to jail. John's confession that he hates school because "everyone in school has new everything" demonstrates that John feels ostracized from his peers by virtue of his lower economic status. His dislike of the "no-name running shoes" purchased by Jessica in lieu of expensive name-brand sneakers underscores John's desire to fit in as well as the difficulty of belonging to a single-income family. The issue comes to a head when Luke allows John to get an ice cream bar from a vending cart. He is embarrassed in front of his son when he searches his pockets and is unable to come up with the money to pay for it. The fact that his ability to provide materially for John is central to his measure of his success as a man is confirmed in a scene with Jessica that takes place in their bedroom. The long take, which begins in a long shot and slowly zooms in to a medium two-shot of Luke and Jessica sitting on the bed, emphasizes Luke's anguish as he relates details of the incident to Jessica. When she tells him that she would have given him the money, Luke responds bitterly, "If I can't give him something as simple as an ice cream, what am I going to give him as a man? What am I going to give my son when he's a man? I gotta give him more than just life." The sentiments expressed by Luke underscore the film's position that drug dealing within the black community is linked to poverty and the economic difficulties faced by young black men. Jessica's reply, however, presented in a shot structure that gives her argument equal weight in the discussion, is a passionate statement that Luke has given John more than just life. Her position implies that Luke's measuring of his masculinity and his contribution as a father in terms of material wealth alone is counterproductive, as there are other far more important ways that he contributes to John's development.

Despite Jessica's assurances, Luke meets with Yankee and negotiates a return to dealing. Virgo illustrates how conflicted Luke is about this decision through a scene that takes place in front of his mural. Luke is depicted in an extreme high-angle shot, leaning against the wall, star-

Rude (Courtesy of The Feature Film Project; photography by Michael Gibson)

Discourses of Blackness in *Rude*

ing down at the ground. In a restatement of the lion motif established at the beginning of the film, the lion walks toward him from a pool of light, disappearing into darkness immediately in front of him. This fantasy sequence suggests that Luke must draw on inner strength in order to fight the temptations of Babylon. Virgo then cuts to a shot of Luke standing on the corner in the rain. A customer approaches him and asks what he has for sale. When Luke does not reply, the customer becomes increasingly agitated, and finally demands, "Are you a dealer or aren't you a dealer?" Luke, portrayed in a medium long shot on the left of the frame with the mural behind him, faces his customer and says, "No. I'm not." The juxtaposition of these two sequences suggests that Luke has drawn on the lion inside of himself to repudiate drug culture once and for all. Virgo develops this premise further in a scene where Luke comes upon Reese in the stairwell doing drugs. Reese, stoned and furious at having been displaced by Luke's return to both Jessica's life and Yankee's operation, pulls a gun on Luke. Luke's demand that Reese put the gun down because "Yankee has your head all fucked up" leads to a struggle for the weapon. Reese backs Luke into a corner, the gun under his jaw, and fires the empty weapon repeatedly as he backs up. As Reese tosses him the gun, then sits back down on the landing to resume preparing his drugs for consumption, Luke, depicted in a medium close-up, stares down at Reese and asks, "When are we going to grow up, Reese? When do we become men?" Luke's question indicates more than the adoption of a new model of black masculinity, it also indicates that Reese mirrors the fate that Luke would have met had he chosen to return to dealing. Hence the valorization of drug culture, for all its promise of economic freedom, is ultimately portrayed as a self-destructive expression of black masculinity. Luke's actions support this view: after Jessica throws him out because she believes that he is dealing, Luke confronts Yankee by throwing his money at him and saying, "You're looking for a nigger. I'm not a dealer." The statement implies that by believing that the only way to advance in Babylon's society is through criminalized activity, black individuals are complicit in creating and perpetuating the devaluation of self promoted by systemic racism. Thus, by refusing the characterization of "dealer," Luke is rejecting the stereotypical role perpetuated by white society.

CHAPTER 9

The climaxes of the story threads suggest that making difficult but constructive individual choices are instrumental in redefining the empowerment of black selves. For example, Maxine destroys the mannequins in her loft, thereby disengaging from preconceived images of who and what she should be. The act, representing a breakdown of her previous identity, allows her to begin redefining herself on her own terms as a black woman. Jordan returns to the scene of the assault and allows himself to be beaten by his victim as a means of penance for his own violence. Although intended as an action to redress Jordan's self-hatred, the act also serves to reinforce a negative connection between self-shame, violence, and homosexuality as his victim in turn victimizes Jordan. Finally, Luke's climax is the most complex: Yankee, having picked up John who was wandering the streets upset at Luke's departure, forces a violent confrontation with Luke on the street in front of his mural. Depicted in a long shot, Luke is positioned on the left side of the frame with a gun to Yankee's head. Yankee, on the right, threatens John with a gun, as he tells Luke that he ought to kill John, saving him the trouble of being shot at twenty. He also suggests that Luke is a fool for believing that he will be able to support John on his own: John is destined, like Luke himself, to become a "dead-end nigger." The scale of the shot allows the spectator to consider the weight of Yankee's commentary. This is visually reinforced by the physical blocking of the scene in which a chain of violence is created as Luke points a gun at Yankee who, in turn, points a gun at John. This suggests that drug violence is a self-fulfilling process that ultimately travels from adult to youth, perpetuating its self-destructive effects on the black community. The standoff is resolved by Jessica's intervention as she empties her gun into Yankee, killing him and saving her family.

Given this context, it is well worth considering the film's position on the issue of what constitutes constructive identities in the black community. The solution to this question lies in the resolution of the film, which does not promote a single, monolithic answer but suggests instead that each individual must take responsibility for her or his life and defeat Babylon according to circumstances specific to her or him. The resolution, signaled by a swell of spiritual music, begins with a long shot depicting Luke, Jessica, and John huddled together in an embrace. The portrayal of a black family unit restored by the death of their oppressor suggests that difficult decisions must be made and actions undertaken in order to resist Babylon's enticements. Thus, Yankee's destruction signifies the ending of disharmony and the establishment of a new order for Luke and his family that reinscribes their identities within "a dignified Black humanity" (Gittings 2002, 261). The position is reified as the resolution progresses, and Rude's face is revealed for the first time in a close-up that portrays her in the center of the frame, thus signaling the restoration of "the fragmented, criminalized body of the community" (257). She comments, "We just heard trumpets disguised as gunshots singing us home. So all aboard the mother ship for those who want a chance at rebirth," thus framing the film as a cautionary tale in which the violence and the oppression of Babylon can only be overcome by making a conscious choice to refuse the constraints of that racist society. This is subsequently reflected in the way in which Maxine and Jordan confront the aftermath of their actions. In Maxine's case, she faces the future alone in her loft amid the ruin of the present. Collapsed on the floor in a sort of numb despair, she is approached by the spirit of her unborn child who holds out her hand to her. As Maxine takes it and rises to her feet, the child smiles, signaling affirmation for Maxine's decision to have an abortion, however much regret she may feel. The results of Jordan's actions are less defined: portrayed alone in a slow-motion long shot, he boxes in the ring, facing the camera. As he is positioned to return the spectator's gaze, it is possible to infer he has faced his homosexuality, but the composition stops short of confirming that he has embraced it. In addition, the length of the shot distances the spectator from Jordan's emotional state, thus reinforcing a certain ambiguity in regard to the specific type of accommodation Jordan has made. The openness of his physical position and his continued pursuit of the sport he loves, however, suggests that Jordan is prepared to continue to fight for his own place within the community.

Critics such as John McCullough have argued that the film *Rude* is "wholly mute on the concept of revolution" (1999, 23).[9] Although revolutionary rhetoric is not foregrounded as an explicit ideological underpinning, the film certainly challenges black individuals to consider the impact of personal decisions on the quality of life within black communities. Furthermore, Rude's final words, which issue an SOS to members of black communities, may be read as a call to continue debate

CHAPTER 9

beyond the screen space. Linked to Canada as a colonial nation through a visual restatement of the Ojibway dancer at the beginning of the film and a final image of the lion, the film advances the establishment of a continuing challenge to Babylon through individual action. Far from a politically neutral ideology, *Rude* reinscribes black subjectivity within a human context that refuses continued self-degradation in a racist society (Gittings 2002, 261). Thus, *Rude*'s valorization of individual choice as a means of community empowerment reflects a profound commitment to revolution intended to decenter the values of Babylon.

NOTES

Introduction

1. I borrow the term *contact zones* from James Clifford as a means of describing the way in which different experiences of the black diaspora are constituted in transcultural contexts.

2. I borrow the term *world-sense* from Oyèrónké Oyěwùmí (1997, 3), who advocates its use as a more "inclusive way of describing the conception of the world by different cultural groups."

Chapter 1

1. For a more detailed discussion, see Countryman (1999), 3–13. As Countryman notes, the North Atlantic slave trade stretched from Montreal to Buenos Aires and "amounted to 9,566,000 people, the largest forced migration in all history," with 4,700,000 taken to South America, 4,040,000 to the West Indies, and 399,000 (roughly 10 percent) to the British and American colonies (4).

2. These three are distinguished as follows: *kin-based slavery* was used to increase labor; *pawnship* generally involved girls whose labor reduced the debts of their fathers or male kin; and *clientage* concerned mostly autonomous individuals who owed labor or a share of crops and political loyalty to free persons or kin (Robertson 1996, 6–7).

3. For a more detailed discussion, see Thornton (1992), 72–97.

4. It should be noted that some schools of Afrocentrism prefer the term "Africentrism." For the purposes of clarity, however, I use Asante's original term, "Afrocentrism."

5. Asante was born Arthur Lee Smith and changed his name to Molefi Kete Asante in 1972 after a visit to Ghana. For more detailed information, see Howe (1999), 230–39.

6. Elmina Castle (called "São Jorge da Mina" [Saint George's of the mine], or simply "Elmina" [the mine]), was one of the first of many slave-trading

NOTES TO CHAPTER 2

posts built by Europeans along the west coast of Africa. Elmina Castle passed through many owners during the course of the slave trade, including the Portuguese, English and Dutch. By the eighteenth century, thirty thousand slaves passed through Elmina each year on their way to the Americas. See the Elmina Castle page at the *Africans in America* web site (Public Broadcasting Service, n.d.). See also Kandé (1998).

7. For a more detailed critique of *Sankofa*'s Afrocentric focus, see Kandé (1998).

8. In many African cultures, the word *griot* is used to describe praise singers who sing the accomplishments of a patron's ancestors. This word has come to have a specific meaning, however, in African cinema, where filmmakers are often described as griots because films create "a 'living' record that could be 'recited' in the future" as a means of preserving tradition (Tomaselli and Eke 1995, 62).

9. Akan is a language group that includes the Twi, Fante, Asante, Ashona, Akim, and Juaben cultures. Grayson argues that Nunu is from the Asante people, based on imagery used in a chant she performs during a secret society initiation (1998, 220–21).

10. The inclusion of the monument in the montage is a direct reference to Afrocentrism and Asante's belief, shared with African philosopher Cheikh Anta Diop, "that until Africa reclaims its ancient civilizations of the Nile Valley and reconnects them to the rest of Africa as Europe connects itself to its classical civilizations of Greece and Rome, we will remain children to the rest of the world" (Asante 1993, 47).

Chapter 2

1. Although the title, *Rue cases-nègres*, has been translated as *Black Shack Alley* in the case of the novel, the translated title of *Sugar Cane Alley* is generally used in reference to the film. I retain that distinction here for clarity.

2. The term *béké* denotes an indigenous individual of all-white heritage in the French Caribbean. See, e.g., Hoetink (1986), 69; Herndon (1996); and Giraud (1995), 79.

3. I am indebted to Sada Niang for an e-mail discussion on this subject, which took place on March 31, 2005. In part, Niang points out that Martinique itself may be regarded as the castle because "one may not get out of it (the castle of Martinique) without the blessing of its owner (France), and only through a bridge across water (boat or plane)."

4. These phrases, which are reflective of African oral tradition, indicate the interactive nature of storytelling in Caribbean societies. The storyteller "initiates the performance by shouting 'Krik?' to which the audience, if it is in the mood to witness a performance, answers 'Krak!'" (Cham 1992, 285n2).

Chapter 3

1. The term *black women's discourses* is used here to indicate a broad category of different discourses dedicated to the exploration of black women's experiences by black diasporic thinkers and writers. To use a more specific term in this context, such as *black womanist, Africana Womanism,* or *black feminism,* is to mistakenly conflate the broad range of discussion that is still unfolding in these very separate and distinct conceptions of black women's experiences.

2. Carole Boyce Davies argues that "historically there have been few avenues for the full hearing of black women's testimonies," citing a broad range of influences from institutionalized racism, "white male paranoia," and even lack of support from black women themselves (1995, 4, 6). For a more detailed discussion, see Boyce Davies (1995), 3–14.

3. bell hooks points out that Western feminism's model of subjectivity was predicated on the struggles of "college-educated, white women who were compelled by sexist conditioning to remain in the home" (1984, 2). This denied the existence of "all non-white women and poor white women" (2). For a detailed examination of this issue, see hooks (1984), 1–15.

4. As Hudson-Weems points out, *Africana Womanism* should not be confused with Alice Walker's *Black Womanism,* which reflects a preference for women's culture (1994, 22–23). For more information on the distinction, see Hudson-Weems (1994), 22–24.

5. Sojourner Truth began life as a slave in New York State and was given the name Isabella (Mabee 1993, ix). As Carleton Mabee notes, after she achieved freedom, she renamed herself Sojourner Truth and, "in the period before and after the Civil War, she became a national figure in the struggle for the liberation of both blacks and women" (ix). One of her most famous speeches, titled, "Ar'n't I a Woman?" was given in Akron, Ohio, in 1851 to a convention of predominantly white suffragettes (67–68). For a more detailed discussion, see Mabee (1993), 67–82.

6. Hudson-Weems argues that an Africana Womanist must be committed to eighteen precepts: self-naming, self-defining, family-centered, genuine in sisterhood, strong, in concert with males in struggle, whole, authentic, a flexible role-player, respected, recognized, spiritual, male compatible, respectful of elders, adaptable, ambitious, mothering, and nurturing (1994, 143). For a more detailed explanation, see Hudson-Weems (1994), 55–74.

7. As Kly notes, by the eighteenth century, "we can use the term 'Gullah' to represent the whole of the imported African population in the regions of South Carolina, Georgia and Florida" (1998, 20).

8. Kly argues that "African involvement [is] not merely . . . a constituent factor in what has been called the Seminole Wars," suggesting that Gullah involvement "can be viewed as part of an ongoing resistance of captured and

NOTES TO CHAPTER 4

enslaved Africans to the institution of slavery" (1998, 20, 21). For example, the Gullah supplied leaders and, in addition, were aligned "through family ties" to "many of the most celebrated Indian leaders" in the conflict (22).

9. This phenomenon has been well documented in previous essays on this film. For example, Lene Brøndum notes that the character of Bilal Muhammed, "the Muslim Sea Islander and member of the extended Peazant family," is based on a nineteenth-century individual who "could not have been a 55-year-old man in 1902" (1999, 155). According to Brøndum, Dash includes Muhammed in order to "present an historical explanation for the existence of Islam in African American culture" (155).

10. Gwendolyn Audrey Foster argues that "Dash began appropriating and refashioning classical soviet montage techniques into her own unique approach to time, space, and the body.... The pacing of the film, which is leisurely and freed of conventions of time and space, is not unlike that of African films" (1997, 68). Furthermore, this experience provided her with the aesthetic grounding necessary to advance beyond Russian montage to a unique expression of "Afrocentric aesthetics" (Dash, quoted in Baker 1992, 157–58).

11. The strongest examples of male oppression are reflected by the fact that both Eula and Yellow Mary have been raped by white men.

12. As Dash explains, "The bottle trees, positioned outside of the Peazants' shanty, were for protection—protection from malevolent or evil spirits. It's my understanding that each bottle would represent a deceased family member or ancestor. The spirits would radiate goodwill, protection, and luck upon the family's house" (Dash 1992, 43).

13. According to Dash, Eula's description of the events at Ibo Landing is a cinematic reworking of a passage from Paule Marshall's 1983 novel *Praisesong for the Widow* (Dash, quoted in Baker 1992, 164).

14. The image of the figurehead has important ideological implications for Dash. She was inspired by first seeing a similar figurehead from a slave ship in an art gallery. The notion that slaves, boarding the ship, would see this image of themselves tied to the prow, encapsulates the horror of slavery (Baker 1992, 164–65).

Chapter 4

1. Other examples of this exchange process are given in later chapters. For example, chapter 5 touches on the influence of Marcus Garvey and W. E. B. DuBois on the Ghanaian leader Kwame Nkrumah. In chapter 7, black British filmmaker Isaac Julien confronts and redefines the works of the Martinican theorist Frantz Fanon.

2. The connection to Senghor creates a link between DuBois and Africa,

as Senghor would become "the first president of the West African nation of Senegal" (Benjamin, 2002, 6). Furthermore, DuBois attended the Pan-African Congress of 1900 in London, where he gave a groundbreaking speech on the need for establishing equal rights for all black peoples from Africa across the black diaspora (107, 108).

3. One of the primary and crucial differences that set slavery apart from colonization is the forced migration of individuals, which totally destroyed cultural connections. Another significant difference is the total dehumanization of individuals as commodities to be sold or traded like farm stock. Thus, although certain aspects of alienation and exploitation are held in common between slavery and colonization, they are not equivalent states.

4. I selected the term *postcolonial* because of its widespread use in current literature. There is considerable debate, however, over its use as a theoretical construct. As Adrian Fielder asserts, the term "falsely posits a teleological movement somehow 'beyond' or 'after' any problematics of colonial domination—and therefore fails to describe a global system which might be more accurately qualified (according to some observers) as 'neocolonial'" (1999).

5. Hargreaves and McKinney argue that *"francisation* [Frenchification] occurs in contemporary France's urban milieux" (1997, 17).

6. A further parallel to double-consciousness can also be drawn. As Benjamin argues, DuBois's work demonstrates "a grasp of how few white Americans have ever believed in the universal humanism voiced in the Declaration of Independence" (2002, 53). In other words, in both the French and American revolutions, access to equality was racially determined.

Chapter 5

1. Ghana was known as the Gold Coast until 1957 when it achieved independence. I will, however, refer to the country as Ghana throughout the chapter in order to provide consistency.

2. Basil Davidson notes that both 1909 and 1912 are given as the year in which Nkrumah was born. For further discussion, see Davidson (1973), 19.

3. The breadth of opinion on Nkrumah ranges from most laudatory to most deprecating. See, in particular, Davidson (1973); Omari (1970); and James (1977b).

4. According to members of the military junta that overthrew Nkrumah, he had amassed large personal assets in Swiss and Ghanaian banks. See, in particular, Davidson (1973).

5. For example, Akomfrah's mother worked as a C.P.P. district organizer in Accra, as did his father until his death in 1966. See Ofori (1990), 625.

6. This represents another autobiographical element, as Akomfrah's fam-

ily belongs to the Ga cultural group and the elements reflecting Ga history are drawn from this context. See Ofori (1990), 625.

7. The film is subtitled *The War Zone of Memories.*

8. The full name of the Institute is Kwame Nkrumah Institute of Ideological Studies. See Simon Baynham (1988), 140.

9. *Nkrumahism* and its allied concept *consciencism*, are described by Baynham as "vacuous" and by Omari as a "vast catch-all, an indiscriminate hotchpotch of sadly familiar concepts" (Baynham 1988, 151n41; Omari 1970, 122). It may be most appropriate, however, to let the theory speak for itself. See Nkrumah (1964).

10. Rashid's revelation that he heard the news on the radio is another example of how Akomfrah interweaves historical fact with *Testament's* fiction as the success of the coup was first formally announced by a radio broadcast at six a.m. that morning (Baynham 1988, 183).

11. Akomfrah is alluding to the continued dispute concerning the role of the United States and other powers in colluding with the military and Nkrumah's downfall (Baynham 1988, 210).

12. Water, in all of its forms, plays an important role in traditional Ga culture as it serves to "mediate relations between man and the gods, between the living and the dead, between the known and unknown" (Parker 2000, 21). Sakumo is a warlike lagoon god and a source of ritual knowledge and power (21).

Chapter 6

1. There are several spellings of this acronym; MEISON is the one most commonly found, but ME'ISON and Mei'sone are also used. See, e.g., Donham (1999), 131; Spencer (1987), 350; and Halliday and Molyneux (1981), 121.

Chapter 7

1. A feature-length (seventy minutes) version of the film is available in the United Kingdom through Normal Films. The version analyzed in this chapter is the fifty-minute television version distributed by California Newsreel in the United States. Julien and Nash write that *Frantz Fanon: Black Skin, White Mask* "originated as a contribution to the 1995 'Mirage' exhibition and conference at the Institute of Contemporary Art, London, curated by David Bailey" (2000, 110n2).

2. The first two images are of patients Fanon will encounter during his psychiatric practice in Algeria. The doorway will be associated with Fanon's early life in Martinique, symbolizing Julien's action of opening Fanon's text up for rereading.

3. The Algerian Revolution (1954–62) is considered one of the most significant post–World War II anticolonial struggles in Africa. The roots of this revolution were the social conditions and economic exploitation of the Algerian people at the hands of the French. Conquered in 1830, Algeria was considered by France to be part of its colonial empire, and a minority French population controlled 90 percent of the industrial and economic activity in the country as well as the most prosperous agricultural areas. The liberation struggle, widely supported by villagers, involved guerilla attacks against all levels of the colonial regime. The FLN was solidly backed in the Casbah, the working-class area of Algiers, a zone forbidden to imperialist forces. By 1960, massive demonstrations swept Algeria, demanding independence from France, which was ultimately attained in 1962 (McCartan 2001).

4. The narration is drawn from chapter 2, "The Woman of Color and the White Man," in *Black Skin, White Masks* (Fanon 1982).

5. For a full discussion of this point, see Fanon (1982), 202–3.

6. Although not necessary for a rich viewing experience, knowledge of Fanon's work can expose deeper layers of meaning in Julien's documentary. For example, the Algerian patient and the French military officer's first-person accounts are taken directly from the case histories of patients offered in Fanon's *The Wretched of the Earth* as a means of illustrating the relationship between colonial war and mental disorders (Fanon 1963, 261–70).

Chapter 8

1. The conspiracy was led by Makandal, a charismatic maroon, who was eventually captured and executed in 1758. His rebellion represented the first widespread attempt to establish black rule in Haiti, and it served as an important precedent in subsequent struggles for freedom in Haiti (Rey 1998, 342).

2. This character is referred to by two names in the film. Prior to his torture by the tonton-makout, the character is referred to as Sorel. After this incident, according to Sarah's narration, he is given the name Gracieux by the town.

3. It is worthwhile considering how Peck's depiction of Sarah differs significantly from Palcy's portrayal of José in *Sugar Cane Alley* (chapter 2). Although José is undeniably affected by the cultural politics of slavery, his childhood, for all its poverty, has an idyllic cast. In contrast, the political violence in Sarah's childhood has an overt effect on her persona because she is a direct subject of Janvier's terrorism and, by extension, a victim of Duvalier's regime. José's oppression seems surmountable through education, as long as he maintains an effective relationship with his African origin, allowing for a blending of European and African cultures. In Sarah's case, however, African origin is not at issue, although the internalized oppression of slavery certainly is. Thus, Sarah

NOTES TO CHAPTER 9

must negotiate the dangers of a racially striated society as an active participant and, unlike José, will find no easy solution or idealism at hand.

Chapter 9

1. It is generally conceded that the first free black person to set foot on Canadian soil was Mathieu da Costa who arrived in 1605 in the employ of Pierre de Gua des Monts, a French entrepreneur. Da Costa also served as a navigator and interpreter of English, French, and Micmac for Samuel de Champlain, who helped found Port Royal in Nova Scotia in the early 1600s (Alexander and Glaze 1996, 38; Mensah 2002, 44).

2. For further discussion on Antillanité, see chapter 2.

3. For further discussion of the Rastafarian Movement, see Clarke (1988).

4. Clarke has also described Babylon as "accused of the heinous crimes of slavery and exploitation which brought about the degradation and humiliation of black people" (1988, 69).

5. Furthermore, the use of fire as an image seems to metaphorically connect the narrative to the legend of Shadrach, Meshach, and Abednego, three men cast into a furnace by King Nebuchadnezzar of Babylon. In this legend, which is popularly told in Jamaica, the three individuals triumph over the king because their faith protects them from the flames. Purgation by fire plays a significant role in Rasta belief as the cleanser of blood, a metaphor closely related to the belief that the Rastas have been cast into the "wretched cities" of Babylon in order to "to come forth, unscathed by flame" (Hausman 1997, 85, 86). This notion is particularly evident in terms of Luke's introduction. For more information, see Hausman (1997).

6. Virgo implies that Maxine and Andre's relationship is long-standing by the fact that he removes the furniture from the loft while Maxine sleeps off a drunk. Jordan's shame concerning his homosexuality is evident in his close-up reaction shots during a scene in which he showers with the other boxers. In a conversation with the mother of his child, Jessica, Luke displays despair at the fact he cannot support his son, suggesting an economic motivation for his drug dealing.

7. For a full discussion of his concerns, see Walcott (1997), 53–69.

8. Walcott offers an interesting alternative reading of this scene, taking into account "the reality of HIV/AIDS and the various ways in which it crosscuts communities" (1997, 67). Arguing that Virgo has not anticipated how his parallel story strands might be read together, Walcott suggests that "even when intravenous drugs are a part of the story, the underlying subtext remains one of a queer culpability" (68).

9. Walcott shares this vision of *Rude* by asserting that "*Rude* fails to produce a politically transfigurative moment" (1997, 59). It is not a position with-

NOTES TO CHAPTER 9

out challenge, however. George Elliott Clarke, for example, takes Walcott and others to task when he points out that the "African-Canadian conservatism" reflected in the social politics of the film might be more correctly viewed as a contemporary expression of the "conservatism" that, alongside more radical black nationalism, "has always influenced African-Canadian life" (2002, 199).

BIBLIOGRAPHY

Adeleke, Tunde. 1998. "Black Americans and Africa: A Critique of the Pan-African and Identity Paradigms." *International Journal of African Historical Studies* 31, no. 3:505–36.

Alessandrini, Anthony C. 1999. "Introduction: Fanon Studies, Cultural Studies, Cultural Politics." In *Frantz Fanon: Critical Perspectives*, edited by Anthony C. Alessandrini, 1–17. London and New York: Routledge.

Alexander, Ken, and Avis Glaze. 1996. *Towards Freedom: The African-Canadian Experience*. Toronto: Umbrella Press.

Appiah, Kwame Anthony. 1986. "The Uncompleted Argument: DuBois and the Illusion of Race." In *"Race," Writing, and Difference*, edited by Henry Louis Gates Jr. and Kwame Anthony Appiah, 21–37. London and Chicago: University of Chicago Press.

Appiah, Kwame Anthony. 1997. "Europe Upside Down: Fallacies of the New Afrocentrism." In *Perspectives on Africa: A Reader in Culture, History, and Representation*, edited by Roy Richard Grinker and Christopher B. Steiner, 728–31. Oxford and Cambridge, MA: Blackwell.

Arroyo, José. 1995. "The Films of Isaac Julien: Look Back and Talk Black." In *Cinemas of the Black Diaspora: Diversity, Dependency and Oppositionality*, edited by Michael T. Martin, 318–38. Detroit: Wayne State University Press.

Asante, Molefi Kete. 1985. "Afrocentricity and Culture." In *African Culture: The Rhythms of Unity*, edited by Molefi Kete Asante and Kariamu Welsh Asante, 3–12. Westport, CT: Greenwood Press.

———. 1987. *The Afrocentric Idea*. Philadelphia: Temple University Press.

———. 1988. *Afrocentricity*. Trenton, NJ: Africa World Press.

———. 1993. *Malcolm X as Cultural Hero: And Other Afrocentric Essays*. Trenton, NJ: Africa World Press.

Auguiste, Reece, and Black Audio Film Collective. 1989. "Black Independents and Third Cinema: The British Context." In *Questions of Third Cinema*, edited by Jim Pines and Paul Willemen, 212–17. London: British Film Institute.

Baker, Houston A., Jr. 1992. "Not without my *Daughters:* Interview with Julie Dash." *Transition* 57:150–66.

Barlet, Olivier. 1996. *Les cinémas d'Afrique noire: Le regard en question.* Paris: L'Harmattan.

Baynham, Simon. 1988. *The Military and Politics in Nkrumah's Ghana.* Boulder, CO, and London: Westview Press.

Beckles, Hilary. 1997. "Capitalism, Slavery, and Caribbean Modernity." *Callaloo* 20, no. 4:777–89.

Benítez-Rojo, Antonio. 1992. *The Repeating Island: The Caribbean and the Postmodern Perspective.* Translated by James E. Maraniss. Durham, NC: Duke University Press.

Benjamin, Playthell. 2002. Contributions to *Reconsidering the Souls of Black Folk: Thoughts on the Groundbreaking Classic Work of W. E. B. DuBois,* by Stanley Crouch and Playthell Benjamin, 6–68; 102–213. Philadelphia: Running Press.

Bergner, Gwen. 1995. "Who Is That Marked Woman? or, The Role of Gender in Fanon's *Black Skin, White Masks.*" *PMLA* 110, no. 1 (January): 75–88.

Berlin, Ira. 1999. "From Creole to African: Atlantic Creoles and the Origins of African-American Society in Mainland North America." In *How Did American Slavery Begin?* edited by Edward Countryman, 19–63. Boston and New York: Bedford/St. Martin's.

Bernabé, Jean, Patrick Chamoiseau, and Raphaël Confiant. 1993. *Éloge de la Créolité/In Praise of Creoleness.* Édition bilingue français/anglais. Translated by M. B. Taleb-Khyar. Paris: Gallimard. Originally published 1989.

Bhabha, Homi. 1994. *The Location of Culture.* London: Routledge.

———. 1996. "Day by Day . . . with Frantz Fanon." In *The Fact of Blackness: Frantz Fanon and Visual Representation,* edited by Alan Read, 186–205. London: Institute of Contemporary Arts; Seattle: Bay Press.

———. 1999. "Remembering Fanon: Self, Psyche, and the Colonial Condition." In *Rethinking Fanon: The Continuing Dialogue,* edited by Nigel C. Gibson, 179–96. New York: Humanity Books.

Blatt, David. 1997. "Immigrant Politics in a Republican Nation." In *Post-colonial Cultures in France,* edited by Alec G. Hargreaves and Mark McKinney, 40–55. London and New York: Routledge.

Bly, Antonio T. 1998. "Crossing the Lake of Fire: Slave Resistance during the Middle Passage, 1720–1842." *Journal of Negro History* 83, no. 3. http://jaah.asalh.net/jaah.htm.

Bobo, Jacqueline. 1995. *Black Women as Cultural Readers.* New York: Columbia University Press.

Boyce Davies, Carole. 1994. *Black Women, Writing and Identity: Migrations of the Subject.* New York: Routledge.

———. 1995. "Hearing Black Women's Voices: Transgressing Imposed Boundaries." In *Moving beyond Boundaries*, vol. 1: *International Dimensions of Black Women's Writing*, edited and introduced by Carole Boyce Davies and 'Molara Ogundipe-Leslie, 3–14. New York: New York University Press.

———. 1999. "Beyond Unicentricity: Transcultural Black Presences." *Research in African Literatures* 30, no. 2 (Summer). http://inscribe.iupress.org/loi/ral.

Brah, Avtar. 1996. *Cartographies of Diaspora: Contesting Identities*. London and New York: Routledge.

Brantlinger, Patrick. 1986. "Victorians and Africans: The Genealogy of the Myth of the Dark Continent." In *"Race," Writing, and Difference*, edited by Henry Louis Gates Jr. and Kwame Anthony Appiah, 185–222. London and Chicago: University of Chicago Press.

Brathwaite, K. 1984. *History of the Voice: The Development of Nation Language in Anglophone Caribbean Poetry*. London: New Beacon Books.

———. 1993. *Roots*. Ann Arbor: University of Michigan Press.

Britton, Celia M. 1999. *Edouard Glissant and Postcolonial Theory: Strategies of Language and Resistance*. Charlottesville and London: University Press of Virginia.

Brøndum, Lene. 1999. "'The Persistence of Tradition': The Retelling of Sea Islands Culture in Works by Julie Dash, Gloria Naylor, and Paule Marshall." In *Black Imagination and the Middle Passage*, edited by Maria Diedrich, Henry Louis Gates Jr., and Carl Pedersen, 153–63. New York and Oxford: Oxford University Press.

Brouwer, Joel R. 1995. "Repositioning: Center and Margin in Julie Dash's *Daughters of the Dust*." *African American Review* 29, no. 1 (Spring): 5–16.

Burnett, Paula. 1999. "'Where Else to Row, but Backward?' Addressing Caribbean Futures through Re-visions of the Past." *ARIEL: A Review of International English Literature* 30, no. 1 (January): 11–37.

Burton, Richard D. E. 1984. "Comment peut-on être Martiniquais? The Recent Work of Edouard Glissant." *Modern Language Review* 79 (April): 301–12.

———. 1995. "The Idea of Difference in Contemporary French West Indian Thought: In Négritude, Antillanité, Créolité." In *French and West Indian: Martinique, Guadeloupe, and French Guiana Today*, edited by Richard D. E. Burton and Fred Reno, 137–66. Charlottesville and London: University Press of Virginia.

———. 1997. *Afro-Creole: Power, Opposition, and Play in the Caribbean*. Ithaca, NY, and London: Cornell University Press.

Bush, Barbara. 1996. "Hard Labor: Women, Childbirth, and Resistance in British Caribbean Slave Societies." In *More than Chattel: Black Women and Slavery in The Americas*, edited by David Barry Gaspar and Darlene Clark Hine, 193–217. Bloomington and Indianapolis: Indiana University Press.

Busia, Abena P. A. 1997. "Preface to *Testimonies of* Exile: On Territories, Tied Tongues, and Translations." In *The Word behind Bars and the Paradox of Exile*, edited by Kofi Anyidoho, 188–200. Evanston, IL: Northwestern University Press.

Cade Bambara, Toni. 1993. "Reading the Signs, Empowering the Eye: *Daughters of the Dust* and the Black Independent Cinema Movement." In *Black American Cinema*, edited by Manthia Diawara, 118–44. New York and London: Routledge.

Campbell, Loretta. 1983. "Reinventing Our Image: Eleven Black Women Filmmakers." *Heresies* 4, no. 4:58–62.

Capécia, Mayotte. 1948. *Je suis Martiniquaise*. Paris: Editions Corréa.

Carby, Hazel. 1999. *Cultures in Babylon: Black Britain and African America*. London: Verso.

Césaire, Aimé. 1972. *Discourse on Colonialism*. Translated by Joan Pinkham. New York: Monthly Review Press.

———. 1976. "Discourse on Colonialism." In *Carifesta Forum: An Anthology of Twenty Caribbean Voices*, edited by John Hearne, 25–34. Carifesta 76. Kingston: Institute of Jamaica.

Cham, Mbye. 1992. "Introduction: Shape and Shaping of Caribbean Cinema," 1–43, and "Interview with Christian Lara," 280–85. In *Ex-Iles: Essays on Caribbean Cinema*, edited by Mbye Cham. Trenton, NJ: Africa World Press.

———. 2004. "Film and History in Africa: A Critical Survey of Current Trends and Tendencies." In *Focus on African Films*, edited by Françoise Pfaff, 48–68. Bloomington and Indianapolis: Indiana University Press.

Chambers, Iain. 1994. *Migrancy, Culture, Identity*. London: Routledge.

Chatterjee, P. 1993. *The Nation and Its Fragments: Colonial and Postcolonial Histories*. Princeton, NJ: Princeton University Press.

Clarke, George Elliott. 1998. "Contesting a Model Blackness: A Meditation on African-Canadian African Americanism, or The Structures of African Canadianité." *Essays on Canadian Writing* 63 (Spring): 1–55.

———. 2002. *Odysseys Home: Mapping African-Canadian Literature*. Toronto and Buffalo: University of Toronto Press.

Clarke, Peter B. 1988. *Black Paradise: The Rastafarian Movement*. San Bernardino, CA: Borgo Press.

Claverie, Chantal. 1998. "Aimé Césaire et la question du métissage." *Présence Africaine* 158:86–98.

Clifford, James. 1992. "Travelling Cultures." In *Cultural Studies*, edited by L. Grossberg, C. Nelson, and P. Treichler, 96–116. New York: Routledge.

———. 1994. "Diasporas." *Cultural Anthropology* 9, no. 3 (August): 302–38.

Cottenet-Hage, Madeleine. 1996. "Decolonizing Images: *Soleil O* and the Cinema of Med Hondo." In *Cinema, Colonialism, Postcolonialism: Perspectives* from the French and Francophone Worlds, edited by Dina Sherzer, 173–87. Austin: University of Texas Press.

Cottenet-Hage, Madeleine. 2004. "Images of France in Francophone African Films (1978–1998)." In *Focus on African Films*, edited by Françoise Pfaff, 107–123. Bloomington: Indiana University Press.

Countryman, Edward. 1999. "The Beginnings of American Slavery." In *How Did American Slavery Begin?* edited by Edward Countryman, 3–13. Boston and New York: Bedford/St. Martin's.

Cruz, Amanda. 2000. "Introduction." In *The Film Art of Isaac Julien*, by David Deitcher and Isaac Julien, with contributions from Amanda Cruz, edited by David Frankel vi–ix. Annandale-on-Hudson, NY: Center for Cultural Studies.

Dash, Julie, with Toni Cade Bambara and bell hooks. 1992. *Daughters of the Dust: The Making of an African American Woman's Film*. New York: New Press.

Davidson, Basil. 1973. *Black Star: A View of the Life and Times of Kwame Nkrumah*. London: Allen Lane.

Davis, Zeinabu Irene. 1995. "The Future of Black Film: The Debate Continues." In *Cinemas of the Black Diaspora: Diversity, Dependency and Oppositionality*, edited by Michael T. Martin, 449–54. Detroit: Wayne State University Press.

Dayan, Joan. 1993a. "France Reads Haiti: An Interview with René Depestre." *Yale French Studies* 83, no. 2:136–53.

———. 1993b. "France Reads Haiti: René Depestre's *Hadriana dans tous mes rêves*," *Yale French Studies* 83, no. 2:154–75.

———. 1995. "Codes of Law and Bodies of Color." *New Literary History* 26, no. 2:283–308.

———. 1996. "Paul Gilroy's Slaves, Ships, and Routes: The Middle Passage as Metaphor." *Research in African Literatures* 27, no. 4 (Winter). http://inscribe.iupress.org/loi/ral.

Depestre, René. 1976. "Problems of Identity for the Black Man in the Caribbean." In *Carifesta Forum: An Anthology of Twenty Caribbean Voices*, edited by John Hearne, 61–67. Carifesta 76. Kingston: Institute of Jamaica.

Diawara, Manthia. 1999. "The 'I' Narrator in Black Diaspora Documentary." In *Struggles for Representation: African American Documentary Film and Video*, edited by Phyllis R. Klotman and Janet K. Cutler, 315–28. Bloomington and Indianapolis: Indiana University Press.

Diop, Cheikh Anta. 1974. *The African Origin of Civilization*. Westport, CT: Lawrence Hill.

———. 1978. *Cultural Unity of Black Africa*. Chicago: Third World Press.

———. 1987. *Precolonial Black Africa*. Westport, CT: Lawrence Hill.

Donham, Donald L. 1999. *Marxist Modern: An Ethnographic History of the Ethiopian Revolution.* Berkeley and Los Angeles: University of California Press; Oxford: James Curry.

DuBois, W. E. B. 1994. *The Souls of Black Folk.* New York: Dover. Originally published 1903.

Edwards, Norval (Nadi). 1994. "Roots, and Some Routes Not Taken: A Caribcentric Reading of the Black Atlantic." *Found Object* 4 (Fall): 27–35.

Ellerson, Beti. 2000. *Sisters of the Screen: Women of Africa on Film, Video, and Television.* Trenton, NJ: Africa World Press.

Ellis, Jack C., and Virginia Wright Wexman. 2002. *A History of Film.* 5th ed. Boston, MA: Allyn & Bacon.

Erhart, Julia. 1996. "Picturing *What If:* Julie Dash's Speculative Fiction." *Camera Obscura* 38 (May): 116–31.

Fanon, Frantz. 1963. *The Wretched of the Earth.* New York: Grove Press.

Fanon, Frantz. 1982. *Black Skin, White Masks.* Translated by Charles Lam Markmann. Evergreen ed. New York: Grove Press.

Farred, Grant. 1996. "You Can Go Home Again, You Just Can't Stay: Stuart Hall and the Caribbean Diaspora." *Research in African Literatures* 27, no. 4 (Winter). http://inscribe.iupress.org/loi/ral.

Fielder, Adrian. 1999. "The Politics of Reading the 'Postnational': Hybridity and Neocolonial Critique in Djibril Diop Mambéty's *Hyènes.*" *Jouvert: Journal of Post-colonial Studies* 3, no. 3. http://social.chass.ncsu.edu/jouvert/v3i3/fielde.htm.

Foster, Cecil. 1996. *A Place Called Heaven: The Meaning of Being Black in Canada.* Toronto: HarperCollins.

Foster, Gwendolyn Audrey. 1997. *Women Filmmakers of the African and Asian Diaspora: Decolonizing the Gaze, Locating Subjectivity.* Carbondale: Southern Illinois University Press.

Fusco, Coco. 1988. *Young, British and Black: The Work of Sankofa and Black Audio Film Collective.* Buffalo, NY: Hallwalls/Contemporary Arts Center.

———. 1995. "Black Filmmaking in Britain's Workshop Section." In *Cinemas of the Black Diaspora: Diversity, Dependency and Oppositionality,* edited by Michael T. Martin, 305–17. Detroit: Wayne State University Press.

Fuss, Diana. 1994. "Interior Colonies: Frantz Fanon and the Politics of Identification." *Diacritics* 24, nos. 2–3 (Summer–Fall): 20–42.

Garvey, Marcus. 1968. *Philosophy and Opinions of Marcus Garvey.* New York: Arno Press and the *New York Times.*

Gates, Henry Louis, Jr. 1986. "Editor's Introduction: Writing 'Race' and the Difference It Makes." In *"Race," Writing, and Difference,* edited by Henry Louis Gates Jr. and Kwame Anthony Appiah, 1–20. London and Chicago: University of Chicago Press.

———. 1987. *Figures in Black: Words, Signs, and the "Racial" Self.* New York and Oxford: Oxford University Press.
———. 1991. "Critical Fanonism." *Critical Inquiry* 17, no. 3 (Spring): 457–70.
Geggus, David P. 1996. "Slave and Free Colored Women in Saint Domingue." In *More than Chattel: Black Women and Slavery in the Americas,* edited by David Barry Gaspar and Darlene Clark Hine, 259–78. Bloomington and Indianapolis: Indiana University Press.
Gerima, Haile, and Pamela Woolford. 1994. "Filming Slavery." *Transition* 64:90–104.
Gikandi, Simon. 1996. "Introduction: Africa, Diaspora, and the Discourse of Modernity." *Research in African Literatures* 27, no. 4 (Winter). http://inscribe.iupress.org/loi/ral.
Gill, June M. 2000. "The Films of Euzhan Palcy: A Voice for Black History." *Quarterly Review of Film and Video* 17, no. 4:371–81.
Gilroy, Paul. 1993a. *The Black Atlantic: Modernity and Double Consciousness.* Cambridge, MA: Harvard University Press.
———. 1993b. *Small Acts: Thoughts on the Politics of Black Cultures.* London and New York: Serpent's Tail.
———. 1996. "Route Work: The Black Atlantic and the Politics of Exile." In *The Post-colonial Question: Common Skies, Divided Horizons,* edited by Iain Chambers and Lidia Curti, 17–29. London and New York: Routledge.
Giraud, Michel. 1995. "Dialectics of Descent and Phenotypes in Racial Classification in Martinique." In *French and West Indian: Martinique, Guadeloupe, and French Guiana Today,* edited by Richard D. E. Burton and Fred Reno, 75–85. Charlottesville and London: University Press of Virginia.
Gittings, Christopher E. 2002. *Canadian National Cinema: Ideology, Difference and Representation.* London and New York: Routledge.
Glassman, Marc. 1995. "Where Zulus Meet Mohawks: Clement Virgo's *Rude.*" *Take One* (Fall), 16–21.
Glissant, Edouard. 1989. *Caribbean Discourse: Selected Essays.* Translated and with an introduction by J. M. Dash. Charlottesville: University Press of Virginia.
Goldman, Anita Haya. 1995. "Comparative Identities: Exile in the Writings of Frantz Fanon and W. E. B. DuBois." In *Borders, Boundaries, and Frames: Cultural Criticism and Cultural Studies,* edited by Mae Henderson, 107–32. New York and London: Routledge.
Gordon, Lewis R. 1995. *Fanon and the Crisis of European Man: An Essay on Philosophy and the Human Sciences.* New York: Routledge.
Gould, L. Virginia. 1996. "Urban Slavery—Urban Freedom: The Manumission of Jacqueline Lemelle." In *More than Chattel: Black Women and Slavery in the Americas,* edited by David Barry Gaspar and Darlene Clark Hine, 298–314. Bloomington and Indianapolis: Indiana University Press.

Gourévitch, Jean-Paul. 2000. *La France africaine: Islam, intégration, insécurité: Infos et intox*. Paris: Le Pré aux Clercs.

Grayson, Sandra M. 1998. "'Spirits of Asona Ancestors Come': Reading Asante Signs in Haile Gerima's *Sankofa*." *CLA Journal* 42, no. 2 (December): 212–27.

Gysin, Fritz. 1999. "The Enigma of the Return." In *Black Imagination and the Middle Passage*, edited by Maria Diedrich, Henry Louis Gates Jr., and Carl Pedersen, 183–90. New York and Oxford: Oxford University Press.

Haley, Marjorie Hall, and Keith Q. Warner. 1997. "Joseph Zobel and Technology: From Novel to Film to Classroom." *CLA Journal* 40, no. 3 (March): 380–91.

Hall, Catherine. 1996. "Histories, Empire and the Post-colonial Moment." In *The Post-colonial Question: Common Skies, Divided Horizons*, edited by Iain Chambers and Lidia Curti, 65–77. London and New York: Routledge.

Hall, Stuart. 1990. "Cultural Identity and Diaspora." In *Identity: Community, Culture, Difference*, edited by J. Rutherford, 222–37. London: Lawrence & Wishart.

———. 1992. "Cultural Identity and Cinematic Representation." In *Ex-Iles: Essays on Caribbean Cinema*, edited by Mbye Cham, 220–36. Trenton, NJ: Africa World Press.

———. 1996. "The After-life of Frantz Fanon: Why Fanon? Why Now? Why *Black Skin, White Masks?*" In *The Fact of Blackness: Frantz Fanon and Visual Representation*, edited by Alan Read, 12–37. London: Institute of Contemporary Arts; Seattle: Bay Press.

Halliday, Fred, and Maxine Molyneux. 1981. *The Ethiopian Revolution*. London: Verso.

Hanchard, Michael. 1990. "Identity, Meaning and the African-American." *Social Text* 24:31–42.

Hargreaves, Alex G., and Mark McKinney. 1997. "Introduction: The Post-colonial Problematic in Contemporary France." In *Post-colonial Cultures in France*, edited by Alex G. Hargreaves and Mark McKinney, 3–25. London and New York: Routledge.

Harris, Joseph E., ed. 1982. *Global Dimensions of the African Diaspora*. Washington, DC: Howard University Press.

Hausman, Gerald, ed. 1997. *The Kebra Nagast: The Lost Bible of Rastafarian Wisdom and Faith from Ethiopia and Jamaica*. New York: St. Martin's Press.

Henderson, Mae, ed. 1995. *Borders, Boundaries and Frames: Essays in Cultural Criticism and Cultural Studies*. New York and London: Routledge.

Herndon, Gerise. 1996. "Auto-ethnographic Impulse in *Rue Cases-Nègres*." *Literature/Film Quarterly* 24, no. 3:261–66.

Hill, John. 1999. *British Cinema in the 1980s: Issues and Themes*. Oxford and New York: Oxford University Press, Clarendon Press.

Hoetink, H. 1986. "'Race' and Color in the Caribbean." In *Caribbean Contours,* edited by Sidney W. Mintz and Sally Price, 55–84. Baltimore, MD: Johns Hopkins University Press.

Hondo, Abid Med. 1987. "The Cinema of Exile." In *Film and Politics in the Third World,* edited by John D. H. Downing, 69–76. New York: Autonomedia.

hooks, bell. 1984. *Feminist Theory: From Margin to Center.* Boston: South End Press.

———. 1989. *Talking Back: Thinking Feminist, Thinking Black.* Toronto: Between the Lines.

———. 1990. *Yearning: Race, Gender and Cultural Politics.* Toronto: Between the Lines.

———. 1991. "States of Desire (Interview with Isaac Julien)." *Transition* 53:168–84.

———. 1992. *Black Looks: Race and Representation.* Boston: South End Press.

———. 1996a. "Feminism as a Persistent Critique of History: What's Love Got to Do with It?" In *The Fact of Blackness: Frantz Fanon and Representation,* edited by Alan Read, 76–85. London: Institute of Contemporary Arts; Seattle: Bay Press.

———. 1996b. *Reel to Real: Race, Sex and Class at the Movies.* New York: Routledge.

Howe, Stephen. 1999. *Afrocentrism: Mythical Pasts and Imagined Homes.* London and New York: Verso.

Hudson-Weems, Clenora. 1994. *Africana Womanism: Reclaiming Ourselves.* Troy, MI: Bedford.

———. 2000. "Africana Womanism: An Overview." In *Out of the Revolution: The Development of Africana Studies,* edited by Delores P. Aldridge and Carlene Young, 205–17. Lanham, MD, and Oxford: Lexington Books.

———. 2001. "Africana Womanism: The Flip Side of a Coin." *Western Journal of Black Studies* 25, no. 3 (Fall). http://www.wsu.edu/~wjbs/.

Inikori, J. E., and Stanley L. Engerman, eds. 1992. *The Atlantic Slave Trade: Effects on Economies, Societies, and Peoples in Africa, the Americas, and Europe.* Durham, NC: Duke University Press.

James, C. L. R. 1963. *The Black Jacobins, Toussaint Louverture and the San Domingo Revolution.* New York and London: Vintage.

———. 1977a. *The Future in the Present: Selected Writings.* London: Allison & Busby.

———. 1977b. *Nkrumah and the Ghana Revolution.* Westport, CT: Lawrence Hill.

———. 1984. *Beyond a Boundary.* New York: Pantheon.

JanMohamed, Abdul R. 1992. "Worldliness-without-World, Homelessness-as-Home: Toward a Definition of the Specular Border Intellectual." In *Ed-*

ward Said: A Critical Reader, edited by Michael Sprinker, 96–120. Oxford: Blackwell.

Johnson-Hill, Jack A. 1995. *I-Sight: The World of Rastafari: An Interpretive Sociological Account of Rastafarian Ethics*. Metuchen, NJ, and London: American Theological Library Association and Scarecrow Press.

Jones, Peter. 1991. "Race, Discourse and Power in Institutional Housing: The Case of Immigrant Worker Hostels in Lyons." In *Race, Discourse and Power in France*, edited by Maxim Silverman, 55–70. Aldershot, England, and Brookfield, VT: Avebury Gower.

Jordan, Winthrop D. 1970. "Modern Tensions and the Origins of American Slavery." In *Slavery and Its Aftermath*, edited by Peter I. Rose, 103–15. Chicago: Atherton Press.

Jules-Rosette, Bennetta. 1998. *Black Paris: The African Writers' Landscape*. With a foreword by Simon Njami. Urbana and Chicago: University of Illinois Press.

Julien, Eileen. 1987. "La Métamorphose du reel dans *La Rue Case-Nègres*." *French Review* 60, no. 6 (May): 781–87.

Julien, Isaac, and Mark Nash. 2000. "Frantz Fanon as Film." In *The Film Art of Isaac Julien*, by David Deitcher and Isaac Julien, with contributions from Amanda Cruz, edited by David Frankel 103–10. Annandale-on-Hudson, NY: Center for Cultural Studies.

Kandé, Sylvie. 1998. "Look Homeward, Angel: Maroons and Mulattos in Haile Gerima's 'Sankofa.'" *Research in African Literatures* 29, no. 2 (Summer). http://inscribe.iupress.org/loi/ral.

Kandé, Sylvie, and Gyasi Kwaku. 1994. "Renunciation and Victory in 'Black Shack Alley.'" *Research in African Literatures* 25, no. 2 (Summer). http://inscribe.iupress.org/loi/ral.

Kanneh, Kadiatu. 1998. "History, 'Africa' and Modernity." *Interventions: International Journal of Postcolonial Studies* 1, no. 1:30–34.

Katz, William Loren. 1968. "A Short History of Black Separatism." In *Philosophy and Opinions of Marcus Garvey*, by Marcus Garvey, i–x. New York: Arno Press and the *New York Times*.

Kesteloot, Lilyan. 1974. *Black Writers in French: A Literary History of Negritude*. Translated by Ellen Conroy Kennedy. Philadelphia: Temple University Press.

Kitson, Thomas J. 1999. "Tempering Race and Nation: Recent Debates in Diaspora Identity." *Research in African Literatures* 30, no. 2 (Summer). http://inscribe.iupress.org/loi/ral.

Klein, Herbert S. 1978. *The Middle Passage: Comparative Studies in the Atlantic Slave Trade*. Princeton, NJ.: Princeton University Press.

———. 1994. "Profits and Causes of Mortality." In *The Atlantic Slave Trade*, edited by David Northrup, 112–20. Lexington, MA: D. C. Heath.

Kly, Y. N. 1998. "The Gullah War: 1739–1858." In *The Legacy of Ibo Landing: Gullah Roots of African American Culture*, edited by Marquetta L. Goodwine and the Clarity Press Gullah Project, 19–53. Atlanta: Clarity Press.

Knight, Franklin W. 2000. "AHR Forum: The Haitian Revolution." *American Historical Review* 105, no. 1 (February): 103–15.

Kruks, Sonia. 1996. "Fanon, Sartre, and Identity Politics." In *Fanon: A Critical Reader*, edited, with an introduction, and translations by Lewis R. Gordon, T. Denean Sharpley-Whiting, and Renée T. White, 122–33. Oxford: Blackwell.

Laforest, Marie Hélène. 1996. "Black Cultures in Difference." In *The Post-colonial Question: Common Skies, Divided Horizons*, edited by Iain Chambers and Lidia Curti, 115–20. London and New York: Routledge.

Lamming, George. 1984. *The Pleasures of Exile*. London: Allison & Busby.

Langley, April. 2001. "Lucy Terry Prince: The Cultural and Literary Legacy of Africana Womanism." *Western Journal of Black Studies* 25, no. 3 (Fall). http://www.wsu.edu/~wjbs/.

Lawrence, Amy. 1994. "Women's Voices in Third World Cinema." In *Multiple Voices in Feminist Film Criticism*, edited by Diane Carson, Linda Dittmar, and Janice R. Welsch, 406–20. Minneapolis: University of Minnesota Press.

Lefort, René. 1983. *Ethiopia: An Heretical Revolution?* Translated by A. M. Berrett. London: Zed Press.

Lewis, Gordon K. 1983. *Main Currents in Caribbean Thought: The Historical Evolution of Caribbean Society in Its Ideological Aspects, 1492–1900*. Baltimore, MD: Johns Hopkins University Press.

Lionnet, Françoise. 1989. *Autobiographical Voices: Race, Gender, Self-Portraiture*. Ithaca, NY, and London: Cornell University Press.

———. 1995. *Postcolonial Representations: Women, Literature, Identity*. Ithaca, NY: Cornell University Press.

Mabee, Carleton, with Susan Mabee Newhouse. 1993. *Sojourner Truth: Slave, Prophet, Legend*. New York and London: New York University Press.

McCartan, Greg. 2001. "Lessons of the Algerian Revolution." *Militant*, vol. 65, no. 23 (June 11). http://www.themilitant.com/2001/6523/652350.html (accessed July 20, 2007).

McCulloch, Jock. 1983. *Black Soul White Artifact: Fanon's Clinical Psychology and Social Theory*. Cambridge: Cambridge University Press.

McCullough, John. 1999. "*Rude*; or, The Elision of Class in Canadian Movies." *Cineaction* 49:19–25.

McCusker, Maeve. 2000. "De la problématique du territoire à la problématique du lieu: Un entretien avec Patrick Chamoiseau." *French Review* 73, no. 4 (March): 724–33.

McKittrick, Katherine. 2002. "'Their Blood Is There and They Can't Throw It

Out': Honouring Black Canadian Geographies." *Topia: A Canadian Journal of Cultural Studies* 7 (Spring): 27–37.

McKoy, Sheila Smith. 1999. "The Limbo Contest: Diaspora Temporality and Its Reflection in *Praisesong for the Widow* and *Daughters of the Dust*." *Callaloo* 22, no. 1:208–22.

McMaster, Neil. 1991. "The 'seuil de tolérance': The Uses of a 'Scientific' Racist Concept." In *Race, Discourse and Power in France*, edited by Maxim Silverman, 14–28. Aldershot, England, and Brookfield, VT: Avebury Gower.

Mensah, Joseph. 2002. *Black Canadians: History, Experiences, Social Conditions*. Halifax: Fernwood.

Mercer, Kobena. 1988. "Diaspora Culture and the Dialogic Imagination." In *Blackframes: Celebration of Black Cinema*, edited by Mbye Cham and Claire Andrade-Watkins, 50–61. Cambridge, MA: MIT Press.

———. 1994. *Welcome to the Jungle: New Positions in Black Cultural Studies*. New York: Routledge.

———. 1996. "Decolonisation and Disappointment: Reading Fanon's Sexual Politics." In *The Fact of Blackness: Frantz Fanon and Visual Representation*, edited by Alan Read, 114–31. London: Institute of Contemporary Arts; Seattle: Bay Press.

Mercer, Kobena, and Chris Darke. 2001. *Isaac Julien*. London: Ellipsis.

Mintz, Sidney W. 1974. *Caribbean Transformations*. Chicago: Aldine.

Mulvey, Laura. 1992. "Visual Pleasure and Narrative Cinema." In *Film Theory and Criticism: Introductory Readings*, edited by Gerald Mast, Marshall Cohen, and Leo Braudy, 746–57. New York and Oxford: Oxford University Press.

Munford, Clarence J. 1991. *The Black Ordeal of Slavery and Slave Trading in the French West Indies, 1625–1715*. Vols. 1 and 2. Lewiston, NY: Mellen.

Murdoch, Adlai. 1992. "(Re)Figuring Colonialism: Narratological and Ideological Resistance." *Callaloo* 15, no. 1:2–11.

Naficy, Hamid. 2001. *An Accented Cinema: Exilic and Diasporic Filmmaking*. Princeton, NJ, and Oxford: Princeton University Press.

Newbury, Michael. 1994. "Eaten Alive: Slavery and Celebrity in Antebellum America." *ELH* 61 (Spring): 159–87.

Nichols, Bill. 1994. *Blurred Boundaries: Questions of Meaning in Contemporary Culture*. Bloomington and Indianapolis: Indiana University Press.

Nkrumah, Kwame. 1964. *Consciencism: Philosophy and Ideology for Decolonization and Development with Particular Reference to the African Revolution*. New York: Monthly Review Press.

———. 1970. *Class Struggle in Africa*. New York: International.

Ofori, Ruby. 1990. "Testament of Faith." *West Africa*, no. 3790, 625–26.

Okpewho, Isidore. 1992. *African Oral Literature: Backgrounds, Character, and Continuity*. Bloomington and Indianapolis: University of Indiana Press.

Omari, T. Peter. 1970. *Kwame Nkrumah: The Anatomy of an African Dictatorship.* London: C. Hurst.

Osagie, Eghosa. 1985. "Socialism in the African Cultural Context." In *African Culture: The Rhythms of Unity,* edited by Molefi Kete Asante and Kariamu Welsh Asante, 141–54. Westport, CT: Greenwood Press.

Oyěwùmí, Oyèrónké. 1997. *The Invention of Women: Making an African Sense of Western Gender Discourses.* Minneapolis and London: University of Minnesota Press.

Parker, John. 2000. *Making the Town: Ga State and Society in Early Colonial Accra.* Portsmouth, NH: Heinemann.

Parry, Benita. 1992. "Overlapping Territories and Intertwined Histories: Edward Said's Postcolonial Cosmopolitanism." In *Edward Said: A Critical Reader,* edited by Michael Sprinker, 19–47. Oxford: Blackwell.

Patterson, Orlando. 1982. *Slavery and Social Death: A Comparative Study.* Cambridge, MA, and London: Harvard University Press.

Peck, Raoul, and Clyde Taylor. 1996. "Autopsy of Terror: A Conversation with Raoul Peck." *Transition* 69:236–46.

Pedersen, Carl. 1993. "Middle Passages: Representation of the Slave Trade in Caribbean and African-American Literature." *Massachusetts Review* 34, no. 2:225–39.

Peters, John Durham. 1999. "Exile, Nomadism, and Diaspora: The Stakes of Mobility in the Western Canon." In *Home, Exile, Homeland: Film, Media, and the Politics of Place,* edited by Hamid Naficy, 17–41. New York and London: Routledge.

Petley, Julian. 1989. "Testament." *Monthly Film Bulletin* 56 (September): 259–61.

Pfaff, Françoise. 1988. *Twenty-Five Black African Filmmakers: A Critical Study, with Filmography and Bio-bibliography.* Westport, CT: Greenwood Press.

———, ed. 2004. *Focus on African Films.* Bloomington and Indianapolis: Indiana University Press.

Pollitzer, William S. 1998. "The Relationship of the Gullah-Speaking People of Coastal South Carolina and Georgia to Their African Ancestors." In *The Legacy of Ibo Landing: Gullah Roots of African American Culture,* edited by Marquetta L. Goodwine and the Clarity Press Gullah Project, 54–68. Atlanta: Clarity Press.

Prochaska, David. 2003. "That Was Then, This Is Now: The *Battle of Algiers* and After." *Radical History Review* 85 (Winter): 133–49.

Public Broadcasting Service. n.d. "Elmina Castle, Trading Outpost and 'Slave Factory,'1481," *Africans in America,* pt. 1: *The Terrible Transformation, 1450–1750.* http://www.pbs.org/wgbh/aia/part1/1p260.html (accessed July 20, 2007).

Rahier, Jean. 1999. *Representations of Blackness and the Performance of Identities.* Westport, CT: Bergin & Garvey.

Rawley, James A. 1981. *The Transatlantic Slave Trade.* New York and London: W. W. Norton.

Reid, Mark A. 1993. *Redefining Black Film.* Berkeley and Los Angeles: University of California Press.

Rey, Terry. 1998. "The Virgin Mary and Revolution in Saint-Domingue: The Charisma of Romaine-la-Prophétesse." *Journal of Historical Sociology* 11, no. 3 (September): 341–69.

Riggs, Marcia Y. 1994. *Awake, Arise and Act: A Womanist Call for Black Liberation.* Cleveland: Pilgrim Press.

Robertson, Claire. 1996. "Africa into the Americas? Slavery and Women, the Family, and the Gender Division of Labor." In *More than Chattel: Black Women and Slavery in the Americas,* edited by David Barry Gaspar and Darlene Clark Hine, 3–40. Bloomington and Indianapolis: Indiana University Press.

Rose, Cynthia. 1989. "Digging the Feeling." *Observer* (September 3), sec. 5.

Rose, Peter I., ed. 1970. *Slavery and Its Aftermath.* Chicago: Atherton Press.

Rosello, Mireille. 1993. "'One More Sea to Cross': Exile and Intertextuality in Aimé Césaire's *Cahier d'un retour au pays natal.*" *Yale French Studies* 83, no. 2:176–95.

Ross, Marlon B. 2000. "Camping the Dirty Dozens: The Queer Resources of Black Nationalist Invective." *Callaloo* 23, no. 1:290–312.

Rotberg, Robert I. 1976. "Vodun and the Politics of Haiti." In *The African Diaspora: Interpretive Essays,* edited by Martin L. Kilson and Robert I. Rotberg, 342–65. Cambridge, MA, and London: Harvard University Press.

Said, Edward. 1983. *The World, the Text, and the Critic.* Cambridge, MA: Harvard University Press.

———. 1990. "Reflections on Exile." In *Out There, Marginalization and Contemporary Cultures,* edited by Russell Ferguson, Martha Gever, Trinh T. Minh-Ha, and Cornel West, 357–66. Cambridge, MA: MIT Press.

Sealy, David. 2000. "'Canadianizing' Blackness: Resisting the Political." In *Rude: Contemporary Black Canadian Cultural Criticism,* edited by Rinaldo Walcott, 87–108. Toronto: Insomniac Press.

Sekyi-Otu, Ato. 1996. *Fanon's Dialectic of Experience.* Cambridge, MA: Harvard University Press.

Sherzer, Dina. 1996. "Introduction." In *Cinema, Colonialism, Postcolonialism: Perspectives from the French and Francophone Worlds,* edited by Dina Sherzer, 1–19. Austin: University of Texas Press.

Signaté, Ibrahima. 1994. *Med Hondo: Un cinéaste rebelle.* Paris: Présence Africaine.

Silverman, Maxim. 1991. "Introduction." In *Race, Discourse and Power in France,* edited by Maxim Silverman, 1–4. Aldershot, England, and Vermont, USA: Avebury Gower.

Snead, James. 1990. "Repetition as a Figure of Black Culture." In *Out There, Marginalization and Contemporary Cultures*, edited by Russell Ferguson, Martha Gever, Trinh T. Minh-Ha, and Cornel West, 213–30. Cambridge, MA: MIT Press.

Socolow, Susan M. 1996. "Economic Roles of the Free Women of Color of Cap Français." In *More than Chattel: Black Women and Slavery in the Americas*, edited by David Barry Gaspar and Darlene Clark Hine, 279–97. Bloomington and Indianapolis: Indiana University Press.

Sooknanan, Renuka. 2000. "The Politics of Essentialism: Rethinking 'Black Community.'" In *Rude: Contemporary Black Canadian Cultural Criticism*, edited by Rinaldo Walcott, 137–58. Toronto: Insomniac Press.

Spencer, John H. 1987. *Ethiopia at Bay: a Personal Account of the Haile Selassie Years*. Algonac, MI: Reference Publications.

Stuckey, Sterling. 1987. *Slave Culture: Nationalist Theory and the Foundations of Black America*. New York and Oxford: Oxford University Press.

Studlar, Gaylyn. 1992. "Masochism and the Perverse Pleasures of the Cinema." In *Film Theory and Criticism: Introductory Readings*, edited by Gerald Mast, Marshall Cohen, and Leo Braudy, 773–90. New York and Oxford: Oxford University Press.

Taylor, Lucien. 1997 "Créolité Bites: A Conversation with Patrick Chamoiseau, Raphaël Confiant, and Jean Bernabé." *Transition* 74: 124–61.

Tembo, Mwizenge S. 1985. "The Concept of African Personality: Sociological Implications." In *African Culture: The Rhythms of Unity*, edited by Molefi Kete Asante and Kariamu Welsh Asante, 193–206. Westport, CT: Greenwood Press.

Thompson, Vincent Bakpetu. 1987. *The Making of the African Diaspora in the Americas, 1441–1900*. New York: Longman.

Thornton, John. 1992. *Africa and Africans in the Making of the Atlantic World, 1400–1680*. Cambridge and New York: Cambridge University Press.

Tomaselli, Keyan, and Maureen Eke. 1995. "Secondary Orality in South African Film." *IRIS* 18 (Spring): 61–69.

Trees, Kathryn, and Mudrooroo Nyoongah. 1993. "Postcolonialism: Yet Another Colonial Strategy." *Journal of the South Pacific Association for Commonwealth Literature and Language Studies*, vol. 36. http://wwwmcc.murdoch.edu.au/ReadingRoom/litserv/SPAN/36/Trees.html.

Triulzi, Alessandro. 1996. "African Cities, Historical Memory and Street Buzz." In *The Post-colonial Question: Common Skies, Divided Horizons*, edited by Iain Chambers and Lidia Curti, 78–91. London and New York: Routledge.

Trouillot, Michel-Rolph. 1990. *Haiti: State against Nation: The Origins and Legacy of Duvalierism*. New York: Monthly Review Press.

Ukadike, Nwachukwu Frank. 1994. *Black African Cinema*. Berkeley and Los Angeles: University of California Press.

———. 2002. *Questioning African Cinema: Conversations with Filmmakers*. London and Minneapolis: University of Minnesota Press.

Vergès, Françoise. 1996a. "Chains of Madness, Chains of Colonialism: Fanon and Freedom." In *The Fact of Blackness: Frantz Fanon and Visual Representation*, edited by Alan Read, 46–75. London: Institute of Contemporary Arts; Seattle: Bay Press.

———. 1996b. "To Cure and to Free: The Fanonian Project of Decolonized Psychiatry." In *Fanon: A Critical Reader*, edited by Lewis R. Gordon, T. Denean Sharpley-Whiting, and Renee T. White, 85–99. Oxford: Blackwell.

———. 1997. "Creole Skin, Black Mask: Fanon and Disavowal." *Critical Inquiry* 23, no. 3 (Spring): 578–95.

———. 1999a. "'I Am Not the Slave of Slavery': The Politics of Reparation in (French) Postslavery Communities." In *Frantz Fanon: Critical Perspectives*, edited by Anthony C. Alessandrini, 258–75. London and New York: Routledge.

———. 1999b. *Monsters and Revolutionaries: Colonial Family Romance and Métissage*. Durham, NC, and London: Duke University Press.

Walcott, Rinaldo. 1997. *Black Like Who?* Toronto: Insomniac Press.

———. 2000. "By Way of a Brief Introduction-Insubordination: A Demand for a Different Canada." In *Rude: Contemporary Black Canadian Cultural Criticism*, edited by Rinaldo Walcott, 7–10. Toronto: Insomniac Press.

Warner, Keith Q. 1995. "On Adapting a West Indian Classic to the Cinema." In *Cinemas of the Black Diaspora: Diversity, Dependency and Oppositionality*, edited by Michael T. Martin, 266–73. Detroit: Wayne State University Press.

Washington Creel, Margaret. 1990. "Gullah Attitudes toward Life and Death." In *Africanisms in American Culture*, edited by Joseph E. Holloway, 69–97. Bloomington and Indianapolis: Indiana University Press.

Weinstein, Brian. 1976. "The French West Indies: Dualism from 1848 to the Present." In *The African Diaspora: Interpretive Essays*, edited by Martin L. Kilson and Robert I. Rotberg, 237–79. Cambridge, MA, and London: Harvard University Press.

West, Cornel. 1997. "The Ignoble Paradox of Western Modernity." In *Spirits of the Passage: The Transatlantic Slave Trade in the Seventeenth Century*, edited by Rosemarie Robotham, 8–10. New York: Simon & Schuster.

Wihtol de Wenden, Catherine. 1991. "North African Immigration and the French Political Imaginary." Translated by Clare Hughes. In *Race, Discourse and Power in France*, edited by Maxim Silverman, 98–109. Aldershot, England, and Brookfield, VT: Avebury Gower.

Williams, Eric. 1994. "Economics, Not Racism as the Root of Slavery." In *The Atlantic Slave Trade*, edited by David Northrup, 3–12. Lexington, MA: D.C. Heath.

Winks, Robin W. 1997. *The Blacks in Canada: A History.* Montreal and Kingston: McGill-Queen's University Press.

Wolff, Cynthia Griffin. 1996. "Passing beyond the Middle Passage: Henry 'Box' Brown's Translations of Slavery." *Massachusetts Review* (Spring), 23–44.

Wynter, Sylvia. 1976. "Talk about a Little Culture." In *Carifesta Forum: An Anthology of Twenty Caribbean Voices,* edited by John Hearne, 129–37. Carifesta 76. Kingston: Institute of Jamaica.

Zéphir, Flore. 1999. "Caribbean Films in the French Curriculum: Strengthening Linguistic and Multicultural Compentency." *French Review* 72, no. 3 (February): 515–28.

INDEX

Note: Italicized page numbers refer to photographs. Film characters' names are followed by (char.).

Abena (char.): betrayal by, 149–51; conflation of personal histories and journalistic observation, 141; conflict between Danso and, 145–47; conflicted personal identity, 142; continued estrangement of, 152; deflection of responsibility by, 147–48; interior dialogue *vs.* psychological state, 143–44; return from exile, 138; and war zone of memories, 141, 153
Abeyhoy, Neburaelid Mekuria, 167–68
acculturation: and betrayal, 120–21; and fragmentation of indigenous societies, 111; migrants, and desires toward, 118–19; and rejection of Africanness, 99–100; of skilled laborers, 21
Adamafio, Tawai, 135
Adane, W. Elfenesh, 173–74
Adjei, Ako, 135
aesthetic syncretism, 202
affranchis, in Haiti, 198–99
Africa: as concept for African slaves in America, 21; estrangement between Afrocentrism and, 25; independence movements in, 136; postcolonial period in, 111; role of, in promulgation of slavery, 18; symbol of, in *Sankofa*, 50
Africana men, 83

African American consciousness, 108
Africana Womanism, 9–10, 82–83, 87, 89, 261n. 4, 261n. 6
African Canadianité, 228–29
African Canadians, 228–29. *See also* black Canadians
African-centered discourse, in *Sankofa*, 28
African cultures: emphasis on community in, 41–42; and evocation of African diasporic consciousness, 21; oral tradition in, 27, 64–65, 69, 166, 174–75, 260n. 3; portrayal of, in *Sankofa*, 33–34, 43; riddles in, 64–65; West African, 85
African embassies, and immigrants, 124–25
Africanisms, 20–21
African slaves. *See also* slavery; slaves: in America, 17, 19, 21; in Canada, 224–26; in the Caribbean, 52; nonperson status of, 19–20
African spirituality: as central element of Afrocentrism, 25; in *Daughters of the Dust*, 89–90, 95–96; as factor in Africana Womanism, 83; in Gullah culture, 85
Afrocentrism, 23–26, 28–29
Akan language, 260n. 9
Akomfrah, John: background of, 137; *Testament*, 11–12, 129–30, 136–53

INDEX

Algeria, 178, 188, 192–95
Algerian Revolution, 265n. 3 (chap. 7)
All Ethiopian Socialist Movement (MEISON), 169–70
American Civil War, 108
Amharic people, in Ethiopia, 159, 167
Andre (char.), 238, 240–42
Angola, 84
Antillanité, 56–58, 60, 79, 196–97, 228
Aristide, Jean Baptiste, 202
Asante, Molefi Kete, 23–26, 259n. 5
Assad (char.), 211–13
assassinations, in Ethiopia, 173–74
Azikiwe, Nnamdi, 130–36

Babylon, 232–34
Back to Africa movements, 7, 22–23
Battle of Algiers (Pontecorvo), 192–93
béké culture, 67, 72–74, 260n. 2
Bernabé, Jean, 58
Bhabha, Homi, 179
Bight of Biafra, 84
black Atlantic concept, 10–11, 104–9, 126
Black Audio Film Collective, 136, 183
black British culture, 136
black Canadian cinema, 229–30
black Canadians, 14, 224, 228–31, 234–35. See also *Rude* (Virgo)
black diaspora: complexities of arrival, 105; as composite formation, united and divided, 127–28; as field of identifications, 128; as global phenomenon, 115; problems in defining, 2–3
black diasporic cinema, 6–7
black diasporic communities: in Canada, 227–28; homophobia in, 243; localizing strategies in, 176; social disintegration of, in hood film genre, 248–49; and strategies of remembrance, 1–2
black diasporic context, 174–75, 234
black diasporic cultures, 5, 22, 106
black diasporic experience, 3–6, 28, 81
black diasporic identities, 105, 155–56
black diasporic space, 128
black diasporic theories, 5–6, 104, 107, 127, 155
black female experience, 9, 81, 86
black identities and identity: African center as defining aspect of, 34, 51; black diaspora and, 106; composite, in *Sankofa*, 36; conflicted, of exiles, 139; constructive, in *Rude*, 256–57; and double-consciousness, 109; expressions of, by African slaves in America, 21; Fanon's preoccupation with construction of, 179–80; power of myth and magic in, 101; Rastafarianism and, 231; representations of, in *Rude*, 234; role of slippage in creation of, 5; slippage in integrating transnational, 175
Black Loyalists, 225–26
black migrants: and Canada's open-door immigration policy, 227; and double-consciousness, 115, 119–20, 126; emancipated African Americans compared to, 118–19; in ex-colonial metropolises, 117–18; in France, 109, 112–13, 115, 124; in postcolonial context, 111, 120–21
blackness: in Canada, 224, 228; and self-loathing, 72; and status, 68; as term, 80
black resistance, as marker of African resilience and heritage, 38
black separatism, 23
Black Skin, White Mask (Fanon), 176–78, 180, 183–84, 190
black women: as arbiters of resistance, 219; discourses of, 9, 80, 261n. 1; identities of, African tradition as locus for, 83; selfhood of, 83, 96
black women's selfhood, 91
black youth culture, 243–44
bottle trees, 262n. 12
Brah, Avtar, 127, 138
Britain, 225

cagoulars, 207
call-and-response exchanges, 66, 68–69

INDEX

Camille (char.), 211–15, 221–22
Canada, 14, 227
Canadian Film Centre, 230
Canadian filmmaking, 230–31
Capécia, Mayotte, 190–91
Caribbean Discourse (Glissant), 57
Caribbean experience, 52, 197
Caribbean identity, 57–59, 203
Carter, Robert "King," 22
Casbah, 265n. 3
Cedras, Raoul, 202
center-periphery dichotomies, 105, 111, 113, 120
Césaire, Aimé, 54–57, 63
Chambers, Iain, 4, 155
Chamoiseau, Patrick, 58, 60
Christianity, and slavery, 92
Christian religious symbolism, in *Rude*, 234
Christiansborg Castle incident, 131–36
Clarke, George E., 228–29
clientage, 259n. 2 (chap. 1)
Clifford, James, 2–3, 5, 12, 154, 156
cocoa prices, collapse of, 135
Code Noir (Black Code), 53–54, 225
colonial gaze, 12–13, 181, 184–86, 191–92
colonialism: defined, 109–10; and double-consciousness, 121–22; legacy of, 110, 136, 201; persistence of, in Caribbean, 197–98; as poisonous, 56; profits of, 117; and refusal of recognition, 189; strategies to maintain power, 117
colonizer/colonized relationship, 176–77, 188, 194
colonizers' metropolises, 111–12, 121
color politics in Martinique, 62, 71
Committee on Youth Organization (C.Y.O.), 132
community: absence of, in black Canadian identity, 225; as central element of Afrocentrism, 25; emphasis on, in African cultures, 41–42, 44–45; in Gullah culture, 85, 87, 89; and problem-solving approaches to social needs, 83
Confiant, Raphaël, 58

consciencism, 264n. 9
contact zones, as term, 259n. 1 (intro.)
Convention People's Party (C.P.P.), 132, 134–35, 138, 152
Creole, conceptions of, 60
Creole language, 58–60, 67–69, 213
Créolité, 58–60, 67, 69
creolization, 58, 196–97
cultural and social ties, destabilization of, 19
Curtis (char.), 247–48

da Costa, Mathieu, 266n. 1
Damas, Léon-Gontron, 54–55
Danso (char.), 138, 142–47
Dash, Julie: background of, 85–86; *Daughters of the Dust*, 86–103
Daughters of the Dust (Dash), 86–103, 88; overview of, 10; African-based spirituality in, 89–90; community, affirmation of, 87, 89; conflicting points of view in, 92–93; generational conflict in, 98–99; male characters in, 93–94; narrative of, 87, 91, 93–94; visual strategies in, 90–91
Davies, Carol Boyce, 261n. 2
de Champlain, Samuel, 266n. 1
Delany, Martin R., 23
Deluge (Mekuria), 154–75, 162; compared to *Testament*, 156; multinarrational approach to, 161–64; narrative and aesthetic elements in, 166; narrative structure and illustrations in, 163–64; as site of slippage, 12, 160, 165; social critique in, 172–73; undelineated boundaries of history and myth in, 165; visual elements, repetition of, 166–67
Depestre, René, 13, 197
Derg regime, 161, 169–71
Dessalines, Jean-Jacques, 200
de Thorail, Jacques (char.), 73–74
dirge singers, 143–44
disappeared, the, 174, 209
domestic-worker crisis in Canada, 227

289

INDEX

double-consciousness: black diasporic identities and, 104–8; black migrant and, 115, 119–20, 126; colonialism and, 121–22; DuBois and, 228; intersection of, with black Atlantic, 10–11; parallels to, 263n. 6; rejection of, as acceptable state, 125; wider definition of, 109
drug culture, 252–53, 255–56
DuBois, W. E. B.: double-consciousness concept, 10–11, 104–9, 119, 228, 262–63n. 2; influence of, on Dash, 91; influence of, on Nkrumah, 130; *The Souls of Black Folk* (DuBois), 107–8
Duvalier, Françoise, 204
Duvalier regime: and culture of terror, 207–9; interrogation of, in *The Man by the Shore*, 202; persistence of, 205; resistance to, successfully reduced, 216–17; and rise of Duvalierism, 204; role of *mulâtre* in power of, 211; sexual victimization during, 221–22; violation of social prohibitions by, 209–10

Edwards, Norval, 196–97
Egypt (Kemet), 25–26
Eli (char.), 87, 95–96, 101
Elide (char.), 221–22
Elmina Castle, 259–60n. 6
Elmina (fortress), 30–31
Éloge de la Créolité (In Praise of Creoleness), 58
emancipation, and betrayal, 108
Emancipation Act of Britain (1833), 226
empowerment of black selves, 256, 258
Ethiopa, 156–59, 167, 169–71. *See also* Red Terror
Ethiopia Armed Forces, 159, 169
Ethiopian Christianity, 156
Ethiopian People's Revolutionary Party (EPRP), 170, 173
ethnicities, obliteration of diversity in, 32, 50
étudiant noir, L' (newspaper), 55
Eula (char.), 87, 100–103

Eurocentrism, 22, 24, 26, 234
exile: black diasporic experience rooted in, 3–4; contradictions of, 161–63; hybridizing power of, 155; nationalism and, 142; political turmoil and, 129
exilic experience: arrested national history of, 147; displacement as locus of, 129; as mediated position, 154–55; origin and, 128–29; and problematics of return, 129–30; trauma of dispersal in, 138–39
exilic identities: formation in the black diaspora, 137; role of conflicting notions of history and memory in, 129

family-centered theoretical practice, 83
Fanon, Frantz: background, 178; binarisms in work by, 181–82; and colonial gaze, 12–13; cultural and political importance of work by, 183–84; examination of theories of, by Julien, 176; and experiences of racism in France, 180–81; in *Frantz Fanon*, 186–87; idealization of Algerian revolutionary, 194; importance of works by, 177–78; influence of, 13; lifetime preoccupation of, 179–80; resurgence in interest in work by, 179
Fanon, Joby, 190
Fanon, Olivier, 195
feminisms, 81–82, 94, 261n. 3
fieldworkers, 20–21
fire, in Rasta belief, 266n. 5
Flora, Miss (char.), 72
flying back stories, 50
Foster, Cecil, 228
Foster, Gwendolyn Audrey, 262n. 10
France: and Atlantic slave trade, 52; colonial possessions of, 52–53; concept of *mission civilisatrice*, 110–11; and political myth of equality, 112, 119–20, 122; racism in, 180; and *seuil de tolérance* theory, 113
François (char.), 205–6, 216–20

INDEX

Frantz Fanon: Black Skin, White Mask (Julien), 176–95, *177;* overview, 13; aesthetic and narrative strategies of, 192–93; *Battle of Algiers* scenes in, 192–94; and Fanon's notion of the gaze, 184–85; newsreel footage in, 187–88; as open text, 195; and tensions in Fanon's work, 182; use of reconstructions in, 185–88, 190, 192
French Antilles, films from (1980s), 61
French Caribbean, 67
French culture, 54, 62, 75–76, 111, 115
French education, in Martinique, 69–71, 74–75
French Revolution, 112
Front de Libération Nationale (FLN), 178–79
Fugitive Slave Act of U.S. (1850), 227

Garvey, Marcus, 23–24, 130, 231
Gates, Henry Louis, Jr., 2, 38, 177
gay bashing, in *Rude,* 243, 246
gaze, the, 12–13, 181, 184–86, 191–92
gens de couleur, 198
Gerima, Haile: background of, 26–27; *Sankofa,* 8–9, 26–51
Ghana, 130–36, 263n. 1
Gilroy, Paul, 2, 5, 10–11, 17, 104–9
Gisèle (char.), 205, 218–19
Glissant, Edouard, 3–4, 56–58, 60, 228
Gold Coast, 84
Gracieux (char.), 206–7, 217–22, 265n. 2
griot, 38, 232, 260n. 8
Groupe d'Etudes et de Recherches de la Créolophonie (GEREC), 58
Gullah, as term, 261n. 7
Gullah culture, 84–86, 89
Gullah War, 84

Haagar (char.), 87, 96–100, 102
Haas, Elsie, 201
Haiti: divisions among black population of, 201; under Duvalier regime, 218; as first black independent state, 13, 197; and fragmentation of colonialism, 210; independence of, 200; as plantation society, 198; slave agriculture and crafts in, 199; social hierarchy, 211; societal disintegration, 219–20; struggle for freedom, 198
Haitian identity, 13–14, 201, 203
Haitian Revolution, 199–200
Hall, Stuart, 188–89, 191
Herzog, Werner, 138
historical dispersals, and pan-diasporic consciousness, 105
historical narratives, mainstream, 227
home, as mythic place of desire, 138
homophobia, 181–83, 243
homosexuality, in *Rude,* 242–48
Hondo, Med (Mohamed Abid): background, 113–14; *Soleil O,* 11, 114–26
Honorine (char.), 72–74
hood film genre, 248
hooks, bell, 81–82, 261n. 3
Hudson-Weems, Clenora, 81–82, 89
hybridization, as model for black culture in Canada, 228

Ibo people, 84, 101
identities and identity. *See* black identities and identity
Illusions (Dash), 86
interracial marriage, 190

"J'ai deux amours" (song), 73
Jamaicans, immigration to Canada by, 227
James, C. L. R., 130–31, 134
JanMohamed, Abdul, 154
Janvier, Madame (char.), 213
Janvier (char.), 206, 208–9, 214–15, 217–23
Jessica (char.), 248–50, 253, 256
Je Suis Martiniquaise (Capécia), 190–91
Joe (char.), 46–49
Johnny (John) (char.), 248, 256
Jordan (char.), 231, 237, 242–48, 256–57
José (char.): education of, 67, 69–70; identity of, as mediation, 62, 78–79; isolation of, from working

291

INDEX

José (char.) (*continued*)
community, 70–71; and Miss Flora, 72; portrayal of, 265–66n. 3; relationship with Médouze, 64; and school in Fort-de-France, 76; story about Médouze, 76–77; and talisman from Médouze, 66
Julien, Isaac: approach to filmmaking, 187–88; background of, 183; Fanon, examination of theories of, 176; *Frantz Fanon: Black Skin, White Mask*, 13, 176–95; use of transgression in work of, 184–85
Junior (char.), 251

Kandé, Sylvie, 33–36, 46–49
kin-based slavery, 259n. 2 (chap. 1)
Kirke, David, 225
Kongo Kingdom, 84
Korsa, Arku, 135
Kruks, Sonia, 180
Kutu (char.), 41–42
Kwame (char.), 42

L.A. Underground (UCLA film school), 86
labor: commodification of, 4
Lafayette (char.), 39–40, 45
language, as marker of authority, 68
la Pointe, Ali, 192–93
laws, and hierarchy of racial superiority, 20
Léopold (char.), 72–74, 77–78
L'etudant noir (newspaper), 55
Liberia, 84
lifetime servitude, hereditary, 19
Lion of Judah, in *Rude*, 231–32, 255
Louverture, François-Dominique Toussaint, 200
Lucy (char.), 47–48
Luke (char.): climax of story of, 256–57; and drug dealing, 253–55; portrayal of, 236; relationship with son, 251–53; structure of story strand of, 249; struggles of, 248–55

Makandal, 265n. 1
Makonnen, Ras Tafari, 156–57. *See also* Selassie, Haile
Man by the Shore, The (Peck), 196–223, 212, 216; overview, 13–14; and Haitian vs. non-Haitian audience, 203–4; narrative structure of, 201–2, 207–8, 218; open ending of, 223; terror of violence in, 206–8; visual strategies in, 205–6; women as arbiters of resistance in, 219
manumission, 18
map and history, concepts of, in Caribbean experience, 197
maroons, 200, 226
Martinican identities, 61, 66–67
Martinique: color politics in, 55, 62, 71; departmentalization of, 56, 63; French education in, 69; race relations in, complexity of, 71–72; subordination of, to France, 54
Maxine (char.), 231, 236–42, 249, 256–57
Médouze (char.), 64–66, 68–69
Mekuria, Salem, 154–75; background and works by, 160; *Deluge*, 154–75; and distance of, from origin, 171–72; and Negist (friend), 169–70, 172–73; and Saamra (daughter), 174–75; self reflexive role played by, 164; and Selomon (brother), 168–70, 172–75; in space between Selomon and Negist, 170–71; as subject/participant, 163
Mekuria, Sehin, 173
memory: Abena and, 146–47; arrested, dissociative effects of, 138; of primary loss, exile as, 161–63; in reconstituting cultural identity, 21; as sole delineator of slavery's time, 38; as system of resistance, 91; violence and, 201
Mengistu, Haile Mariam, 169–70
Mensah, Joseph, 224
menticide, 47
Mercer, Kobena, 181–82
métissage, 196–97, 203
Middle Passage, 8, 16–17, 26, 52

migration, forced, 3–4, 263n. 3
miscegenation, 20
mission civilisatrice, 54, 110–11
mixed race individuals, and white-power apparatus, 67
M'man Tine (char.), 71, 73, 77–78
Mona (char.), 30–32, 34, 42, 49–50. *See also* Shola (char.)
Muhammed, Bilal, 262n. 9
mulâtre, 14, 198–99, 210–11, 213, 216
mulattos, 46–49, 62, 67, 72–74

Napoleonic code, 112
Nash, Mark, 192–93
natal alienation, 19
Négritude movement: Césaire's involvement in, 54–57; conceptual roots of, 55; contemporization of Zobel's ideology by Palcy, 62; and Créolité, 59; Fanon and, 179–80; origins of, 8; overtones of, in *Sugar Cane Alley*, 64
Negro, as term, 19
New France, 225
New Queer Cinema, 182
Nkrumah, Kwame, 130–36, 142, 150, 263n. 4 (chap. 5)
Nkrumah Ideological Institute, 141–42
Nkrumahism, 264n. 9
noiriste, 14, 210–11, 213, 216
Normal Films, 183
North Atlantic slave trade, 21–22, 259n. 1 (chap. 1)
Nova Scotia, 225–26
Nunu (char.), 38–43, 48

Ontario, 227
orality, 21, 25, 38, 43, 86. *See also* African cultures, oral tradition
origin, and exilic experience, 128, 138

Padmore, George, 131
Palcy, Euzhan: background, 61; *Sugar Cane Alley*, 8–9, 60–79
Pan-African conferences, 108
pan-Africanism, 130
pawnship, 259n. 2 (chap. 1)
Peazant, Nana (char.), 87, 90–91, 95–96, 98–102
Peazant family, 91
Peck, Raoul: background of, 201–2; *The Man by the Shore*, 13–14, 196–223
Peters, John Durham, 128–29
plantation economy, 66, 198
poétique de la relation (cross-cultural poetics), 57
Pontecorvo, Gillo, 192–93
postcolonialism, 111, 263n. 4 (chap. 4)

quadroons, defined, 67

racial polarization, in Haiti, 14, 210
racism: and dehumanization of colonized people, 110, 188–89; and desire, 191–92; DuBois's exploration of, 107–8; in France, 180; ideology of, 53–54; systemic, 3, 36, 112, 119–22
Rankin, Virginia, 230
rape, as metaphor, 221–22
Raphael, Father (char.), 45, 47–49
Rashid (char.), 138, 147–48, 150
Rastafarianism, 231
Red Terror, 160–61, 171, 173, 175
Reese (char.), 248, 250, 255
Regent Park projects, Toronto, 231
Rogers, Tania, 141
Rude (char.), 232–33, 235–36, 241, 245, 249, 257
Rude (Virgo), 224–58, 233, 254; overview, 15–16; awards for, 230–31; crosscutting as organizing principle, 237; emphasis on personal choice in, 238; ethnicities in, 248; gay bashing in, 246; individual responsibility in, 251, 258; lack of character backstory, 237–38; narrative motifs in, 231–32; personal trials of characters, 234–35; plot structure and plotlines, 235–36; and revolutionary rhetoric, 257–58; sparring session in, 247–48
Rue cases-nègres (Black Shack Alley) (Zobel), 61–62, 260n. 1

293

INDEX

sacred drummer, in *Sankofa*, 29, 49–50
Sagoe, Sally, 141
Said, Edward, 128–29, 154
Saint-Domingue (Haiti), 53, 198
Saint Louis (char.), 68–69, 76
Sakumo, 264n. 12
Salmon, Colin, 186–87
sankofa, meaning of, 26, 29
Sankofa (char.), 30–31, 41
Sankofa Film and Video Collective, 183
Sankofa (Gerima), 26–51, *27*, *33*; overview of, 8–9; African context of slave resistance, 45; backgrounds of characters, 36; as black diasporic imaginary, 26; community solidarity abandoned in, 41–42; confessional scene, 47; focus on women in, 40–41; Lafayette plantation location, 35–36; narrative structure of, 28; slave rebellion, 49; universalized portrayal of African cultures in, 33–34; use of multiple time lines in, 34–35
Sarah (char.): as a child, 205–6; at the convent, 208–9; depiction of, 265–66n. 3 (chap. 8); dream sequence of, 220; and Duvalierism, 202–4; flashback to birthday party, 215; memories of, 204, 218; narration by, 204–5, 218; as symbol of Haitian identity, 201; trauma of, 222–23
satire, in African oral tradition, 69
Sea Islands, 83–85
Selassie, Haile, 157–59, 167–68
self, devaluation of, 255–56
Seminole Wars, 261–62n. 8
Senegambia, 84
Senghor, Léopold, 54–55, 262–63n. 2
seuil de tolérance theory, 113, 124
Shango (char.), 37, 42–46
Shango (theater company), 114
Shola (char.), 35–37, 39–40, 43–45, 49–51
Sierra Leone, 84
Sierra Leone Company, 226
Sister Suzanne (char.), 208–9
slave cultures, rise of, 20–21
slavery: abolition of, in Martinique, 66; in Africa, 18; aftermath of, in *Daughters of the Dust*, 86; black diasporic experience rooted in, 3–4; in Canada, 224–26; in the Caribbean, 52; Christianity and, 92; colonialism compared to, 109–10; destruction of colonizer and colonized through, 56; evolution of institution of, in New World, 20; and forced migration, 263n. 3; Gullah and challenge to, 84; hierarchical structure in, 20–21; kin-based, 259n. 2 (chap. 1); legacies of, 9, 53, 197–98, 201; rise and evolution of, in America, 18–19
slaves: in America, 17; diversity in backgrounds, 36; forced assimilation of, 47; hierarchy of, 36–37; as livestock commodities, 19; of mixed race, 21; resistance by, 45, 49, 199–200; skilled laborers, acculturation of, 21
slave ship figurehead, 262n. 14
slave trade, 18, 21–22, 52, 259n. 1 (chap. 1)
slippage: *Deluge* as site of, 12, 160; between personal and national histories, 164–65, 174; role of, in creation of black identities, 5, 175
Sojourner Truth, 82, 261n. 5
Soleil O (Hondo), *110*, 114–26; overview, 11; awards won by, 114; Christian baptism scene in, 115–17; depiction of colonizer's metropolis, 118; effects of colonization on Africa, 115–16; focus on migration of Africans to France, 109; housing for migrants, 124; narrative ambiguity in, 121–22; narrative of, 114–15, 123; visual strategies in, 116, 121
Souls of Black Folk, The (DuBois), 107–8
spirituality. *See* African spirituality
St. Pierre rebellion, 66
Stono Rebellion (1739), 84
storytelling, 38, 43
Studio Museum in Harlem, 85
Sugar Cane Alley (Palcy), 60–79, *63*,

294

75; overview of, 8–9; compared to Zobel's novel, 62–64, 69; depiction of race relations in, 71–72; grounding of, in Antillanité, 79; narrative locus of, 64; reception of, by Martinican audiences, 62; response to, 61–62
sugar cane industry, 52–53, 63
symbolic imagery in African oral tradition, 69
Syrians, as term, 212
systemic racism, 3, 36, 112, 119–22

tableau vivant, as interrogative device, 192
Takoradi strike, 134–35
Testament (Akomfrah), 136–53, *139–40*; overview, 11–12; aesthetic strategies in, 139–41; autobiographical fragments in, 137; exilic experience and problematics of return in, 129–30; film characters, and Nkrumah's regime, 130; narration of, 141–42; narrative structure of, 142; separation of conjoined twins, 148–49; visual strategies, 141, 152
third Seminole War (1858), 84
tonton-makout, 203, 207–8, 214–15
Toronto, as extension of Babylon, 233–34
Tortilla (char.), 70–71, 76–77
Triangle Trade, 17
triple caste system, 23
Tubman, Harriet, 226

unborn child, in *Rude*, 240–42, 257
Unborn Child (char.), 87, 94–95, 97, 101–3

Underground Railroad, 226
United Gold Coast Convention (U.G.C.C.), 131–32
United States blockade of Haiti, 200

Van Der Zee, James, 86
Vergès, Françoise, 182, 190–92, 194
victim/victimizer, 219–20
Viola (char.), 87, 92–93, 102
violence, effect of, 246–47
Virgo, Clement: *Rude*, 15–16, 229–58
vulture, as messenger of the ancestors, 29–30

Walcott, Rinaldo, 5, 243, 247, 266–67n. 8–9
water, in Ga culture, 264n. 12
West, Cornel, 3
West African cultures, 85
Western Europe blockade of Haiti, 200
West Indian Domestic Scheme, 227
West Indians, 59, 198
whiteness, 72, 210
white-thinking blacks, 122
Worke, Ato Mola, 174
world-sense, as term, 259n. 2
Wossene, W. Asegedeich, 174
Wretched of the Earth (Fanon), 192–93

Yankee (char.), 248, 250–51, 256
Yellow Mary (char.), 87, 92–93, 100–103
Yeshewawork, W. Negede, 174
Young Soul Rebels (Julien), 183

Zobel, Joseph, 61–62
zombification, 217–19

www.ingramcontent.com/pod-product-compliance
Lightning Source LLC
Chambersburg PA
CBHW070301240426
43661CB00057B/2611